South-Ea...

Land above 500 metres

LUZON

Manila

PHILIPPINE
ISLANDS

Legaspi

SAMAR

PANAY

PACIFIC
OCEAN

Cebu

NEGROS

MINDANAO

Davao

BRITISH
NORTH
BORNEO

EAST   INDIES

ECONOMIC CHANGE IN
SOUTH-EAST ASIA, c.1830–1980

Economic Change in South-East Asia, c.1830–1980

IAN BROWN

KUALA LUMPUR
OXFORD UNIVERSITY PRESS
OXFORD SINGAPORE NEW YORK

Oxford University Press

Oxford New York

Athens Auckland Bangkok Bogotá Buenos Aires
Calcutta Cape Town Chennai Dar es Salaam Delhi
Florence Hong Kong Istanbul Karachi
Madrid Melbourne Mexico City Mumbai
Nairobi Paris São Paulo Shah Alam Singapore
Taipei Tokyo Toronto Warsaw

and associated companies in
Berlin Ibadan

Oxford is a trade mark of Oxford University Press

Published in the United States
by Oxford University Press, New York

© Oxford University Press 1997
First published 1997
Second impression 1999

British Library Cataloguing in Publication Data
Data available

Library of Congress Cataloging-in-Publication Data
Brown, Ian (Ian George), 1947–
Economic change in South-East Asia, c. 1830–1980/Ian Brown.
p. cm.
Includes bibliographical references and index.
ISBN 983 56 0014 7 (boards)
1. Asia, Southeastern—Economic conditions. 2. Asia,
Southeastern—History—19th century. 3. Asia, Southeastern—
History—20th century. I. Title.
HC441.B75 1997
301.959—dc20
96-43168
CIP

Typeset by Indah Photosetting Centre Sdn. Bhd., Malaysia
Printed by Printmate Sdn. Bhd., Kuala Lumpur
Published by Penerbit Fajar Bakti Sdn. Bhd. (008974-T),
under licence from Oxford University Press,
4 Jalan Pemaju U1/15, Seksyen U1, 40150 Shah Alam,
Selangor Darul Ehsan, Malaysia

For Andrew, Alasdair, Raj

Preface

THIS book provides an introduction to the modern economic history of South-East Asia. It is intended principally for undergraduates and for people with a professional interest in the region who seek to understand the historical origins of its modern economic condition.

In the preparatory planning of the book, I identified one particularly serious problem. I now wish to share it, not in a bid for the reader's sympathy, but because the problem and the way in which eventually I decided to deal with it explains the structure and approach of the finished work.

Like all introductory texts, this one rests almost entirely on the published literature, on a reading of specialized published research. However, the secondary literature on the modern economic history of South-East Asia is very unevenly spread. In part this reflects the vastness of the subject, and the fact that it has been the focus of extensive scholarly research for barely three decades. Many important aspects of the modern economic history of South-East Asia still await their Ph.D. student. But it also reflects the fact that each economy in the region has its own distinctive historiography. For a range of reasons—the influence of contemporary economic problems, ease of access to research materials, the scholarly legacy of the colonial relationship—the issues which have most attracted the interest of economic historians working on, say, Java, have been quite different from the issues which have attracted those working on Burma. In my planning I therefore concluded that it would not be possible to be comprehensive. In the treatment of any particular theme—for example, demographic change in the nineteenth century—I could not write about the whole of South-East Asia with equal thoroughness. I certainly could not explore all major themes across the entire region.

I have therefore focused on just a number of key themes, each of which I have explored with reference to just one, two, or three economies. These are the thirteen chapters which, as Part II, comprise the heart of the book. Other economic historians would almost certainly have chosen differently: another time, another place, my choice may well have been different. And I am fully aware that in choosing as I have, important themes have been ignored and some of the region's economies have received less attention than their importance demands. At the same time I am confident that the thirteen offer an essential insight into South-East Asia's modern economic experience.

These core explorations are preceded by four chapters, comprising Part I, which provide a basic outline of economic change in the region between roughly 1830 and 1980, and are intended for those coming to the subject with little prior knowledge. Inevitably, there is occasional overlap and repetition between Parts I and II, but sometimes it does no harm to say important things twice. An opening chapter provides a context for the main discussion by looking briefly at the economy of South-East Asia in the period prior to the nineteenth century and an epilogue offers two perspectives on the distinctiveness of South-East Asia's economic experience.

In the thirteen core chapters, I have not aimed at a smooth summary of the present state of knowledge. Rather I have attempted to draw the reader into the specialized literature, to emphasize divergent views, and, where appropriate, to admit ignorance. Above all, I have sought to kindle curiosity and enthusiasm, to encourage the reader to explore further. (There are initial suggestions for further reading at the end of each chapter.) It is in this spirit that I have not resisted the temptation to mount some of my own hobby-horses as circumstances allowed, although I hope that I have been sufficiently gracious also to represent the views of those who, foolishly, would attempt to unseat me. Finally, some readers may feel that on occasions the discussion becomes too focused on narrow detail for an introductory text. But complex issues often demand exploration of the detail if their complexity is to be fully grasped: and even in those passages, this book remains the first, not the last, step.

I end on a small technical point. The changing names of the countries of South-East Asia in the period covered by this book may cause confusion for those new to the region. I am sure to have added to that confusion by using for each country the name in

common use at the time about which I am then writing: thus the
Netherlands East Indies before 1949, but Indonesia thereafter;
Siam until the late 1930s, and then Thailand. There is a map of
South-East Asia around 1930 in the endpapers.

London   IAN BROWN
November 1996

Acknowledgements

A book of this scope could not be written without the assistance of many individuals. Two stand out. Clive Dewey and Vic Lieberman read each chapter as it was completed. Both are masters of the sharp criticism wrapped in warm encouragement. It is a rare gift, and I am deeply indebted to them for the time and care which they gave to my work. Anne Booth, Raj Brown, Peter Carey, Gervase Clarence-Smith, Nigel Crook, John Drabble, Bob Elson, Hal Hill, Roger Knight, Paul Kratoska, Jonathan Rigg, Ralph Smith, Philip Stott, and Bob Taylor each read one or two chapters, bringing much-needed expertise to bear. To each I am very grateful. Catherine Lawrence very kindly drew the map. Finally, I must acknowledge the contribution made to this book by my under-graduate and postgraduate students, first at the University of Birmingham from 1974, and then, from 1979, at the School of Oriental and African Studies in London. Their ideas, perspectives, and reading of the literature greatly deepened my own understanding. I learnt with them.

Contents

Tables

Figure

1
Introduction: The Legacy of
an Earlier Past

THIS book begins in 1830, the year in which the Dutch introduced the Cultivation System to Java, so initiating the massive expansion in primary production and export which dominates the modern economic history of South-East Asia. However, it clearly makes no sense simply to plunge in at that point. Some chronological background is essential.

This requirement is demanded, of course, of all histories, whether introductory texts such as this or specialist studies. The reader needs either a brief summary of 'the story so far' or a concise statement of the position at the point of departure. However this requirement is particularly important in the present case, for many of the major changes which took place in the economy of South-East Asia in the century and a half after 1830, the period covered by this book, were shaped less by immediate influences, such as the ambitions of colonial rulers or the changing structures of contemporary world markets, than by the legacy of a distant past. So often, a full explanation of the economic experience of South-East Asia in the nineteenth and twentieth centuries will lie further back.

That earlier legacy could be captured, of course, if the time-frame of the book were to be extended backwards. But this is hardly practical. Even with the present dates there is simply too much complex ground to cover within the space allowed. And in any event, a book which took as its starting point, say, 1450, would still require an introductory background chapter, summarizing the story so far! The solution adopted here is to examine just two important features of the South-East Asian economy in the period prior to the nineteenth century. This will provide at least some insight into the processes of economic change in that earlier period. More importantly, it will illustrate the ways in which its legacy could profoundly shape the modern economic experience of the region.

An Age of Commerce

In two recently published books and a string of articles, Anthony Reid (1988; 1990a; 1990b; 1992; 1993a; 1993b) has identified the fifteenth to the seventeenth centuries in South-East Asia, more specifically the period 1450–1680, as an 'age of commerce'. From the early fifteenth century, the region experienced a long period of export growth, sustained, with inevitable interruptions, for more than two centuries. The most visible early commodities were the valuable spices—cloves, nutmeg, and mace—cultivated uniquely in Maluku in the eastern part of present-day Indonesia, but trade in this period also embraced many other primary articles, including resins, tortoise-shell, aromatic woods, deerskins, and, by far the most important, pepper. In return, South-East Asia imported finely woven cloth from India, silver from the Americas and from Japan, and, from China, copper cash, ceramics, and silk. This was trade on a substantial scale. Reid (1992: 465–6, 469) has calculated that the production of pepper, concentrated principally in Sumatra, the Malay peninsula, and southern Borneo, rose from about 2500 tonnes a year around 1510 to a peak of about 8500 tonnes around 1670. In that last year, pepper cultivation would have engaged some 40,000 families, at least 200,000 individuals, which was equivalent to around 5 per cent of the population of Sumatra, Borneo, and the Malay peninsula at that time. Annual imports of fine Indian cloth into South-East Asia probably exceeded 20 million square metres in the period 1620–50, virtually a square metre for each inhabitant each year. In the fifteenth and sixteenth centuries, China was the most important market for South-East Asia's exports. European demand became increasingly insistent from the beginning of the sixteenth century, growing most rapidly in the late sixteenth and early seventeenth centuries.

The sustained growth in trade created a string of flourishing commercial capitals across the region, accessible to sea-going vessels and highly dependent on long-distance commerce. Those cities compared favourably in size to the cities of contemporary Europe. Reid (1992: 473) suggests that in the middle of the seventeenth century there were probably six cities in South-East Asia with populations of 100,000 or more, sometimes very substantially more: Thang-long (modern Hanoi), Ayutthaya, Aceh, Banten, Makassar, and Mataram. The populations of these commercial centres were remarkably cosmopolitan: each had important communities of traders, merchants, sailors, and craftsmen not only from outside the region, from China, India, the Middle East, and Europe, but from other parts of South-East Asia itself, notably Mons from Burma and Javanese from that island's north coast. These foreign communities, with their own commercial practices, commercial legal systems, and technical innovations, decisively shaped the urban-commercial structures of South-East Asia. The point has been well put by Reid (1992: 481): 'Chinese technology, weights and coins, Indian financial methods, Islamic commercial laws, and European technology and capital, all played a major part in creating the character of Southeast Asian urban and commercial life in this period.'

The long trade boom clearly generated very considerable wealth in the port-capitals of South-East Asia and, to a smaller degree, in the hinterlands which serviced them. Contemporaries described the vigour of the commercial quarters and the splendour of the courts. And yet, crucially, this great expansion generally failed to create powerful indigenous merchant communities, or see the accumulation of independent capital, craftsmanship, and entrepreneurial skill and experience in indigenous hands. Commerce, and in particular long-distance commerce, was largely commanded by foreigners.

It is commonly argued that a strong indigenous merchant class failed to emerge in this period principally because powerful ruling élites feared the challenge which wealthy traders might pose to them. It is evident, for example, that the institutions of state and society in early modern South-East Asia possessed few formal mechanisms to prevent autocratic rulers from seizing the wealth of any subject who appeared to be growing too strong. There was little or no protection in law for individual property against the power of the state. The practice of escheat, in which the ruler inherited at least part of the estate of an official, particularly in those cases where the deceased had no identified heirs, appears to have been widespread. In these circumstances it was clearly difficult, in fact exceptional, for an indigenous trader to accumulate private capital independently. Indeed it was foolish to try.

The emergence of an independent indigenous merchant class was further blocked by the fact that in this period, the most valuable articles of trade were commonly traded through state monopolies. Using forced labour and forced deliveries, the ruler secured valuable commodities from agricultural and forest hinterlands, including the aromatic woods, skins, and resins noted above, which were then traded at the capital through his officials or agents. There was clearly only limited opportunity in this structure for indigenous traders to gain business experience, build long-distance networks or accumulate capital, in either the port-cities or the hinterlands. Royal authority may have suppressed indigenous commercial initiative in one further way. In the absence of protection through the law or through formal institutional mechanisms, individuals secured property and position principally through the cultivation of patronage ties. Almost inevitably this involved a considerable investment in conspicuous gift-giving and displays of wealth, including the possession of large numbers of retainers. This, of course, did little to promote the frugal habits which are conducive to successful commercial endeavour.

At the same time, South-East Asian rulers frequently favoured foreign merchants at the expense of their own subjects. Foreigners—Chinese, a Turk, a Greek, Persians, Indian Muslims, and Tamils are clearly identified—were often appointed to important commercial positions in port-capitals, notably the positions of *syahbandar* (harbourmaster) and *laksamana* (admiral; court official), to the governorships of provinces and, on occasions, to ministerial posts. These appointments clearly facilitated trade with the foreign merchants who came to the realm. But they also had the effect of excluding potentially powerful domestic rivals from positions which enriched the holder, and which provided a possible base from which rulers might be challenged, in combination with internal political allies. Foreigners, on the other hand, could be driven out, imprisoned, or executed with relative impunity if they grew too powerful in their appointed position, because they were outside local power alliances. Therefore, as long as they were not drawn too deeply into internal politics, foreign merchants possessed a considerable commercial advantage in the absolutist states of South-East Asia. They came to command the commercial centres, while local traders were largely stuck in peripheral roles, as pedlars and petty brokers.

According to Reid, the divide between foreign and indigenous capitalist in South-East Asia was decisively reinforced by a severe commercial crisis in the middle decades of the seventeenth century. The crisis can be seen as part of a world-wide contraction, also felt particularly strongly in Europe and China. In China, recurrent crop failures led to famines and epidemics, following a prolonged reduction in rainfall and increased instability in weather conditions: these in turn may have had their origins in a reduction in world temperatures during the seventeenth century, as a consequence of diminished solar activity. It has also been argued that the crisis was exacerbated by a marked reduction from around 1630 in the output of silver from mines in the Americas and in Japan, in that it hampered the conduct of international commerce. Across the world, trade volumes contracted and commodity prices fell.

But there were also local factors. The most important in island South-East Asia was a decisive advance in European power, as the Dutch inflicted a series of military defeats on local rulers, and sought, largely successfully, to secure a stranglehold over some of the most important elements in the region's trade. The forces of the Dutch East India Company, the VOC, seized Batavia in 1619 and the tiny Banda archipelago in 1621. Almost the entire population of Banda, some 15,000, was massacred, taken as slaves or left to starve, while the Company repopulated the islands with Dutch planters and their slave workers, who were to deliver all their production of nutmeg to it. The Dutch then took three crucial ports: Melaka from the Portuguese in 1641, Makassar in 1666–9, and Banten in 1682. Aceh was blockaded in the 1650s, while by 1680 almost all the remaining ports in the archipelago had been coerced into exclusive, and oppressive, trading arrangements with the Dutch. Finally, in order to create a monopoly in the highly valuable trade in cloves, the VOC destroyed all clove trees outside Ambon, which it directly controlled. With Dutch control of production and trade secure, the prices paid to cultivators were set at low levels and Asian intermediaries were eliminated from the trading system.

The result, argues Reid, was a decisive retreat on the part of South-East Asians from international commerce. A number of rulers in the Malay archipelago brought the cultivation of spices and pepper to a halt, in the hope that this would spare their domain the attention of the marauding Dutch. States were driven to reduce cash-cropping severely and switch to the cultivation of food for subsistence, either under pressure of a Dutch blockade of their coast or in response to the soaring prices of imported food where the Dutch had taken control of supplies. Across the region, rulers and cultivators, faced with a sharp fall in export prices, simply lost faith in the market and returned to subsistence crops.

Some rulers reacted to the dismal prices imposed by the Dutch by squeezing the profits of their cultivators to the point where supply dried up completely. The retreat from long-distance commerce was not always a consequence of Dutch assault and monopoly, certainly not in mainland South-East Asia which was largely spared Dutch aggression. There Reid draws attention to a series of major domestic crises in the seventeenth century which, he argues, led to disengagement from foreign, but particularly European, trade. With respect to Burma, in 1599 the capital, Pegu, which was located near the coast and which had long commanded a vigorous external trade, fell to internal enemies and was destroyed. In 1635, under a new dynasty, the capital was removed to Ava, in the agrarian heartland of Upper Burma. In these changed circumstances, European commerce struggled against quite considerable hostility. The English East India Company withdrew from Burma in 1657, the Dutch in 1679. Meanwhile, in Siam, a severe political crisis in 1688, in essence a crisis over the succession to the throne, resulted in the immediate expulsion of all French merchants and in the inauguration of a long period of restricted contact with all European traders, although, it is important to note, the same period saw a considerable expansion in Siam's trade with China. If there is a single image which most effectively illustrates the retreat of South-East Asians from long-distance commerce in the seventeenth century, it is the disappearance by around 1620 of the distinctive, 500-ton, South-East Asian junk, which had been the most important trading vessel in local seas during the long boom.

The retreat divided South-East Asians and the immigrant populations, notably the Chinese, in a number of ways. Once the Dutch were in control of the principal trading ports in maritime South-East Asia, they separated off the Chinese communities both physically and administratively, in order to reduce the opportunities for alliance between the Chinese and the indigenous populations aimed against them, but also to enhance the effectiveness of the Chinese in their role as commercial intermediaries. In each Dutch enclave, the Chinese were allocated their own quarter and were governed through their own administration. They serviced these European-controlled urban enclaves, not only in their roles as traders, middlemen, and moneylenders, tying the port into its commercial networks, but also as craftsmen, gardeners, provisioners, and labourers. And foreign domination of the urban centres discouraged local migration from the rural hinterlands.

The retained distinctiveness, the diminishing assimilation of the Chinese, reflected not simply European intervention but also important changes within the Chinese communities themselves. The final decades of the seventeenth century saw a considerable surge in Chinese migration to South-East Asia, largely the result of a decision by the Chinese authorities in 1684 to remove a long-enforced ban on overseas trade. Earlier generations of migrants had commonly been cut off from their homeland by that ban, and therefore had been driven towards assimilation. Now, replenished by waves of new migrants, the pressures on the overseas Chinese to assimilate slackened, the capacity to maintain a distinct Chinese identity and role grew.

A rather different configuration of forces was at work in the mainland states. As noted above, the crises of the seventeenth century had largely driven European merchants from the commerce of Burma and Siam, as well as Cambodia and Vietnam. The Chinese were therefore left in large part unchallenged, their position being further strengthened by the expansion which took place in the trade of China with South-East Asia from the 1680s. To some extent the Chinese in mainland South-East Asia, under local rulers, found it necessary to assimilate and, on occasions, to take official posts in order to protect their commercial position. But these communities were sufficiently large, at least in the major urban centres, to retain a considerable measure of distinctiveness. As Reid (1992: 497) notes: 'The ethnic identification of Chinese with trade and Southeast Asian with office-holding was ... never so sharp under indigenous rule, but it did slowly take hold nevertheless.'

The increasing identification of the Chinese with economic power in South-East Asia in this period was secured, finally, by their near-exclusive command of revenue-farming, first in the Dutch territories and then in the indigenous states. In revenue-farming, the monopoly right to collect a particular tax, sell a regulated commodity (usually salt or opium), or provide a specific service (for example, the operation of gambling establishments) was sold by the state, normally at competitive auction, to an individual or syndicate for a specified period of time, commonly three years. The revenue-farmer kept all the revenues he collected. As that income commonly far exceeded the sum the farmer had contracted to pay the state, the revenue-farm became an important source of economic power for the Chinese in South-East Asia, an essential factor in their domination of the region's commerce. Moreover, by largely absolving the state from responsibility for the collection of revenues, including harbour duties and toll-gate fees, and for the administration of many revenue-generating mono-polies, that is, opium dens and gambling houses, the revenue-farm facilitated the further withdrawal of rulers from commercial con-cerns. Again, Reid (1993a: 319) puts the point clearly: 'In the long term ... Chinese revenue farming undoubtedly widened the gulf between the indigenous population and large-scale commerce.'

The analysis presented here has been dangerously compressed. It sweeps over the subtleties of the literature on this subject and ignores the disagreements within it. But a crucial point has been established. The final chapter of this book will identify two im-portant common elements in the modern economic history of the states of South-East Asia, elements which establish South-East Asia as a distinct region with a considerable measure of internal unity. One of those elements was the ubiquitous presence in the modern period of a pronounced ethnic separation of economic roles, in which immigrant communities, but particularly the Chinese, provided the core entrepreneurial skills, the commercial networks, and the capital that secured rapid economic growth in the region from the early decades of the nineteenth century. The immigrant command of large expanses of the economic heights undoubtedly reflected the ambitions and policies of colonial administrations, as will be brought out in later chapters. But it was not *created* by colonial rule, and it would be entirely misleading to look to the period from the early nineteenth century for its origin. That lay in the long boom of the sixteenth century and the turmoil of the seventeenth.

Rural Settlements

Historians have long held sharply divergent views over the organ-ization of production and the nature of socio-economic relations in pre-colonial South-East Asia. At various times, colonial officials and, if only by implication, nationalist leaders have also had firm opinions on this subject. At one extreme, many Dutch colonial writers maintained that rural settlements in the pre-colonial period had a high degree of administrative and economic self-sufficiency. They were largely closed to the outside world. Every settlement possessed its own internal government and resisted the interven-tion of higher authorities. Each settlement, even each household, produced from its own resources virtually all the items of daily existence, notably food and clothing but also household implements and agricultural tools. There was, therefore, little need to trade or exchange outside the settlement's boundaries. A further important characteristic, in this view, was that each settlement possessed a high degree of socio-economic homogeneity. This meant not simply that there were no major disparities in income and power within the settlement. It also implied that every inhabitant was imbued with an understanding that, as part of the natural order, the economic ambitions of the settlement's élite would be constrained and the material position of the more vulnerable would be protected. Social and economic mechanisms, levelling devices, supposedly secured those outcomes. In other words, the settlement was a community, not only in the sense of possessing clearly defined physical boundaries and a precise knowledge of who belonged to it, but also in the sense of being bound together by a corporate moral responsibility. Communal identity was reinforced, it was argued, by the settlement's enduring attachment to a specific location, which it had occupied, unchanging, from the mists of time.

At the other extreme was a view which, in all respects, was the direct opposite. Far from being unchanging, timeless, rooted in a single place, settlements were almost constantly in a state of flux. They decayed, relocated, broke up: in other words, rural populations were highly mobile. Again, settlements were marked by a substantial degree of socio-economic inequality. There was little sense of community in the pre-colonial settlement, little sense of collective unity, of corporate responsibility. (It is for this reason that the word 'village' has been studiously avoided in this section. To the European mind at least, 'village' carries heavy connotations of community or collectivity. The word 'settlement' is free from such connotations.) In the view of a number of scholars, the settlement as a community was a later creation of the colonial state, to serve its own administrative needs. Lastly, the settlement was not administratively and economically closed but was open to extensive relations with the outside world. It did not produce all it needed but to a degree specialized in the production of particular commodities or household crafts, which it then traded in order to secure those it could not produce itself.

It must be emphasized that these are the two extreme positions, and that most of the writers on this subject have sought to refine and qualify them. There is space here for just three observations. It has been argued that individual elements in the two positions are in fact interchangeable. It would be possible, for example, for a closed settlement to harbour a marked degree of socio-economic inequality, and, in contrast, for the inhabitants of an open settlement to be bound by a powerful sense of community. Second, there is the argument that settlements were never simply open or closed but that each was located at a particular point on an open-closed continuum, and, crucially, would shift its position, in one direction or the other, in response to changing external circumstances. For example, during periods in which a strong central state had imposed stability and security, the settlement would seize the opportunity to trade more extensively. But in periods of turmoil it would be driven to rely increasingly on its own resources: it would close against the outside world. And finally, although many of these opposites remain the subject of considerable debate, notably the assertion that the inhabitants of the pre-colonial settlement were bound together by a corporate moral responsibility, there are those on which scholarly opinion is now, in general, no longer divided. For example, it is now abundantly clear that rural settlements in pre-colonial South-East Asia were commonly specialized in production and extensively engaged in trade. There is ample evidence that the region's provincial towns invariably possessed a vigorous market, commonly at work each day, which drew in traders and customers from a deep hinterland; that transactions were commonly conducted in coin; that particular settlements or districts were widely known for a specific craft or crop specialization; that itinerate traders, moving from settlement to settlement, were a prominent feature of rural life. This was a market economy.

The importance of this discussion in the present context is as follows. Our view of the pre-colonial rural order profoundly informs our understanding of the economic and social change which took place in rural South-East Asia during the colonial period. If pre-colonial settlements had been closed, self-sufficient communities, then their commitment to extreme specialization in production and their full engagement with the external economy under colonial rule would mark a fundamental break with the past, the imposition of a radically different economic order. But if, as seems clear, settlements had long practised a marked degree of occupational and crop specialization, produced surpluses, and exchanged and sold in local and regional markets, their later commitment to export production merely involved a change of scale, albeit a very marked one, rather than a sharp break with old structures. Moreover, if pre-colonial settlements had been characterized by substantial socio-economic inequalities, in other words, if élite households had commanded a major part of the settlement's land and labour, then the later transition to large-scale cultivation for export was almost certainly more easily achieved. The élite had the resources, the dispossessed the need, to respond to changing opportunities.

SUGGESTED READING

Anthony Reid's analysis of South-East Asia's 'age of commerce', the crisis of the seventeenth century, and the historical origins of Chinese economic power in the region, is most concisely presented in Anthony Reid (1992), 'Economic and Social Change, c.1400–1800', in Nicholas Tarling (ed.), *The Cambridge History of Southeast Asia*, Vol. 1, *From Early Times to c.1800*, Cambridge: Cambridge University Press, pp. 460–507. The fullest statement of his views appears in two extremely fine volumes: Anthony Reid (1988), *Southeast Asia in the Age of Commerce, 1450–1680*, Vol. 1, *The Lands below the Winds*, New Haven: Yale University Press; Anthony Reid (1993a), *Southeast Asia in the Age of Commerce, 1450–1680*, Vol. 2, *Expansion and Crisis*, New Haven: Yale University Press, but particularly the final substantive chapter, 'The Origins of Southeast Asian Poverty', pp. 267–325. Parts of his analysis have also appeared in articles: Anthony Reid (1990a), 'An "Age of Commerce" in Southeast Asian History', *Modern Asian Studies*, 24(1): 1–30; Anthony Reid (1990b), 'The Seventeenth-century Crisis in Southeast Asia', *Modern Asian Studies*, 24(4): 639–59. Finally a volume of essays, Anthony Reid (ed.) (1993b), *Southeast Asia in the Early Modern Era: Trade, Power, and Belief*, Ithaca: Cornell University Press, contains not only a further valuable statement by Reid, 'Introduction: A Time and a Place', pp. 1–19, but also two papers which are critical of his views on the seventeenth-century crisis, Victor Lieberman, 'Was the Seventeenth Century a Watershed in Burmese History?', pp. 214–49, and Dhiravat na Pombejra, 'Ayutthaya at the End of the Seventeenth Century: Was There a Shift to Isolation?', pp. 250–72, as well as a valuable paper by Jeyamalar Kathirithamby-Wells, 'Restraints on the Development of Merchant Capitalism in Southeast Asia before c.1800', pp. 123–48, which explores some of the reasons for the failure of a substantial, independent indigenous merchant class to emerge in the region in the early modern period.

A major part of the literature on the pre-colonial rural order in South-East Asia, on patterns of production and trade and, in particular, on the nature of socio-economic relations, has focused on Java. A valuable introduction, concentrating on the communal character of the Javanese village in and before the nineteenth century, is provided by Peter Boomgaard (1991a), 'The Javanese Village as a Cheshire Cat: The Java Debate against a European and Latin American Background', *Journal of Peasant Studies*, 18(2): 288–304. For the view that the pre-colonial settlement was politically and economically open, and marked by a considerable degree of socio-economic inequality, see Jan Breman (1982), 'The Village on Java and the Early-Colonial State', *Journal of Peasant Studies*, 9(4): 189–240, and Jan Breman (1988), *The Shattered Image: Construction and Deconstruction of the Village in Colonial Asia*, Centre for Asian Studies Amsterdam, Comparative Asian Studies, No. 2, Dordrecht: Foris Publications. Breman strongly denies that the pre-colonial settlement was in any way a community: the settlement as a community was purely a creation of colonial rulers. R. E. Elson (1986a), 'Aspects of Peasant Life in Early 19th Century Java', in David P. Chandler and M. C. Ricklefs (eds.), *Nineteenth and Twentieth Century Indonesia: Essays in Honour of Professor J. D. Legge*, Centre of Southeast Asian Studies, Clayton: Monash University, pp. 57–81, provides a valuable insight into the economic and social structures of rural Java in the period immediately before the introduction of the Cultivation System, and, in its final pages, a firm rebuttal of Breman's views on the settlement as a community. Finally, Peter Boomgaard (1991b), 'The Non-agricultural Side of an Agricultural Economy, Java, 1500–1900', in Paul Alexander, Peter Boomgaard, and Ben White (eds.), *In the Shadow of Agriculture: Non-farm Activities in the Javanese Economy, Past and Present*, Amsterdam: Royal Tropical Institute, pp. 14–40, demonstrates the remarkable diversity and scale of non-agricultural production in pre-colonial and early colonial rural Java.

Reference should also be made to two important studies of rural society in South-East Asia in the modern period, on the grounds that they are underpinned by, and explore at some length, strongly contrasted understandings of the pre-colonial rural order: James C. Scott (1976), *The Moral Economy of the Peasant: Rebellion and Subsistence in Southeast Asia*, New Haven: Yale University Press; and Samuel L. Popkin (1979), *The Rational Peasant: The Political Economy of Rural Society in Vietnam*, Berkeley: University of California Press.

PART I

2
Economic Change, 1830–1920:
The Expansion of Production and Trade

THE century from around 1830 saw a remarkable increase in agricultural and mineral production in South-East Asia. Hundreds of
thousands of cultivators right across the region, together with a
vast influx of migrant labourers from China and India, committed
themselves to the production of rice, tin, rubber, sugar, coffee,
tobacco, abaca, coconuts, and in so doing transformed both the
economy and the physical landscape of the region. This chapter
will provide a straight description, commodity-by-commodity,
country-by-country, of that process. Why South-East Asian cultivators engaged in this vast enterprise, and with what consequences
for their immediate and longer-term economic circumstances, are
important questions that will be addressed later.

This description begins in the mainland states of Burma, Siam,
and Vietnam, and with the cultivation and export of rice. Around
1900, an average of 2.6 million short tons of rice were exported
each year from the deltas of the Irrawaddy, the Chao Phraya, and
the Mekong. Four decades earlier, recorded exports had been neg-
ligible. In the Irrawaddy and Mekong deltas, the commitment to
rice cultivation for export followed the imposition of European
rule, Britain annexing Lower Burma on the conclusion of the
Second Anglo-Burmese War in 1852, France seizing the three
eastern provinces of Cochin-China in 1862 and then, in 1867, the
three western provinces. In the Chao Phraya Delta, the expansion
of rice cultivation and export followed the commitment of the
Siamese Court, through a series of treaties with each of the major
Western powers, beginning with the Bowring Treaty of 1855 with
Britain, to freedom of international trade.

Cultivation itself was undertaken almost exclusively by the

indigenous populations, the important exception being the employment of Indian work-gangs to assist in planting and harvesting the crop in the Irrawaddy Delta from the final decades of the nineteenth century. The methods of wet-rice cultivation were those which had been used in the region for countless generations. In other words, the remarkable increase in rice production was achieved not through changes in agricultural practices that implied a more intensive cultivation of the land but simply by a dramatic extension of the cultivated area. In 1850, huge expanses of the deltas, particularly those of the Irrawaddy and the Mekong, were simple jungle, grassland, and swamp, with few human inhabitants. The creation of the mainland rice industry involved bringing those vast uncultivated tracts into cultivation, a massive endeavour built upon the migration of tens of thousands of pioneer cultivators and their families into the frontier wildernesses.

The expansion of the area under rice is recorded in Tables 2.1–2.3. The increases in export volumes were, of course, comparably dramatic. In brief, the volume of rice exports from mainland South-East Asia rose six times over the period 1863–71 to 1902–11, the area under rice cultivation increasing roughly fourfold over the period 1870–1920, with the most rapid growth occurring in the decades from around 1890. It is also important to note that, in terms of both export volume and area under cultivation, the rice industry of Burma was commonly twice or more the size of those in Siam and Cochin-China throughout this period of

TABLE 2.1
Lower Burma: Area under Rice Cultivation,
1855–1920 ('000 hectares)[a]

Year	Area	Year	Area
1855	402	1890	1 780
1860	539	1895	2 124
1865	582	1900	2 662
1870	702	1905	2 923
1875	963	1910	3 160
1880	1 255	1915	3 353
1885	1 497	1920	3 476

Source: Calculated from Cheng Siok-Hwa (1968), The Rice Industry of Burma, 1852–1940, Kuala Lumpur: University of Malaya Press, pp. 241–2.
[a]Acres converted to hectares at the rate of 1 hectare = 2.471 acres.

TABLE 2.2
Siam: Area of Rice Cultivation, 1860–1920 ('000 hectares)

Year	Area	Year	Area
1860	813	1895	1 270
1865	778	1900	1 293
1870	907	1905	1 542
1875	1 003	1910	1 755
1880	995	1911–15	1 964
1885	1 046	1916–20	2 295
1890	1 192		

Source: Sompop Manarungsan (1989), *Economic Development of Thailand, 1850–1950: Response to the Challenge of the World Economy*, Institute of Asian Studies, Monograph No. 42, Bangkok: Chulalongkorn University, p. 51.

TABLE 2.3
Cochin-China: Land under Rice Cultivation,
1873–1920 ('000 hectares)

Year	Area	Year	Area
1873	274	1900	1 174
1880	753	1910	1 528
1890	854	1920	1 752

Source: Martin J. Murray (1980), *The Development of Capitalism in Colonial Indochina (1870–1940)*, Berkeley: University of California Press, p. 417.

growth (Table 2.4). This may have been a reflection of the natural advantages of the Irrawaddy Delta over the Chao Phraya and the Mekong, in terms, for example, of the security of the monsoon rains. But it may also have reflected the heavy involvement of Indian capital and labour in the cultivation of rice in Lower Burma from around 1880, but the virtual absence of immigrant Asian labour from involvement in rice cultivation in Siam and Cochin-China. This is one aspect of an important, recurrent theme in this book: the crucial role of immigrant Asian communities in shaping the modern economic experience of South-East Asia.

Most of the rice exported from the mainland deltas was shipped to markets elsewhere in Asia, that is, to India (an important market for Burma's rice), to China through Hong Kong, and, of particular

TABLE 2.4

Mainland South-East Asia: Rice Exports by 10-year Averages,
1863–1911 ('000 short tons)

Years	Burma	Siam	Cochin-China	Total
1863–71	417	124	157	698
1872–81	907	198	315	1,420
1882–91	1,095	329	496	1,920
1892–1901	1,645	572	646	2,863
1902–11	2,411	954	793	4,158

Source: Norman G. Owen (1971b), 'The Rice Industry of Mainland Southeast Asia, 1850–1914', Journal of the Siam Society, 59(2): 95.

interest in this context, to other parts of South-East Asia itself, commonly through Singapore. In the years 1902–11, 36 per cent of Siam's rice exports went to Singapore, while 32 per cent of the rice exported from Cochin-China went to the Netherlands East Indies and the Philippines. Increasingly heavy imports of rice into the Malay States, the Netherlands East Indies, and the Philippine Islands reflected the rapid expansion there of other forms of commodity production and trade, for the food requirements of the vast numbers of indigenous cultivators now committed to the production of industrial raw materials and food crops for Western markets, together with the rapidly growing local Chinese and Indian populations, now had to be made good from external sources.

Nowhere was this more evident than in the Malay States. The Malayan export economy was built on two commodities, tin and, from the beginning of the twentieth century, rubber. The modern expansion of tin production and export began in the 1840s, substantially before the imposition of British rule. The volume of tin imported from the Malay Peninsula into the Straits Settlements, that is, Singapore, Penang, and Melaka, rose from an annual average of 1,252 tons in 1845–9 to 2,997 tons in 1865–9. Following the imposition of British rule, introduced state-by-state from 1874, production simply soared, as Table 2.5 illustrates. In the last year of the table, 1910, Malaya accounted for no less than 40 per cent of world production of tin.

Until the very first years of the twentieth century, Malayan tin was extracted almost entirely by Chinese enterprise, using rather simple, highly labour-intensive mining methods. Therefore, as production soared, there was heavy recruitment of labour from

TABLE 2.5
Malaya: Tin Production, 1875–1910 (tons)

Year	Volume	Year	Volume
1875	8,566	1895	49,592
1880	11,735	1900	43,111
1885	17,319	1905	50,991
1890	27,200	1910	45,918

Source: Wong Lin Ken (1965), *The Malayan Tin Industry to 1914*, Association for Asian Studies, Monographs and Papers No. 14, Tucson: University of Arizona Press, p. 246.

China. In 1900, for example, there was a net inflow of 41,306 Chinese males into the two main tin states of Perak and Selangor. In 1905, 209,014 coolies were employed in mining in the Federated Malay States. (This was part of the very substantial immigrant labour force in Malaya which could be fed only through increased rice imports.) Chinese domination of tin mining was broken principally by the increasing exhaustion of the richest, most accessible seams from the closing years of the nineteenth century. In those circumstances, to maintain the existing high rate of extraction required the introduction of technologically more sophisticated, capital-intensive mining methods, and these appeared to be the prerogative of Western enterprise. As a result, Western firms, which had produced only 10–15 per cent of the total output of the Federated Malay States in the mid-1900s, accounted for 23 per cent in 1910, and 36 per cent in 1920.

At the same time as Western capital was beginning to take a major share in tin production, it was also acting as the pioneer in a new primary industry, the cultivation of rubber. Production was concentrated in the west coast states of the peninsula, principally to take advantage of the communications infrastructure—the roads, ports, and railways—that had been created to service the tin industry. In 1898 there were a mere 2,000 acres under rubber in Malaya. But the expansion in acreage was explosive, to 46,000 acres in 1905, 541,000 in 1910, and to 2,181,000 in 1920. Because newly planted rubber took six or seven years to produce latex, the growth in output, comparably spectacular, occurred after a lag (Table 2.6). In that last year, 1920, Malaya accounted for 51 per cent of world exports of rubber.

The labour force for the Western rubber plantations largely comprised migrants from south India. In 1920, 160,966 Indians

TABLE 2.6
Malaya: Rubber Exports, 1905-1920 (tons)

Year	Volume
1905	130
1910	6,500
1915	70,200
1920	181,000

Source: J. H. Drabble (1973), *Rubber in Malaya, 1876-1922: The Genesis of the Industry*, Kuala Lumpur: Oxford University Press, p. 220.

were employed on estates in the Federated Malay States, while between 1900 and 1920, net Indian immigration to Malaya exceeded 600,000. (This was a further important component of Malaya's immigrant population which, committed to export production, could be fed only with increased rice imports.) Large-scale Malay smallholder planting of rubber, to challenge the supremacy of the Western plantations, began in 1909, and expanded extremely rapidly. By 1922, smallholdings accounted for 39 per cent of total rubber acreage in Malaya.

The first great expansion in commodity production and trade in South-East Asia in the modern period had taken place on the Dutch-ruled island of Java, from the beginning of the 1830s. The Dutch had come to the archipelago in the closing years of the sixteenth century, to exploit the rich production of spices in Maluku and then, over a much wider territory, the archipelago's very considerable cultivations of pepper. Masters of Java by the mid-eighteenth century, in the opening decades of the nineteenth the Dutch sought in various ways to release the island's vast potential for the cultivation of bulk commercial crops. Success came in 1830 with the introduction of the *Kultuurstelsel*, the Cultivation System. The principles and practices of the Cultivation System were so complex, its impact on the economy of rural Java in the nineteenth century a matter of such fierce scholarly argument, that a full chapter of this book, Chapter 7, has been devoted to it. It is sufficient to say here that the Cultivation System was a series of administrative arrangements by which the Dutch colonial state, acting through local élites, instructed the rural population of Java to cultivate designated crops for export. In brief, the *Kultuurstelsel* involved government-directed coercion. In this respect, the expansion of commodity production and trade on Java from the mid-nineteenth century stood in strong contrast to the expansions elsewhere in the region—rice cultivation in mainland South-East Asia, tin and rubber in the Malay States, but also rubber and tobacco in Sumatra, sugar, abaca, and copra in the Philippines—where increased production was achieved not through state coercion but largely reflected the responses of individual cultivators, landowners, moneylenders, and traders to sharply increased market opportunities.

The designated crops of the Cultivation System included tobacco, tea, pepper, and cinnamon, but the important ones were indigo and, in particular, coffee and sugar. In 1870, for example, coffee and sugar accounted for 64 per cent of the total value of commodity exports from Java and Madura. The spectacular expansion in exports is made clear in Table 2.7.

The Dutch colonial administration began to dismantle the Cultivation System in the early 1860s, not because output had begun to falter (the continued growth of sugar and coffee exports, illustrated in Table 2.7, makes that clear) but essentially as a result of increasing opposition within the Netherlands itself to the arbitrary oppression and vast corruption which were said to accompany it, as well as a growing belief that releasing the Javanese cultivator from government coercion would now produce a more efficient

TABLE 2.7

Java and Madura: Sugar and Coffee Exports, 1830–1870[a]

	Sugar		Coffee	
Year	Volume	Value	Volume	Value
1830	6.78	1,575	17.74	4,552
1835	26.51	5,707	28.83	14,090
1840	62.11	13,577	69.84	37,318
1845	88.63	20,093	62.13	20,118
1850	84.80	16,918	50.76	18,785
1855	102.01	20,320	78.06	32,396
1860	126.44	32,399	57.28	30,598
1865	131.65	32,272	50.38	33,624
1870	145.41	31,599	74.86	37,291

Source: *Changing Economy in Indonesia: A Selection of Statistical Source Material from the Early 19th Century up to 1940* (General Editor, P. Boomgaard), Vol. 12a, 1991, *General Trade Statistics, 1822–1940*, edited by W. L. Korthals Altes, Amsterdam: Royal Tropical Institute, pp. 138–47.

[a]Values in thousands of guilders; volumes in millions of kilograms.

and benevolent exploitation of Java's agricultural resources. The decisive measure was the Sugar Law of 1870 which provided for the phasing out of the forced cultivation of sugar over the period 1879–90. Government-directed cultivation of coffee, the most profitable of the state cultivations, did not finally disappear until 1918–19.

The dismantling of the Cultivation System left the Javanese cultivator, now like his counterparts elsewhere in South-East Asia, to decide which crops to cultivate and in what quantities. Although the total value of Java's commodity exports stagnated in the final decades of the nineteenth century, this was largely the result of a world-wide depression in primary prices. Around the turn of the century, the rapid expansion in commodity exports was firmly re-established, spectacularly so in the case of sugar (Table 2.8).

The period from around 1870 also saw a major expansion in agricultural and mineral production in the outer islands, notably Sumatra. This took place as Dutch administration was extended into the outer territories, usually behind but occasionally in advance of it. The expansion involved a diversification into new commodities. The commercial cultivation of high quality tobacco, soon to establish an unrivalled reputation on world markets as a cigar wrapper leaf, began on Sumatra's east coast, prominently in the Deli district around the town of Medan, in the mid-1860s. Cultivation and processing of the harvested leaf was restricted to Western-owned estates, which employed immigrant labour, first

TABLE 2.8
Java and Madura: Sugar Exports, 1875–1920[a]

Year	Volume	Value
1875	209.7	52,435
1880	222.2	48,893
1885	420.4	84,079
1890	367.8	51,490
1895	575.7	80,593
1900	736.6	73,661
1905	1 049.9	83,993
1910	1 182.2	139,615
1915	1 205.8	213,239
1920	1 513.8	1,049,812

Source: As for Table 2.7, pp. 137, 152–62.
[a]Volume in millions of kilograms; value in thousands of guilders.

Chinese but then increasingly Javanese. The growth of the industry into the twentieth century was again spectacular, despite occasional reverses (Table 2.9).

The opening years of the twentieth century saw the first commercial planting of rubber on Sumatra's east coast. The early initiative lay firmly with Western-owned plantations, for British, Dutch, French, Belgian, and American capital was soon pouring into the industry. The strong surge of local interest in rubber came around 1910, but, once established, smallholder production increased dramatically. Rubber became the major smallholder crop in Sumatra, with particularly extensive cultivation in Jambi, in the south-central part of the island. The rapid expansion of rubber planting in East Sumatra in the first two decades of the twentieth century is caught in Table 2.10.

Two non-agricultural commodities, tin and petroleum, also came to occupy important positions in the exports of the Netherlands East Indies in this period. In 1920, for example, together they accounted for almost 17 per cent of the total value of commodity exports from the Dutch territories. The commercial extraction of tin had begun on the large island of Bangka, off the south-east

TABLE 2.9
East Sumatra: Tobacco, 1865–1920[a]

Year	Production Volume	Approximate Total Revenue
1865	189	40
1870	2,868	450
1875	15,355	3,900
1880	64,965	11,250
1885	124,911	26,976
1890	236,323	26,000
1895	204,719	28,350
1900	223,731	38,000
1905	225,369	54,500
1910	234,133	47,800
1915	323,911	64,700
1920	145,507	64,500

Source: Thee Kian-wie (1977), Plantation Agriculture and Export Growth: An Economic History of East Sumatra, 1863–1942, Jakarta: National Institute of Economic and Social Research (LEKNAS–LIPI), p. 9.

[a]Production volume in number of bales; approximate total revenue in thousands of guilders.

TABLE 2.10
East Sumatra: Area under Rubber, 1902–1920 (hectares)

Year	Area	Year	Area
1902	176	1912	86 196
1904	651	1914	99 147
1906	2 078	1916	106 413
1908	13 090	1918	120 331
1910	29 471	1920	150 156

Source: As for Table 2.9, p. 14.

coast of Sumatra, in the first decades of the eighteenth century.
The working of tin deposits on the adjacent, but smaller island
of Belitung began in the 1850s. The colonial state had had a
central role in the industry from the early nineteenth century,
imposing increasingly rigorous regulation on the Chinese mining
co-operatives which worked the seams on Bangka, and, from 1892,
taking a majority interest in the company which had worked the
Belitung deposits since 1860. Tin export volumes and values rose
firmly through the last quarter of the nineteenth century and into
the twentieth (Table 2.11). In 1910, the Dutch territories accounted for just over 18 per cent of world tin production.

TABLE 2.11
Netherlands East Indies: Export of Tin, Annual Averages,
1875–1914[a]

Years	Volume	Value
1875–9	8 351	6,892
1880–4	9 151	8,035
1885–9	10 516	11,937
1890–4	11 550	11,022
1895–9	13 707	10,827
1900–4	17 950	23,335
1905–9	13 041	16,935
1910–4	15 250	30,081

Source: J. A. M. Caldwell (1964), 'Indonesian Export and Production from the
Decline of the Culture System to the First World War', in C. D. Cowan (ed.),
The Economic Development of South-East Asia: Studies in Economic History and
Political Economy, London: George Allen & Unwin, p. 90.
[a]Volume in thousands of kilograms; value in thousands of guilders.

The extraction of oil, in contrast, was a new industry, the first commercial concession being taken out in 1883. The main oilfields were in south-east Borneo and south Sumatra. This highly capital-intensive industry was entirely in Western hands, attracting very considerable investment from not only the Netherlands but also Britain, the United States, and France. Royal Dutch–Shell, a fusion created in 1907, controlled by far the major part of a rapidly expanding output. In 1920, petroleum and petroleum products were the second most valuable export of the Netherlands East Indies, behind sugar, accounting for almost 14 per cent of total export value (Table 2.12).

The expansion of tin production on Bangka and Belitung, the exploitation of oil deposits in south Sumatra and south-east Borneo, the establishment of major tobacco and rubber cultivations in east and south Sumatra, all from the mid-nineteenth century, produced a fundamental shift in the relative economic importance of Java and the outer territories. In 1877–9, the latter accounted for 21.7 per cent of the total value of private merchandise exports from the Netherlands East Indies: in 1910–14, the share of the outer territories had risen to 43.5 per cent.

The remaining major export economy in the region was the Philippines, a Spanish colony until 1898 and then a colony of the United States. Like the Netherlands East Indies, the Philippines produced a notable range of primary commodities, the relative importance of which changed over time. In the first decade of the twentieth century, the single most valuable Philippine export was abaca, or Manila hemp: indeed, it accounted for well over half of total export value. This is a fibre obtained by stripping the stalk of the abaca plant, a modestly sized member of the banana family. Its remarkable strength and resistance to salt water established its high

TABLE 2.12

Netherlands East Indies: Exports of Petroleum and
Petroleum Products, 1890–1920 ('000 guilders)

Year	Value	Year	Value
1890	6	1910	37,651
1895	2,906	1915	141,927
1900	4,593	1920	310,202
1905	21,507		

Source: As for Table 2.7, pp. 155–61.

reputation in the manufacture of ship rope in the nineteenth century. Abaca was unique to the Philippines. The most intense cultivation took place in the Bikol region, the south-east extremity of Luzon, where typically the crop was grown on lands owned by local élites, using labour employed in share-cropping arrangements. The first consignment of abaca was shipped from the Philippines in 1818, but the main expansion in production and export took place from the mid-nineteenth century, with a striking acceleration towards the century's end (Table 2.13).

The other leading Philippine primary export in the colonial period was sugar. If its relative position had slumped in the first decade of the twentieth century (there had been a particularly sharp fall in sugar export volumes from the mid-1890s), for much of the second half of the nineteenth century and again in the decades between the wars, sugar was the single most valuable of the colony's exports. The principal sugar-producing regions of the Philippines were the province of Pampanga, to the north-west of the capital, Manila, on the island of Luzon, and, to a lesser degree, neighbouring central Luzon provinces; and much of the western part of the island of Negros, in the Visayas. The earliest cultivation for export took place on Luzon, and was firmly established there by 1830. Production on Negros began in the mid-1850s, following the opening of the port of Iloilo, on the neighbouring island of Panay, to international trade. In the early 1890s, Negros supplanted Pampanga as the premier sugar region in the Islands. The growth of Philippine sugar exports in this period is captured in Table 2.14.

TABLE 2.13
The Philippines: Exports of Abaca, 1855–1920 (million pesos)

Year	Value	Year	Value
1855	1.4	1890	8.4
1860	1.8	1895	12.7
1865	2.4	1900	26.6
1870	n.a.	1905	43.5
1875	3.7	1910	33.0
1880	5.4	1915	42.7
1885	6.6	1920	71.7

Source: Norman G. Owen (1984), *Prosperity without Progress: Manila Hemp and Material Life in the Colonial Philippines*, Berkeley: University of California Press, pp. 258–62.

TABLE 2.14

The Philippines: Sugar Exports, 1850–1920 (metric tons)

Year	Volume	Year	Volume
1850	29 090	1890	149 297
1855	49 194	1895	233 694
1860	55 126	1900	65 191
1865	56 062	1905	108 499
1870	79 469	1910	121 472
1875	128 225	1915	211 013
1880	183 698	1920	180 341
1885	205 933		

Source: John A. Larkin (1993), *Sugar and the Origins of Modern Philippine Society*, Berkeley: University of California Press, p. 249.

In Luzon, sugar cultivation for export was organized principally on a share tenancy basis. The landowner contributed the land, cuttings, milling facilities, and cash loans, the tenant cultivator provided his labour, while the harvest was divided between them, sometimes equally, often not. On Negros, from the late 1880s, cultivation commonly took place on plantations, and involved the use of wage labour, frequently engaged on a daily basis. The late Spanish and early American periods saw important advances in sugar milling technology, notably the arrival of steam-powered mills in the 1860s and then centrifugal milling from the 1910s. Both innovations required substantial capital investment, which commonly could be undertaken only by Western concerns. The principal markets for Philippine sugar towards the end of the nineteenth century were Britain and the United States: in the mid-1880s, together they absorbed around 80 per cent of the total. But with the imposition of American rule, and in particular with the establishment of free trade between the colony and the United States in 1909, the American market became the main, indeed from the late 1920s virtually the sole, destination for Philippine sugar.

Two final commodities, tobacco and coconuts/coconut products, completed the major exports of the Philippines in this period, although neither came near to matching the importance of either sugar or abaca. Late in the eighteenth century, the Spanish colonial administration imposed a monopoly on the cultivation of tobacco, on the collection of the harvested tobacco leaf, and on the manufacture and domestic sale of cigars. The principal region of cultivation, producing the finest quality leaf, was the Cagayan Valley, in north-east Luzon. The tobacco monopoly was, above all, an instrument of domestic taxation, and indeed, from the point of view of the Spanish administration, a highly successful one. But in addition, from the 1830s substantial quantities of leaf tobacco were requisitioned for delivery to the royal cigar factories in Spain, and there was also a modest private export of both manufactured and leaf tobacco, as supplies allowed. The tobacco monopoly was abolished in 1882, leaving tobacco cultivation, manufacture, and trade to private interest. Export values rose substantially in the final years of Spanish rule, and throughout the 1890s, tobacco never accounted for less than 10 per cent of total export value. The arrival of the Americans appears to have provided a major stimulus to production and trade: the average annual volume of manufactured and leaf tobacco exports rose from 55 000 metric tons in 1900–4 to 115 000 in 1910–14.

Coconuts/coconut products emerged as a significant export only in the final years of Spanish rule, but, again, the arrival of the Americans, and strong demand from soap and margarine manufacturers in the United States, provided a major stimulus. Copra exports rose from 15,000 tons in 1899 to 119,000 tons in 1910: in 1919, the copra equivalent of all coconut product exports was 237,000 tons, and coconuts/coconut products accounted for 37 per cent of total export value. The principal coconut provinces were Quezon Province (Tayabas) and Laguna, to the south-east of Manila, but there was also substantial cultivation throughout southern Luzon and in parts of the Visayas and Mindanao.

This description of the expansion of commodity production and trade in South-East Asia in the century from around 1830 is far from comprehensive. A considerable number of important commodities, for example, teak in Burma and Siam, rubber, coal, zinc, and tin in French Indo-China, indigo, tea, and copra in the Netherlands East Indies, have been omitted. Yet the principal purpose of this description has simply been to establish in general terms the sheer scale of the expansion. Although precise comparisons with other parts of the non-European world are difficult, it is hard to imagine that any region of similar size in South Asia, Africa, or Latin America matched South-East Asia in the scale and range of its commodity production and trade in this period. This was a spectacular growth.

Two important caveats must immediately be added. First, the

expansion was certainly not uninterrupted or infallibly secure. Across the region, throughout this period, many new crops failed outright or enjoyed only a brief, modest success. Before Malay smallholders threw themselves at rubber towards the end of the first decade of the twentieth century, many had been hit disastrously by a collapse of coffee in the mid-1890s. When Siam was opened to international trade in the 1850s, it was confidently anticipated that sugar, then well-established, would dominate the kingdom's exports. But low prices killed that prospect, and after 1880, exports of sugar virtually disappeared. But even the great successes could run into serious difficulties from time to time, as a result of over-production, the emergence of rival producers, market collapse, an outbreak of crop disease, or political turmoil. The crisis in the Philippine sugar industry from the mid-1890s was noted earlier. Second, it is important to recognize that commodity production for export in South-East Asia was geographically concentrated, in, to give a few examples, the lower deltas of the mainland, the west coast of the Malay peninsula, Sumatra's east coast, much of the western part of the island of Negros, the Bikol region of Luzon. It did not extend, for example, to Siam's north-east plateau, the east coast of the Malay peninsula, north-west Sumatra. These areas remained largely outside the major economic changes which swept through South-East Asia in the nineteenth century, and therefore, rightly or wrongly, largely beyond the interest of most economic historians of the region.

SUGGESTED READING

From an extensive literature, it is possible here to note only a few texts. This guide proceeds by country and then by commodity.

An excellent overview of the rice industries of mainland South-East Asia, essentially a synthesis of published material, is provided by Norman G. Owen (1971b), 'The Rice Industry of Mainland Southeast Asia 1850-1914', *Journal of the Siam Society*, 59 (2): 75-143. For Burma, see Cheng Siok-Hwa (1968), *The Rice Industry of Burma, 1852-1940*, Kuala Lumpur: University of Malaya Press; and Michael Adas (1974), *The Burma Delta: Economic Development and Social Change on an Asian Rice Frontier, 1852-1941*, Madison: University of Wisconsin Press, Part 2. For Siam, see James C. Ingram (1971), *Economic Change in Thailand, 1850-1970*, Stanford: Stanford University Press, Chapters 3 and 4; Sompop Manarungsan (1989), *Economic Development of Thailand, 1850-1950:*

Response to the Challenge of the World Economy, Institute of Asian Studies, Monograph No. 42, Bangkok: Chulalongkorn University, Chapter 2; David Feeny (1982), *The Political Economy of Productivity: Thai Agricultural Development, 1880–1975*, Vancouver: University of British Columbia Press. For French Indo-China, see Guy Gran (1975), 'Vietnam and the Capitalist Route to Modernity: Village Cochinchina 1880–1940', Ph.D. dissertation, University of Wisconsin-Madison; Martin J. Murray (1980), *The Development of Capitalism in Colonial Indochina (1870–1940)*, Berkeley: University of California Press; Pierre Brocheux (1995), *The Mekong Delta: Ecology, Economy, and Revolution, 1860–1960*, Center for Southeast Asian Studies, Monograph No. 12, Madison: University of Wisconsin-Madison; Charles Robequain (1944), *The Economic Development of French Indo-China*, London: Oxford University Press.

The standard texts on the tin industry of Malaya in the late nineteenth and early twentieth century are Yip Yat Hoong (1969), *The Development of the Tin Mining Industry of Malaya*, Kuala Lumpur: University of Malaya Press; and Wong Lin Ken (1965), *The Malayan Tin Industry to 1914*, Association for Asian Studies, Monographs and Papers No. 14, Tucson: University of Arizona Press. The core work on the early history of rubber in Malaya is J. H. Drabble (1973), *Rubber in Malaya, 1876–1922: The Genesis of the Industry*, Kuala Lumpur: Oxford University Press. For a focus on the smallholder commitment to rubber in this period, see Lim Teck Ghee (1977), *Peasants and Their Agricultural Economy in Colonial Malaya, 1874–1941*, Kuala Lumpur: Oxford University Press. There is much useful information on both rubber and tin, but only limited analysis, in Lim Chong-Yah (1967), *Economic Development of Modern Malaya*, Kuala Lumpur: Oxford University Press.

Our understanding of economic change in the Netherlands East Indies from the early nineteenth century has been greatly enhanced since the mid-1970s by the production, by the Royal Tropical Institute in Amsterdam, of a series of volumes of statistical source material, under the general title *Changing Economy in Indonesia*. Each volume deals with one aspect of the colonial economy: the most useful one in the present context is Volume 12a, 1991, *General Trade Statistics, 1822–1940*, edited by W. L. Korthals Altes. [A full list of the volumes is given in the bibliography.] The literature on the Cultivation System is very extensive (see Chapter 7) but two texts in particular provide valuable accounts of the expansion of Java's main cultivations, coffee and sugar, in this period: R. E. Elson (1984), *Javanese Peasants and the Colonial Sugar Industry: Impact and Change in an East Java Residency, 1830–1940*, Southeast Asia Publication Series No. 9, Singapore: Oxford University Press/Asian Studies Association of Australia; R. E. Elson (1994), *Village Java under the Cultivation System, 1830–1870*, Southeast Asia Publication Series No. 25, Sydney: Allen & Unwin/Asian Studies Association of Australia. The plantation cultivation of tobacco and rubber in East Sumatra is examined in Thee Kian-wie (1977), *Plantation Agriculture and Export Growth: An Economic History of East Sumatra, 1863–1942*, Jakarta: National Institute of Economic and Social Research (LEKNAS–LIPI). For tobacco, see also Karl J. Pelzer (1978), *Planter and Peasant: Colonial Policy and the Agrarian Struggle in East Sumatra, 1863–1947*, 's-Gravenhage: Martinus Nijhoff. A valuable account of the Indies tin industry in this period can be found in Mary F. Somers Heidhues (1992), *Bangka Tin and Mentok Pepper: Chinese Settlement on an Indonesian Island*, Singapore: Institute of Southeast Asian Studies. A useful, if somewhat dated, survey of commodity production and trade in the Netherlands East Indies in the late nineteenth and early twentieth century is provided by J. A. M. Caldwell (1964), 'Indonesian Export and Production from the Decline of the Culture System to the First World War', in C. D. Cowan (ed.), *The Economic Development of South-East Asia: Studies in Economic History and Political Economy*, London: George Allen & Unwin, pp. 72–101.

The two principal export commodities of the colonial Philippines, sugar and abaca, are examined in two core texts: John A. Larkin (1993), *Sugar and the Origins of Modern Philippine Society*, Berkeley: University of California Press; Norman G. Owen (1984), *Prosperity without Progress: Manila Hemp and Material Life in the Colonial Philippines*, Berkeley: University of California Press. For the Spanish administration's tobacco monopoly, see Ed. C. de Jesus (1980), *The Tobacco Monopoly in the Philippines: Bureaucratic Enterprise and Social Change, 1766–1880*, Quezon City: Ateneo de Manila University Press. Useful introductions to those, and other, aspects of the colonial export economy of the Philippines can be found in Thomas Perry Storer (1970), 'The Philippines', in W. Arthur Lewis (ed.), *Tropical Development, 1880–1913*, Evanston: Northwestern University Press, pp. 283–308; Jonathan Fast and Jim Richardson (1979), *Roots of Dependency: Political and Economic Revolution in 19th Century Philippines*, Quezon City: Foundation for

Nationalist Studies; Vicente B. Valdepenas, Jr. and Gemilino M. Bautista (1977), *The Emergence of the Philippine Economy*, Manila: Papyrus Press. And finally, a number of essays in Alfred W. McCoy and Ed. C. de Jesus (eds.) (1982), *Philippine Social History: Global Trade and Local Transformations*, Quezon City: Ateneo de Manila University Press; Sydney: George Allen & Unwin: each focuses on a specific export commodity, for example, abaca or sugar.

3
Economic Change, 1830–1920:
Structural Features

HAVING established the scale of the expansion of primary production and trade in South-East Asia in the century or so from 1830, the present chapter focuses on a number of important structural features of the region's economy in that period, features that were crucial in shaping or underpinning that expansion.

The starting point must be the observation that, taking the region as a whole, South-East Asia in the nineteenth century had a markedly low population relative to the extent of its cultivable land. Statistics in this area, particularly for the earlier decades, are rather flimsy. But Tables 3.1 and 3.2 offer population estimates for 1830 and for the early twentieth century.

TABLE 3.1
South-East Asia: Population in 1830 (million)

Country	Population
Indonesia[a]	11.0
Philippines	2.5
Siam	2.7
Indo-China	5.2
Malay Peninsula[b]	0.4
Burma	4.0
Total	25.8

Source: Charles A. Fisher (1964), 'Some Comments on Population Growth in South-East Asia, with Special Reference to the Period since 1830', in C. D. Cowan (ed.), The Economic Development of South-East Asia: Studies in Economic History and Political Economy, London: George Allen & Unwin, p. 51.
[a]Java = 6.0 million; Outer Islands = 5.0 million.
[b]Figure is for the period 1835–9.

TABLE 3.2

South-East Asia: Population in the Early Twentieth Century (million)

Country	Population
Indonesia[a] (1900)	40.2
Philippines (1903)	7.6
Siam (1911)	8.3
Indo-China (1901, 1911)	16.2
Malay Peninsula (1911)	2.7
Burma (1901)	10.5
Total	85.5

Source: Charles Hirschman (1994), 'Population and Society in Twentieth-century Southeast Asia', *Journal of Southeast Asian Studies*, 25(2): 387.
[a]Java = 29.0 million; Outer Islands = 11.2 million.

A population of approximately 26 million in 1830 and of, say, around 80 million in 1900, implies an average annual rate of growth of 1.6 per cent. To put the early twentieth-century figure in perspective, at that time the continent of Europe (excluding Russia), with a land area only slightly larger than that of South-East Asia, had more than three times the population. Moreover, the population of South-East Asia was distributed very unevenly. There were, on the one hand, a number of major urban concentrations (in 1910 the region had eleven cities with populations in excess of 100,000) as well as densely settled rural areas, notably on Java and in the Red River Delta of northern Vietnam. But even in the early twentieth century, most of South-East Asia, including many vast, highly fertile tracts, was still sparsely populated. It need only be noted that at that time, over one-third of the region's population was concentrated on the island of Java. (See Chapter 6 for an examination of the reasons for the low density of population in South-East Asia in this period, and for the acceleration of population growth which took place in the nineteenth century.)

Those demographic features had a profound impact on the nature of economic change in nineteenth and early twentieth century South-East Asia. They implied, for example, that the great expansions in agricultural production commonly took place in lightly settled tracts or vast frontier wildernesses—the lower deltas of the Irrawaddy, the Chao Phraya and the Mekong, large areas of the Luzon Central Plain, the east coast of Sumatra, even districts in East Java—the clearing of which required the toil of vast streams of pioneer cultivators moving in from areas of more dense settlement. They also implied, obviously, the presence of marked labour shortages in this period of rapid growth, which in turn suggests that wage rates and cultivator incomes may at times have been high in comparison with those prevailing in other, heavily populated parts of Asia. Of central importance, the low density of population in South-East Asia goes a long way to explain why, in this period, the region received a massive influx of labour from its densely populated neighbours, China and India. It is the formidable presence of Chinese and Indians which is the second important structural feature of the South-East Asian economy to be considered.

It was established in the opening chapter that substantial communities of Chinese and Indians, but also of other minorities, had grown up in South-East Asia, concentrated in the main trading ports, during the boom of the long sixteenth century. The cosmopolitan character of the region's population, certainly of its urban population, was firmly established in that period. However, the influx of migrants in the nineteenth century was on a vastly greater scale, and of a fundamentally different character. The statistical data is rather insecure. With respect to Chinese migration, by far the most substantial stream, estimates of the numbers embarking at ports along the south China coast in this period must be viewed with great caution. Until 1894, emigration was forbidden under Chinese law, with severe punishments ordered for those who ignored the prohibition and for those who assisted them. Of course it was almost impossible to enforce the law. But the important point in this context is that port officials were extremely unlikely to record and report these movements, even when they were aware of them. A further difficulty arises from the fact that there was a high incidence of repeated migration: that is, an individual might journey to South-East Asia a number of times, working out short-term contracts, before finally settling permanently in the region, or indeed returning to his home community in China for good. In these circumstances, the number of embarkations was clearly a poor guide to the scale of permanent migration. In contrast, administrations in South-East Asia, which welcomed, and indeed on many occasions actively assisted immigration, did record landings from China, and elsewhere. But again, repeated migrations confuse the data. And finally, although census data from South-East Asia is clearly an important source in this context, it too presents problems. Apart from the fact that acceptably accurate census enumeration was not achieved in most parts of the region until the second or third decade of the twentieth century, almost insuperable difficulties arise in determining ethnicity accurately in those parts of South-East Asia, and Siam is a particularly strong example, where marriage between immigrant Chinese and the local population was common. Precisely who was Chinese and who was Siamese was near impossible to answer. In fact the question was misdirected. With that firm warning, Table 3.3 presents census data on the Chinese populations in South-East Asia in the early 1930s, slightly beyond the period covered in this chapter.

The statistical data on Indian migration to South-East Asia is firmer. With respect to departures from India, from the late 1830s the British authorities regulated, and therefore recorded, all assisted migration, that is the migration of labourers under contract whose passage was being paid by a recruiter or employer. Moreover, the census identification of Indians in South-East Asia, unlike that of the Chinese, was reasonably straightforward, as relatively few Indian immigrants married outside their community. Burma and the Malay States/Straits Settlements were by far the most important destinations in the region for migrants from South Asia. According to 1931 censuses, the Indian population of Burma (excluding Arakan) was 800,024, that of the Malay States and Straits Settlements, 621,847.

The above figures also give some indication of the distribution of the Chinese and Indian populations in South-East Asia in this period. But more needs to be said. Substantial Chinese

TABLE 3.3
South-East Asia: Ethnic Chinese, c.1930

Country	Population
Burma (1931)	194,000
Siam (1929)	445,000
French Indo-China (1931)	418,000
Malay States and Straits Settlements (1931)	1,704,000
Netherlands East Indies (1930)	1,233,000
Philippines (c.1933)	72,000

Source: Victor Purcell (1965), *The Chinese in Southeast Asia*, 2nd edn., London: Oxford University Press, p. 3.

communities were found in all the countries of the region, concentrated in the urban centres and in rapidly growing rural districts. Even in Burma, way off the main Chinese migration routes and far more important as a destination for Indian migrants, there were almost 200,000 Chinese in the early 1930s. Moreover, as will later be made clear, whatever the numerical size of the community, the Chinese invariably had a much greater economic importance than mere numbers might suggest. At the same time, there were important differences across South-East Asia. First, as noted earlier, in many parts of the region, notably in Siam but also in Cochin-China, the Philippines, and, to a degree, the Netherlands East Indies, the immigrant Chinese achieved a measure of assimilation into the local population. But elsewhere, in the Malay States and Straits Settlements, little intermarriage took place, and the Chinese remained a distinct community. Second, across the region there were obviously major differences in the relative sizes of the immigrant and local populations. The overall demographic impact of large-scale Chinese immigration into the vastness of the Netherlands East Indies was obviously much less than its impact in the far smaller Malay States. In 1930 Chinese accounted for 2 per cent of the population of the Dutch territories, although there were marked concentrations in the main towns and in some rural areas, for example, on the tin island of Bangka and in the tobacco districts of East Sumatra. In contrast, Chinese comprised no less than 33.9 per cent of the population of the Malay States, Penang, and Malacca in 1931, 74.3 per cent of the population of Singapore. Large-scale Indian immigration, on the other hand, was concentrated in just two territories, Burma and the Malay States/ Straits Settlements, although substantial Indian commercial communities were also found elsewhere in South-East Asia, notably Siam and Cochin-China. In 1931 Indians comprised 5.4 per cent of the population of Burma, 14.3 per cent of the population of the Malay States/Straits Settlements. As with the Chinese, there were substantial concentrations of Indians in urban centres. In 1931 almost one-third of all Indians in Burma (excluding Arakan) were in the capital, Rangoon, where they comprised over half the population. Colonial Rangoon was an Indian city.

It is also important to note the great diversity within the streams of Chinese and Indian migrants to South-East Asia in this period. For example, the flood of Chinese migrants, almost all from the southern coastal provinces, embraced a number of dialect groups, of which the most important were the Hokkien, Cantonese,

Hakka, Teochiu, and Hainanese. Commonly one, perhaps two dialects dominated the flow of migrants to a particular territory. The largest element in the Chinese population in the Malay States/Straits Settlements were the Hokkiens, followed by the Cantonese: the majority of the Chinese in Siam were Teochiu. In addition, particular dialect groups were commonly drawn into particular occupations. Teochiu and Hokkien dominated pepper and gambier cultivation in mid-nineteenth century Singapore, Hakka were particularly numerous in the tin district of Kinta in Perak, while a major proportion of the tin miners in southern Siam in the late nineteenth century was Hokkien. The divisions within the stream of Indian migration were still more sharply drawn. Over 90 per cent of the Indian migrants to the Malay States/Straits Settlements in the period from the late eighteenth to the mid-twentieth century were from South India, overwhelmingly Tamils from the south-east districts of Madras Presidency. There was also a modest immigration of Tamils from northern Ceylon. The remaining Indian migrants to the Malayan territories, those from North India, were principally from the Punjab, mostly Sikhs. The majority of Indian migrants to Burma in the late nineteenth century were also from Madras Presidency, but mainly Telegus from the northern districts, although there was also a substantial inflow of Tamils from further south. The other important source of migrants for Burma was Bengal Presidency, mainly Chittagong but also parts of Orissa and Bihar, as well as Calcutta and its surrounding districts. Like the Chinese, particular Indian communities were drawn into particular occupations. Indian labourers on the rubber plantations of the Malay States from the beginning of the twentieth century were overwhelmingly Tamils from South India; Tamils from Ceylon commonly found employment as government clerks; Sikhs were prominent in the police and as night-watchmen; and across the region, the Chettiars, from Madras, were an important force in moneylending.

The streams of Chinese and Indian migrants to South-East Asia were divided in one further important respect, that is, by economic standing. The majority of migrants were impoverished, forced into migration by the harshness of economic conditions at home, lured by the prospect, frequently unfulfilled, of advantage overseas. These migrants were in no position to meet the cost of their passage, which in many cases was therefore paid by a recruiter or by the future employer. A number of different mechanisms were used here. In the second half of the nineteenth century, a few thousand

Indian labourers entered the Malay States/Straits Settlements each year under indenture, that is, under contract to a single employer for a period of between one and three years. The contract was usually a written one but verbal agreements were quite common. Undoubtedly, many migrants signed or nodded in ignorance of the terms or under coercion. Breaches of written contracts, even relatively trivial misdemeanours, were regarded as criminal, not civil, offences. At the end of his contract, the labourer had to repay the cost of his passage and all advances received before he was released. Having been paid extremely low wages, many could not do so, and were therefore reindentured. The recruitment of indentured labour in India for the Malay States/Straits Settlements was brought to an end in 1910.

For most of the colonial period, the single most important mechanism for the recruitment of labour in India for the Malayan territories was through the *kangani*. This accounted for 62.2 per cent of total Indian assisted immigration into the Malay States/Straits Settlements in the period 1844–1938, compared with 13.0 per cent brought in under indenture. The *kangani* was a senior labourer, a foreman, who, having secured the confidence of his plantation manager in the Malay States, was sent back to India to recruit additional workers in his home district, commonly from among his own relations and friends. He was paid a commission on each labourer recruited. On his return to the Malay States, he usually acted as plantation foreman for the labourers he had engaged. The contractual position of these labourers was less harsh than those under indenture. Most importantly, desertion was regarded as a civil, not a criminal, offence. In any event, the labourer had the right to abandon his contract, which was usually a verbal rather than a written agreement, at a month's notice. The peak of *kangani* recruitment came in the 1910s, when, in almost every year, between 50,000 and 80,000 Indian labourers arrived in the Malay States/Straits Settlements. It began to decline in the late 1920s, was suspended in the early 1930s under the impact of the world depression, and formally abolished in 1938.

The main mechanism for recruiting Indian labour for Burma in this period was, in important respects, closely similar to *kangani* recruitment in the Malayan territories. Here it was the *maistry*, the established labourer, who recruited labour gangs in India, organized their passage to Burma, and then acted as overseer of their work on the Rangoon wharves or in the lower delta rice fields. The *maistry*'s earnings came principally from the interest which he charged on his advances to his labour gangs, from the commission paid by the firms to which he supplied labour, and from his manipulation of bulk purchases of steamship tickets. A long-established *maistry* could finance recruitment from his own resources.

The assisted migration of impoverished Chinese to South-East Asia was organized on a rather different basis. In essence, there was no Chinese equivalent of the *maistry/kangani*, the recruiter-foreman, simply because the opposition of the Chinese authorities to assisted migration made it impossible to use open, regulated, recruitment arrangements. Rather the migrant labourer was recruited by a local agent, who directed him into a chain of brokers and coolie shipowners which eventually brought him, at the chain's expense, into a South-East Asian port. In many cases this was either Singapore or Penang, for much of this period the main regional distribution ports for labourers bound ultimately for the Malay States, the Dutch territories of East Sumatra, Bangka, and Belitung, and southern Siam. There the migrant was held in a lodging house until an employer came forward to pay off the costs of his recruitment and passage. The landed immigrant was then tied to that employer, working at low wages until the latter had recovered his outlay. As might be expected, employers used numerous devices to prevent their labourers from absconding before they had worked off their recruitment costs, or indeed to ensure that they had little chance of working themselves clear at all. In some territories, the position of employers was buttressed by fierce labour laws. In the tobacco districts of East Sumatra and on the tin islands of Bangka and Belitung, the penal sanction, that is the treatment of breaches of labour contracts as criminal offences, to be harshly punished, was still in use in the inter-war years.

There is a final point on this particular subject. For the Malay States/Straits Settlements at least, a substantially lower proportion of Chinese than Indian immigrants came on assisted passages. Secure comparisons are extremely difficult to produce, but while in the period 1844–1941, no less than 70 per cent of Indian labour immigration into the Malayan territories was assisted, in 1881 only 36 per cent of Chinese immigrants landed in Penang and Singapore had come on credit-tickets, a mere 12 per cent in 1896. In other words, a clear majority of impoverished Chinese, as well as a substantial minority of the poorest Indians, paid their own passage, either from their own resources or with the help of loans from relatives and friends.

But then, to return to the central theme, by no means all Chinese and Indian migrants were poor, forced from their homeland by economic failure. A significant minority in both communities possessed considerable economic standing, and migrated not as a result of material distress at home but in order to exploit the greater commercial or employment opportunities available to them in South-East Asia. Prominent in that minority were traders and merchants, moneylenders, artisans and, in the Indian migrations to Burma and the Malayan territories, government employees. Many individuals, particularly traders and merchants, constantly moved back and forth between China or India and South-East Asia, reinforcing the commercial and financial networks which in this period increasingly bound the region to South Asia and to East Asia. But eventually, perhaps for the majority, the principal focus of their livelihood, their home, firmly shifted to South-East Asia, and their migration was completed.

The preceding paragraphs have indicated, almost in passing, the principal occupations taken by the immigrant Chinese and Indians in colonial South-East Asia. But given the importance of those communities in shaping the modern economic experience of the region, that information must now be firmly restated. The large majority of immigrants worked as labourers, as coolies, almost their sole economic asset being their capacity for physical toil. Many worked directly in agriculture or in mining. Chinese provided the labour force for the tin mines in the Malay States and on the Indies islands of Bangka and Belitung, and also, particularly in their early decades, for the tobacco plantations of East Sumatra. Indians were prominent as tappers on the Malayan rubber estates and in agricultural gangs in the rice delta of Lower Burma. But larger numbers of immigrant labourers were found, not directly in agriculture or mining, but in the processing and handling of primary commodities, as well as in construction work. Across much of the region, immigrant labour gangs, principally Chinese, built the physical infrastructure that was essential for the functioning of the export economy and modern administration—canal, rail, and road networks, docks, and wharves, and the imposing official and commercial buildings which came to dominate the major urban centres. In commodity processing, Chinese laboured, for example, in the rice mills and teak mills of Bangkok, in the rice mills of Saigon–Cholon, and with tin smelters in the Malay States and Straits Settlements. Indians provided the labour for the Rangoon teak mills and rice mills. In each of the region's great ports—

Singapore, Batavia, Rangoon, Saigon–Cholon, Bangkok—Chinese or Indian labour gangs moved vast consignments of primary commodities, commonly in sacks, panniers, or bales, carried across the shoulders or slung across the back, from inland barge or freight wagon, into godowns, across wharves, into lighters, and down into the holds of ocean steamers, returning to unload the latter of their consignments of imported manufactures. In brief, in many important sectors of the economy, the Chinese and Indian immigrant made good the shortage of indigenous labour.

Many immigrants, particularly among the Chinese, found employment in South-East Asia as urban artisans, of various levels of skill and refinement. In a book first published in 1879, *The Manners and Customs of the Chinese of the Straits Settlements*, J. D. Vaughan, a long-term resident, produced a simple list of Chinese occupations in the Straits. The following *brief* extract vividly conveys the extraordinary range.

The Chinese are everything ... bakers, millers, barbers, blacksmiths, boatmen, bookbinders, boot and shoemakers, brickmakers, carpenters, cabinet makers, carriage builders, cartwrights, cart and hackney carriage drivers, charcoal burners and sellers, coffinmakers, confectioners ... painters, paper lantern makers ... soap boilers, stone cutters, sugar boilers, tailors, tanners.... (Vaughan, 1971: 15.)

Finally, across South-East Asia, Chinese and Indians had a high profile in trade and in moneylending. Three points need to be emphasized. Although these immigrant commercial communities were very prominent in the region's urban centres, Chinese or Indian traders and moneylenders were also found in virtually every rural district of economic importance, even deep in the interior. They were ubiquitous. Second, Chinese and Indian traders and moneylenders did not operate as individuals. Indeed, to a considerable degree, the commercial influence of the Chinese and Indians in South-East Asia in this period was built on the fact that each business concern was part of a network that commonly extended across the region, as well as back to India or China. The Chinese rice exporter in Bangkok almost invariably had close ties, commonly kinship ties, with importers in Singapore and Hong Kong. The business of each Chettiar firm in Burma was sustained by caste and kinship networks that extended back to Madras. Third, it was common for Chinese businesses, but not Indian, to develop diverse interests. The middleman, dealing in rice, strengthened his commercial position by making loans to the cultivators who sold to him: the export–import merchant took a major stake in a revenue-farm syndicate: and later, the merchant–revenue farmer moved into banking or manufacturing. The final part of this chapter will return to the Chinese and Indian commercial communities, to explore their relationship with Western enterprise in South-East Asia in this period, for in that relationship resides one of the central influences that shaped the modern economic history of the region.

The final important element in South-East Asia's population in this period were the Europeans. In fact there is a temptation to see the Europeans as *the* important element, as standing at the very centre of the economic changes which took place in South-East Asia from the middle decades of the nineteenth century. After all, the root cause of those changes clearly lay in Europe, in that it was Europe's industrial revolution which created the vast demands for the primary commodities—the tin, rubber, abaca, rice, tobacco, coffee, and sugar—which were at the heart of South-East Asia's economic transformation. The instruments that secured the closer integration of the region into the economy of the Western world in the nineteenth century—the shipping companies, trading houses, and banks—were overwhelmingly in European hands. European-owned estates, mines, and mills were commonly to the fore in production and processing. And behind Western commercial interests stood Western colonial administrations. Europeans occupied the commanding heights of the South-East Asian economy in the late nineteenth and early twentieth century. Or so it seems.

The reality was more complex. It should first be noted that, even in the late colonial period, Europeans formed only an extremely small proportion of the population. The largest European community in South-East Asia, in absolute terms and possibly in relative terms as well, was in the Netherlands East Indies. But in 1920 there were just under 170,000 Europeans in the Dutch colony, a mere 0.34 per cent of the population. In Burma, the European community towards the end of the 1930s numbered less than 10,000, roughly 0.07 per cent of the total. And in the Federated Malay States, in 1921 the European population stood at a mere 5,686. The occupational breakdown of that last figure is particularly interesting. Of the total, 3,200 were employed men, of whom 1,493 worked in agriculture (the vast majority as rubber estate managers), 225 in mining (tin), and 349 in commerce and finance. Within that last group, 173 were proprietors and managers of businesses, and 32 were bankers or bank officers. And yet, despite such small numbers, the Federated Malay States accounted for around half of the world's output of tin and rubber, Western capital occupied a dominant position in Malayan production of both commodities, and Malayan exports went principally to markets in the West.

The argument which is being developed here is that Western commercial power in South-East Asia in this period rested to a considerable degree on effective collaboration with immigrant Asian, principally Chinese and then Indian, intermediaries. The clear majority of Western commercial and financial concerns in South-East Asia were located in the urban centres. For a number of reasons, they rarely established a physical presence in the rural hinterlands, which were, of course, the source of the region's vastly increased production. The heavy overhead costs of Western businesses—high salaries for expatriate European staff and imposing offices and residential accommodation—ruled out the location of branches in distant interiors where the aggregate volume of business was usually relatively modest and where each transaction, commonly with an individual cultivator, was very small. More importantly, European staff did not possess the detailed knowledge of either local commercial and agricultural conditions or the circumstances and standing of local cultivators to conduct business at that level. Few, if any, had an easy command of local languages, in particular of the highly colloquial variants; working for an international company, the European employee was frequently being reassigned to a new, unfamiliar area; and, obviously, in local society, Europeans were irredeemably alien. In other words, at the local level, Chinese and Indian commercial and financial enterprise had all the advantages: overhead costs were usually extremely low; long residence gave individuals an intimate knowledge of local conditions and local inhabitants; most spoke local languages; many married locally.

In brief, across much of rural South-East Asia in the period from the mid-nineteenth century, Chinese and Indian networks provided the crucial link between the local cultivator and the wider economy. In the rice plain of central Siam, it was the small Chinese trader who purchased the crop from the cultivator and brought it, perhaps through further intermediaries, down to Bangkok for sale to the large European or Chinese miller and exporter. In the Malay States at the beginning of the twentieth century, smallholder producers of rubber usually sold their output to a local Chinese dealer, the entry point to a collection network that would end, as far as South-East Asia was concerned, with the large European export firms in the Straits Settlements. There was also an important trade in the opposite direction. In Singapore, Chinese and Indian traders took delivery of consignments of Western consumer manufactures, of which the most important was cotton textiles, from the port's European import merchants. The consignments were then broken up, and distributed down through networks of provincial and local dealers, for eventual sale in stores and by itinerant traders in even the most distant rural district. There were, finally, comparable, and comparably important, links between local Chinese and Indian moneylender networks and the major Western banks in the region. For example, Chettiar firms in Burma and in the Malay States borrowed extensively in this period from, notably, the Chartered Bank of India, Australia, and China, and from the Mercantile Bank, to relend, at a higher rate of interest, either to local cultivators or to indigenous money-lenders, who themselves lent on to the cultivator.

In other words, of central importance in tying the rural districts of South-East Asia into the Western economy from the middle of the nineteenth century was the creation of a mutual dependence between local European enterprise, as extensions of the trading and financial networks of the West, and Chinese and Indian commercial and financial intermediaries, who penetrated deep into the local economy. It is important to emphasize that this was not an unchanging dependence. Over time, substantial realignments took place in the relationship between the immigrant Asian and the European commercial–financial communities. In the case of the Chinese, this also commonly involved realignments in their relationship with the state. Indeed those realignments were to be a central theme in the economic experience of South-East Asia for much of the twentieth century, as the following two chapters will begin to explore.

SUGGESTED READING

A guide to the literature on the demography of nineteenth-century South-East Asia appears at the end of Chapter 6, to the literature on the economic role of the Chinese and Indian immigrant communities, at the ends of Chapters 11 and 13. For the latter subject, a few further references need to be included here. For a long period, the standard text on the Chinese in South-East Asia was Victor Purcell (1965), *The Chinese in Southeast Asia*, 2nd edn.,

London: Oxford University Press. First published in 1951, this
substantial volume, over 600 pages, remains a highly informative
source. J. D. Vaughan, *The Manners and Customs of the Chinese of
the Straits Settlements*, first published in 1879, was republished by
Oxford University Press in Kuala Lumpur in 1971. For an excellent study of the Chinese community on the tin island of Bangka
from the early eighteenth century, see Mary F. Somers Heidhues
(1992), *Bangka Tin and Mentok Pepper: Chinese Settlement on an
Indonesian Island*, Singapore: Institute of Southeast Asian Studies.
The export of Indian labour overseas in the nineteenth century, to
many parts of the world, not simply South-East Asia, is author-
itatively treated by Hugh Tinker (1974), *A New System of Slavery:
The Export of Indian Labour Overseas, 1830–1920*, London: Oxford
University Press. The economic role of the Indians in colonial
Burma is discussed, in a rather partisan manner, in Nalini Ranjan
Chakravarti (1971), *The Indian Minority in Burma: The Rise and
Decline of an Immigrant Community*, London: Oxford University
Press. For the Indians in colonial Malaya, see Kernial Singh
Sandhu (1969), *Indians in Malaya: Some Aspects of Their Immigra-
tion and Settlement (1786–1957)*, Cambridge: Cambridge Univer-
sity Press, and Sinnappah Arasaratnam (1979), *Indians in Malaysia
and Singapore*, rev. edn., Kuala Lumpur: Oxford University Press.
For a pioneering attempt to study a European community in colo-
nial South-East Asia, in much the same way as the Chinese and
Indian minorities have been studied, see John G. Butcher (1979),
*The British in Malaya, 1880–1941: The Social History of a European
Community in Colonial South-East Asia*, Kuala Lumpur: Oxford
University Press.

4
Economic Change, 1920–1950

AROUND 1920, after close to a century of the most impressive expansion in commodity production and trade, although of course not without reverses and failures, South-East Asia entered three decades of economic turmoil. The 1920s and 1930s saw the region caught in the violent oscillations of the world economy that marked those decades, notably the severe depression which took hold at the end of the 1920s. In the war years, 1941–5, South-East Asia was completely cut off from the Western economies, crucially important as markets for the region's primary exports, and as sources of both investment capital and manufactured imports. Moreover, the war saw the physical destruction of production capacity and infrastructure throughout much of the region. After the war, although economic rehabilitation was quickly underway in most of South-East Asia, there was further destruction and dislocation in Indo-China and the Netherlands East Indies where the French and Dutch, determined to re-establish their pre-war possession, met fierce local resistance. In short, these were difficult decades. But they also saw the emergence of many of the central conditions that were to underpin the dramatic economic changes of the post-war, post-independence period.

The Inter-war Decades

The volatility of commodity trade and production in South-East Asia in the 1920s and 1930s is vividly captured by the extraordinary fluctuations in the price of rubber, by this time one of the region's most important exports. The rubber price had hit its peak just before the First World War, when demand was rising rapidly but the vast new planting which had taken place, in the Malay States, from around 1905 had still to mature. As that acreage came into production, the price fell, standard quality rubber on the

London market dropping from an average of 8/9 per pound in 1910 to between 2/- and 3/- per pound in the years 1913–19. A further, dramatic fall took place from 1920, shown in Figure 4.1, as the post-war reconstruction boom in the industrial economies broke. By 1922, with the rubber price in London well under 1/- per pound, there was widespread doubt whether the European plantations in the Malay States, which had enjoyed extremely good profits just a few years earlier, could survive in the long term. In November of that year, the British government introduced restriction on rubber exports from its producing territories, that is the Malay States and Ceylon. Prices then recovered, somewhat erratically, partly under the impact of the Stevenson restriction scheme, as it was known, but also as a result of marked growth in world consumption of rubber, driven largely by a major economic boom

FIGURE 4.1

Average Price of Standard Quality Rubber on the London Market, 1920–1940[a]

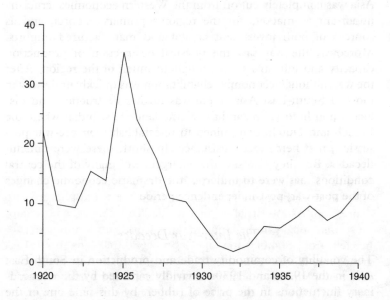

Source: Calculated from John H. Drabble (1991), *Malayan Rubber: The Interwar Years*, London: Macmillan, pp. 306–7.

[a]Price in old pence per pound.

in the United States which was sustained until the closing years of the 1920s. It is important to note, however, that in two important respects the Stevenson restriction increased the volatility of the world rubber market. First, in the opening years, miscalculations in the operation of the scheme led world rubber stocks to fall well below what the market saw as a normal level. With consumption rising strongly, notably in the United States, buyers began to fear a rubber shortage, panicked, and urgently increased their purchases. As a result, in 1925 the price soared far above the scheme's pivotal level, until more generous export quotas brought more rubber on to the market. More importantly, by raising prices, Stevenson encouraged a major wave of new planting in the Netherlands East Indies, which of course lay outside the British restriction scheme, greatly exacerbating what was now clearly a long-term problem of overproduction. Official estimates indicate that between 1924 and 1929, native producers in the outer territories of the Dutch colony planted some 1.5 million acres with rubber, although it is possible that the actual figure was more than twice that amount.

The Stevenson scheme was abandoned in November 1928, as the British authorities came to accept that the restriction of exports from the Malay States and Ceylon alone could no longer have a decisive influence on the world rubber market, indeed that it was merely handing the commercial advantage to unrestricted rival producers, principally the Netherlands East Indies. As restriction ended, the rubber market was hit by three blows which drove the price down to extremely low levels. First, released from restriction, Malayan exports soared, from 294,446 tons in 1928 to 455,545 tons in 1929. Second, the extensive new planting which had taken place in the Netherlands East Indies in the 1920s, under the stimulus of higher prices, began to come into production. Exports from the Dutch territory rose from 90 678 metric tons in 1920 to 301 441 metric tons in 1929. And finally, the world plunged into depression. As industrial activity in the West contracted, perhaps most dramatically in the United States, world consumption of rubber fell, from 804,000 tons in 1929 to 680,000 tons in 1931. A great surge of exports at the end of the 1920s, the near prospect of vast new plantings reaching maturity, declining world consumption, and soaring stocks, put the price on the floor. At its lowest point, in 1932, the price of standard quality rubber on the London market was less than one per cent of its peak in 1910.

With the beginnings of recovery in the industrial economies, the fall in world consumption of rubber was halted. Indeed by 1933 consumption had climbed slightly above the pre-depression peak of 1929. The price now edged off the floor. This was sufficient to encourage a major increase in tapping by smallholders in the Malay States and the Netherlands East Indies in late 1933 and early 1934, although the price was still too low for many plantations to tap at a profit. Fearing that the burgeoning smallholder sector, whose production capacity, although huge, was near impossible to gauge precisely, would now destabilize the market, the British and Dutch governments, with the plantation interests in close attendance, returned to restriction. The International Rubber Regulation Agreement (IRRA) came into force in June 1934. It was considerably more effective than the Stevenson scheme. Most importantly, the IRRA was comprehensive, the participating territories being the Malay States, North Borneo, Sarawak, Ceylon, India, and Burma, on the British side, together with the Netherlands East Indies, French Indo-China, and Siam. Together they accounted for 98.7 per cent of world rubber exports in 1934. In addition the IRRA recognized that production capacity in the industry was now running far ahead of current consumption, and indeed that a rise in price secured by restricting exports was almost certain to encourage still further expansion. Therefore the Agreement included a ban on new planting, and limited replanting to 20 per cent of the existing planted area. A renewed agreement, in 1938, allowed for new planting equivalent to 5 per cent of the existing planted area, and removed all restrictions on replanting. Finally, the calculation of quarterly export quotas was conducted in a considerably more flexible manner by the International Rubber Regulation Committee than had been the case with the Stevenson scheme in the 1920s. Thus the period of the IRRA saw a sustained rise in the world price of rubber, interrupted only in 1938 when a sharp recession in the industrial economies drove down consumption, and there was a marked rise in the level of world rubber stocks.

Dominating these two volatile decades was, of course, the collapse of the late 1920s and early 1930s, the Great Depression. This is clearly evident in the behaviour of the rubber price (see Figure 4.1), but in fact rubber's descent was matched by almost all the region's major commodity exports, as Table 4.1 demonstrates. The collapse in export values was indeed dramatic. Yet the impact of the depression crisis on the economies of South-East Asia was far more complex, and less crippling, than the devastating figures

TABLE 4.1

South-East Asia: Commodity Exports in the Great Depression
(1932 figures as a percentage of 1928 figures)

Commodity (Country)	Value	Volume
Rubber (Malay States)	24	141
Rubber (Netherlands East Indies)	12	88
Tin (Malay States)	29	45
Tin (Netherlands East Indies)	20	44
Sugar (Netherlands East Indies)	26	59
Coffee (Netherlands East Indies)	43	99
Rice (Siam)	54	113
Abaca (The Philippines)	19	61

Sources: Calculated from Lim Chong-Yah (1969), *Economic Development of Modern Malaya*, Kuala Lumpur: Oxford University Press, pp. 319 and 325; John H. Drabble (1991), *Malayan Rubber: The Interwar Years*, London: Macmillan, p. 309; *Changing Economy in Indonesia: A Selection of Statistical Source Material from the Early 19th Century up to 1940* (General Editor: P. Boomgaard), Vol. 12a, 1991, *General Trade Statistics, 1822–1940*, edited by W. L. Korthals Altes, Amsterdam: Royal Tropical Institute, pp. 161–4; David Feeny (1982), *The Political Economy of Productivity: Thai Agricultural Development, 1880–1975*, Vancouver: University of British Columbia Press, pp. 128–9; Norman G. Owen (1984), *Prosperity without Progress: Manila Hemp and Material Life in the Colonial Philippines*, Berkeley: University of California Press, p. 263.

above might suggest. A full chapter in this book, Chapter 15, is devoted to this subject. Although it makes little sense to probe too deeply here, the main lines of that later argument need to be stated. There are three main points.

First, the crisis in primary production and trade in South-East Asia in the late 1920s and early 1930s was not exclusively of external origin, not simply the result of the collapse in international demand as the industrial economies plunged into depression. There were also internal causes. First, for a number of the region's most important primary exports, including rubber and sugar, production was now running well ahead of current consumption. It was also in this period that in many parts of South-East Asia, after half a century or more of rapid extension of the area under cultivation, the open land frontier began to close. A physical limit was being reached. This had an important impact on agrarian structures and conditions. In some of the rice districts of mainland South-East Asia, cultivators who still sought to expand production were now increasingly driven to clear more marginal land, which commonly implied a decline in average yield per acre and in the cultivator's income. At the same time, as uncleared prime land became increasingly hard to locate, land prices and rents rose, forcing marginal owner-cultivators into tenancy, and many tenants into harsher tenancy arrangements or into wage labour. In summary, in many parts of rural South-East Asia, the inter-war decades were marked by an internal agrarian crisis of some severity, quite distinct from the crisis in the world economy.

Second, the economic experience of South-East Asia during the depression crisis was remarkably diverse. That diversity is explored in Chapter 15, but a number of the more dramatic contrasts can be noted here. There were cases in which production of the same primary export took sharply divergent paths in different territories. Thus in the early 1930s, Philippine sugar exports soared, in both value and volume, while Java's sugar exports collapsed. The economic distress experienced in the rice districts of Lower Burma in this period, measured by the rate of land alienation as a result of debt foreclosure, was substantially greater than that experienced in the rice districts of central Siam. There were also, apparently, major differences in the economic fortunes of the different classes of cultivator, although in the present state of research, the details are not fully clear. Michael Adas (1974) suggests that in the Burma Delta, the crisis of the early 1930s was felt most severely by the tenant cultivator, while Norman Owen (1989) argues that in Bikol, it was the smallholder who was most vulnerable. Both are agreed, however, that the landless labourer may have lost relatively little: and, most interestingly, that the major landowner, far from suffering, commonly used the depression crisis to improve his socio-economic position. It is also possible that, in general, urban populations were less severely hit by the crisis than rural-dwellers. It is clear, for example, that Manila's substantial population of government officials, teachers, and middle-class pensioners, whose salaries were left untouched or cut only slightly, enjoyed a very substantial increase in real income as prices collapsed. In brief, the crisis of the late 1920s and early 1930s appears to have caused a significant redistribution of wealth and socio-economic power within both rural and urban South-East Asia, but also possibly between them.

The final argument is that even in those parts of rural South-East Asia most severely hit by the depression crisis, the deterioration in economic conditions may well have been relatively modest. In other words, faced with a sharp drop in money income as commodity prices collapsed, rural populations, even those heavily committed to market production, could find a number of ways in which to defend their material circumstances. To a considerable extent, independent cultivators, but also plantation and mine labourers, could switch from production for the market, to establish or expand subsistence cultivation for their own consumption. In addition, rural populations in many parts of South-East Asia were able to evade or repulse at least part of the tax demands of the state, as well as rent and debt payments due to landowners and moneylenders. In fact, it was not uncommon for governments, recognizing the potentially difficult circumstances of rural populations facing a sharp drop in money income, to grant tax remissions, and many landowners and moneylenders may similarly have thought it prudent not to press their claims too harshly. And finally, in much of rural, and urban, South-East Asia, real incomes were protected during the depression crisis by heavy imports of cheap Japanese manufactures, which pushed aside many long-established, more expensive Western goods. While it is rather difficult to provide firm statistical data to sustain the view that the depression crisis, in general, inflicted only limited damage on the material circumstances of the indigenous populations of the region, some support can be found in the figures in Table 4.2.

TABLE 4.2

Netherlands East Indies: Real Per Capita Income of the Indigenous Population, 1921–1939 (1929=100)

Year	Per Capita Income	Year	Per Capita Income
1921	92	1931	96
1922	96	1932	95
1923	94	1933	94
1924	97	1934	93
1925	99	1935	95
1926	98	1936	95
1927	104	1937	103
1928	105	1938	103
1929	100	1939	107
1930	98		

Source: *Changing Economy in Indonesia: A Selection of Statistical Source Material from the Early 19th Century up to 1940*, Vol. 5, 1979, *National Income*, initiated by W. M. F. Mansvelt, re-edited and continued by P. Creutzberg, The Hague: Martinus Nijhoff, p. 81.

A brief account of economic change in South-East Asia in the inter-war decades will almost inevitably, as here, concentrate on the volatility of primary production and trade, focusing in particular on the depression crisis. But those decades also saw important changes in the structure of the South-East Asian economies which, if perhaps less immediately visible, were undoubtedly of greater long-term significance. Four will be noted here, of which the first three were, in important respects, closely related.

The first was a marked expansion in modern industry, not simply the initial processing of agricultural and mineral commodities for export but also, more significantly, the manufacture of finished consumer goods, usually for the domestic market but on occasions for export as well. Prominent here were building materials, foodstuffs and beverages, and textiles. A full chapter in this book, Chapter 14, is devoted to South-East Asia's early industrialization.

Second, the inter-war decades, more broadly the period from the beginning of the twentieth century, saw important changes in the economic interests of the Chinese entrepreneurial class in South-East Asia. A central element in that process was the swift abolition of revenue farming in all parts of the region around the turn of the century. As was explained in Chapter 1, the revenue farm was an arrangement in which government granted a private individual or syndicate the monopoly right to collect a specific tax, sell a particular article of consumption (notably opium and liquor in this context), or provide a specific service (the operation of gambling dens, or of slaughter houses), in a designated territory for a fixed term (usually three years). The individual or syndicate, that is the revenue farmer, paid the government for that monopoly right: commonly he bid for it at auction. The income over and above that payment which the farmer received from the collection of the tax or from the sale, for example, of opium, was his profit. In the second half of the nineteenth century, the revenue farm was an extremely important instrument of state revenue collection in all parts of South-East Asia, principally because the state did not yet possess the administrative structures to collect all taxes itself. But the important point in the present context is that the vast majority of revenue farmers and farming syndicates were Chinese, and indeed, that for Chinese entrepreneurs throughout South-East Asia, the revenue farms were a source not only of great profit but also of wider commercial power and leverage. (See Chapter 13 for an exploration of this last point.)

Yet this extremely important fiscal and commercial instrument was dismantled in all parts of South-East Asia in a remarkably brief period around the turn of the century. The opium farm, to take a prominent example, was abolished in Cochin-China in 1883, in Java and Madura from 1894, in the outer territories of the Netherlands East Indies from around 1905, in Siam from 1907, and in the Straits Settlements in 1909, in each case to be replaced by state administration of the revenue. No significant revenue farm was left in South-East Asia after 1920. While the particular circumstances which led to abolition obviously differed from case to case, a number of common factors were clearly at work. Most importantly, by the late nineteenth and early twentieth century, government administrative structures, in almost all parts of the region, were much stronger than they had been just a few decades earlier. This meant not simply that the state could now consider taking over the administration of revenues which previously it had been forced to farm out, but also that it now increasingly saw the farms, which as well as controlling the state's revenue income had in addition often assumed responsibility for local administration, as an affront to its authority. Abolition was also frequently driven by a wish, arising from a variety of reasons, to strike at a bastion of Chinese commercial power. In the case of the opium, liquor, and gambling farms, abolition sometimes reflected pressure from both within and outside government to remove trade in that vice from private hands, with opium, perhaps as a prelude to complete suppression. Finally, by the first decade of the twentieth century, many of the region's most prominent revenue-farming syndicates were in serious financial difficulties. They had been driven to collapse, paradoxically, by the fact that the potential profits to be made from the major farms were now huge, a reflection of the region's continuing rapid economic growth: for as the potential profits rose, the capital resources required to bid for a contract also increased, and, perhaps more importantly, so too did the ferocity with which the syndicates fought for control of the most lucrative farms. Syndicates now resorted to destructive, often illegal, manoeuvres to defeat rivals, which only invited retaliation. Unstable farming syndicates implied an unacceptable threat to the security of the state's revenues.

Deprived of the revenue farms, but also threatened by the advance of Western capital into a number of its other economic bastions, for example, in the Malay States, the mining and smelting of tin (see Chapter 13), the Chinese entrepreneurial class sought new fields. Thus the opening decades of the twentieth century saw the Chinese in South-East Asia invest, for the first time, in modern banking. Between 1903 and 1932, no less than 15 Chinese banks were established in the Malay States and Straits Settlements, 13 in Siam, and 5 in the Netherlands East Indies. There are many examples of the movement of Chinese capital from revenue farming into banking. The 1907 Penang opium farm syndicate was closely involved in the Deli Bank of North Sumatra, established in that year: two senior partners in the 1907–9 Singapore and affiliated farms had taken a leading role in the establishment of the Kwong Yik Bank in 1903. Considerable Chinese capital also went into steamship companies, including the Eastern Shipping Company (1907), in which the Khaw family of Penang and southern Siam, with interests not only in revenue farming but also commercial insurance, tin mining, and tin smelting, was particularly prominent; and the shipping concerns of Oei Tiong Ham, the last and most wealthy of Java's opium farmers, acquired from the first years of the twentieth century. And finally, Chinese capital moved into manufacturing. Prominent here was Tan Kah-kee in Singapore, whose business interests had initially been built on the import of rice from mainland South-East Asia. During the 1920s and early 1930s, he was widely acknowledged to be the leading industrialist in Singapore and the Malay States, being involved in the manufacture of biscuits, bricks, soap, leather, cosmetics, toothpaste, and, most importantly, rubber goods, including canvas rubber shoes and soles, tyres and tubes.

Not all these ventures were successful. Indeed the failure rate among Chinese banks, steamship lines, and manufacturing concerns in these decades was notably high. The Kwong Yik Bank failed in 1913, the Deli Bank in 1921; the last of the Khaw ships were sold to the Straits Steamship Company in 1922; Tan Kah-kee's businesses failed in 1934. The reasons were complex, but excessive diversity of commercial interests, together with serious weaknesses in financial and managerial control within the Chinese family business, may have been part of the problem. Yet even with the failures, it is clear that a major realignment of Chinese capitalist endeavour was taking place.

Third, the inter-war period saw a marked increase in the level of government intervention in the economy. In part this was an immediate response to the economic problems brought by those troubled decades. Thus government was forced to take a central role in the negotiation and implementation of the international commodity restriction agreements, for rubber, tin, and sugar, which were erected in this period. Implementation of rubber restriction in the 1920s and 1930s required the Malay States administrations to assess the production capacity and ensure restriction of output for each producer, in both the estate and smallholder sectors. When the Netherlands East Indies became party to the Chadbourne International Sugar Agreement in 1931, which sought to reduce world production, the Dutch administration undertook to secure a very substantial contraction in the colony's sugar acreage. Or again, when a great wave of cheap Japanese manufactures hit South-East Asia in the early 1930s, threatening the position of many Western imports, a number of governments felt compelled to intervene. From mid-1933, the Netherlands East Indies administration, acting under a Crisis Import Ordinance, imposed quotas, allocated by country of origin, on a wide range of imports, including cement, beer, textiles, pottery, bicycle and car tyres, and electric lamps. Even the Straits Settlements, whose prosperity had long been built upon a proud adherence to the principles of free trade, in mid-1934 imposed quotas on the import of foreign cotton and rayon piece goods for local consumption.

But increased government intervention also had more deepseated origins. It commonly reflected a largely new acceptance on the part of government that fundamental, long-term economic problems, now perhaps more clearly in focus, could be solved only by state action. What those problems were perceived to be differed from country to country. In the second half of the 1930s, the Philippines administration, having secured internal self-government in 1935 with a promise of full independence in 1946, was deeply concerned that the country's primary export trade would be devastated when, on independence, it lost privileged access to the huge American market. It therefore embarked on a substantial programme of import-substitution industrialization, in which a government company, the National Development Company, took a leading role. An industrialization drive in Siam in the 1930s, which saw the state invest in the manufacture of paper, textiles, spirits, and cigarettes, as well as take a substantial interest in rice milling, was largely inspired by a determination to reduce the domination of important sectors of the economy by foreign, in particular Chinese, interests. In the Netherlands East Indies, by the mid-1930s it was clear to important elements within the colonial administration that if the material condition of the local population was to be improved, a public concern of the Dutch from the beginning of the twentieth century, the colony's industrial base would need to be greatly strengthened, and, moreover, that this could be achieved only by substantial state action. Consequently, in a major break with previous economic management, the Dutch administration not only regulated imports to protect new domestic manufacturing but also took powers to regulate local industrial production, even to the point where government officials had discretion to control capacity and, in some cases, fix prices. The state was now a major player indeed.

The inter-war decades also saw, as briefly indicated above, a major expansion in Japan's economic interests in South-East Asia. Its most dramatic aspect was a sharp increase in imports of inexpensive Japanese manufactures, principally textiles, reflecting, at heart, the final emergence of Japan as a major industrial power around the time of the First World War, but enormously stimulated by the heavy devaluation of the yen in late 1931. The Netherlands East Indies was a particularly important market for Japanese manufactures. While Japan had accounted for just 3.4 per cent of the Dutch colony's imports in 1915, only 10.4 per cent in 1929, in 1934 the figure was 31.9 per cent, exceeding the shares of the Netherlands, Britain, and the United States combined. The previous year Japan had accounted for no less than 75 per cent of cotton piece goods imports into the Netherlands East Indies. The expansion of Japan's economic interests in South-East Asia also involved substantial investment in rubber plantations, iron ore mines, timber concessions, oil fields, and in commercial fishing. Major gains were made by Japanese shipping lines in a number of the region's most valuable routes while Japanese banks, import and export houses, wholesale merchants and retailers, even hotels and restaurants, established a substantial presence in many parts of South-East Asia in this period. From the mid-1930s, however, Japan's economic position in the region weakened somewhat, in part because the colonial powers, certainly the Dutch, mounted a vigorous defence of Western interests against the Japanese commercial advance, but also because, with international tension increasing, and then the outbreak of war with China in 1937, the Japanese economy was strongly directed towards military production. In 1939, Japan's share in the imports of the Netherlands East Indies had fallen to 17.8 per cent. But even with these reverses, an important structural change had clearly taken place. In the post-war decades, Japan was to establish itself as the dominant foreign economic power in South-East Asia.

The War Years

But what Japan was later to secure by peaceful means, it now sought by force. On 8 December 1941, as the Japanese attacked the American naval base at Pearl Harbor, they simultaneously struck against installations in the Philippines, Singapore, the Malay States, and Siam. The Japanese military advance was extraordinarily rapid. Manila fell on 2 January 1942, Kuala Lumpur on 11 January, Singapore on 15 February, Rangoon on 7 March, and the entire Netherlands East Indies on 9 March. Only the colonial administration in Indo-China remained in place, the French sharing power with the Japanese until dismissed by a Japanese coup in March 1945.

For most South-East Asians, the three years or more of Japanese rule brought much greater economic hardship than the crisis of the late 1920s and early 1930s. In many parts of the region, notably Burma and the Philippines, there was large-scale destruction of production capacity and communication infrastructures. When Japanese troops landed in Luzon, General Douglas MacArthur ordered the destruction of railway lines and rolling stock, bridges, and storage tanks. Some three years later, the retreating Japanese blew up most of the large buildings in Manila, together with the capital's dock piers, bridges, power stations, warehouses, and factories. Eighty per cent of the land area of Manila was in ruins. As the Japanese advanced into Burma in early 1942, the retreating British sabotaged the large oil fields worked by the Burmah Oil Company. By 1944, Allied bombing had brought Burma's railway network to a virtual standstill. But even where physical destruction was slight, the disruption of economic life could still be immense. The removal of the colonial powers broke all ties between South-East Asia and the Western economies. The principal markets for the region's commodity exports, and the major sources of its imports of manufactures, were all lost. Inflows of Western capital disappeared. And many among the region's European business community, the plantation and mine managers, the bankers, traders, and merchants, caught by the speed of the Japanese military advance, were interned. In conditions of total war, the Japanese could not fill this void. Acute shortages of shipping space, as Allied submarines struck, meant that it was virtually impossible for the Japanese to transport the region's exports in bulk to new markets within their empire. The commitment of the Japanese domestic economy to the production of war materials made it impossible for Japan to supply South-East Asia with the consumer manufactures that would secure the local population's involvement in commodity production. Large-scale disruption also occurred when the Japanese authorities requisitioned rice and other commodities, and forcibly conscripted labour for construction work. Across the region, monetary systems were in collapse, as the Japanese brought huge volumes of occupation currency into circulation. At its worst, the disruption of the local economy had truly devastating consequences. In northern Vietnam, the forcible conversion of large areas of land from rice to jute, and the requisitioning of rice supplies for the war effort, together with American bombing of the railway lines from the south, preventing the shipment of relief food from Cochin-China, brought a famine in 1944–5 that claimed perhaps 2 million lives.

But despite the economic hardship and devastation, it is difficult to see the brief period of Japanese rule as an important turning point in the modern economic history of South-East Asia. The decisive structural changes which took place in the first half of the twentieth century, and which were to dominate the second, that is the creation of modern industry, the restructuring of the economic role and ambitions of the Chinese entrepreneurial class, the increase in the power of the state, and the emergence of Japan as a major economic power in South-East Asia, were, as has been shown, firmly established in the 1920s and 1930s, well before the Japanese military advance in late 1941. In only one respect may the period of Japanese rule have had an important impact on long-term economic change, and then only in parts of the region, and only indirectly. For Indo-China and the Netherlands East Indies, the Japanese Occupation made it almost inevitable that the process of decolonization would be violent. In other words, it condemned those territories to continued war and fierce political instability. After 1945 there was to be a sharp divergence in the economic experiences of the different parts of South-East Asia. Here was an important element in that divergence.

SUGGESTED READING

An introduction to the literature on the inter-war crisis appears at the end of Chapter 15. One further reference should be included here: a calculation of the national income of the Netherlands East Indies between 1921 and 1939, undertaken in the early 1940s by J. J. Polak, was subsequently published in *Changing Economy in Indonesia: A Selection of Statistical Source Material from the Early Nineteenth Century up to 1940*, Vol. 5, 1979, *National Income*, initiated by W. M. F. Mansvelt, re-edited and continued by P. Creutzberg, The Hague: Martinus Nijhoff. Chapter 14 of the present book includes a guide to the literature on early industrialization.

The importance of control of the revenue farms for Chinese business interests in South-East Asia through to the early twentieth century, and the restructuring of those interests on the demise of the farms, are thoroughly explored in John Butcher and Howard Dick (eds.) (1993), *The Rise and Fall of Revenue Farming: Business Élites and the Emergence of the Modern State in Southeast Asia*, London: Macmillan. Considerable discussion of the fortunes of Chinese business in the region in the inter-war decades can be found in Rajeswary Ampalavanar Brown (1994), *Capital and Entrepreneurship in South-East Asia*, London: Macmillan. C. F. Yong (1989), *Tan Kah-kee: The Making of an Overseas Chinese Legend*, Singapore: Oxford University Press, is a fine study of one of the region's most important pioneer industrialists.

Japan's commercial expansion into South-East Asia between the wars is explored in a number of papers in Sugiyama Shinya and Milagros C. Guerrero (eds.) (1994), *International Commercial Rivalry in Southeast Asia in the Interwar Period*, Southeast Asia Studies, Monograph No. 39, New Haven: Yale University, including, notably, Anne Booth, 'Japanese Import Penetration and Dutch Response: Some Aspects of Economic Policy Making in Colonial Indonesia', pp. 133–64. See also Howard Dick (1989), 'Japan's Economic Expansion in the Netherlands Indies between the First and Second World Wars', *Journal of Southeast Asian Studies*, 20(2): 244–72; and Peter Post (1995), 'Chinese Business Networks and Japanese Capital in South East Asia, 1880–1940: Some Preliminary Observations', in Rajeswary Ampalavanar Brown (ed.), *Chinese Business Enterprise in Asia*, London: Routledge, pp. 154–76, which, focusing on the Netherlands East Indies, shows the importance of overseas Chinese networks for Japan's economic expansion in the pre-war period.

Most historians of the period of Japanese rule in South-East Asia have concentrated on political and military issues, in general providing only passing reference to the economic impact: see, for example, most of the essays in Alfred W. McCoy (ed.) (1980), *Southeast Asia under Japanese Occupation*, Southeast Asia Studies, Monograph No. 22, New Haven: Yale University. An important exception is Shigeru Sato (1994), *War, Nationalism and Peasants: Java under the Japanese Occupation, 1942–1945*, Southeast Asia Publication Series No. 26, Sydney: Allen & Unwin/Asian Studies Association of Australia. An excellent examination of the wartime famine in northern Vietnam is provided by Bùi Minh Dung (1995), 'Japan's Role in the Vietnamese Starvation of 1944–45', *Modern Asian Studies*, 29(3): 573–618.

5
Economic Change, 1950–1980

IN the century or so before the Second World War, the major
economies of South-East Asia, under colonial rule, had each followed the same path of fuller integration into the world economy.
In the post-war decades, as the colonial regimes were withdrawn or
evicted from the region, the majority remained on that path. Some,
however, moved off in a radically different direction. The states
which remained committed to integration into the world capitalist
economy were the Philippines, which saw the final departure of
American administration in 1946, Malaya, which became independent in 1957, Singapore, which secured full independence from
Britain when it became part of the new Federation of Malaysia in
1963, becoming a separate state in 1965, and Thailand, which of
course had never come under Western rule. The position of
Indonesia, which secured independence in 1949 following a four-
year war against the Dutch, was considerably more complex. In
the 1950s and the first half of the 1960s, under Sukarno, the new
state pursued a strongly nationalist economic strategy, that commonly involved fierce attacks on western interests. For example, in
1957–8, all Dutch enterprises—plantations, factories, mines,
banks, and shipping lines—were expropriated. In one oft-quoted
incident, Sukarno told the United States, 'To hell with your aid.'
However, with the fall of Sukarno from power in the mid-1960s,
and the establishment of Suharto's New Order, Indonesia became
firmly integrated into the world capitalist economy, a realignment
dramatically marked by the establishment of a permanent World
Bank mission in Jakarta in 1968.

The states which took the radically different path, rejecting integration into the capitalist order and committing themselves to
state-ownership and control, were Burma from 1962, having
secured independence from Britain in 1948, and North Vietnam,
the French having been finally removed in 1954. It is important

to add that the economic experience of Burma in this period was shaped to a considerable degree by armed conflict, that of Vietnam, both the communist North and the pro-west South, profoundly so. From independence in 1948, Burma suffered endemic communist and ethnic insurgency, that not only drained the resources of the central government but also placed extensive parts of the country outside its administrative reach. In Vietnam, the determination of the communist government in the north to secure unification led to serious insurgency in the south from the beginning of the 1960s, and then, from the middle of the decade, direct military intervention by the United States in support of the regime in Saigon. The war brought great loss of life and physical destruction, not only in Vietnam but also in Laos and, in particular, in Cambodia. It diverted crucial domestic resources away from productive investment. And it left the economies of both North and South Vietnam dependent on, and distorted by, massive external support, from the Soviet Union and the United States respectively.

For the purposes of clear exposition, this brief outline of economic change in post-war, post-independence South-East Asia will treat the two groups separately.

The State-commanded Economy

The economic paths followed by Burma from 1948 into the 1980s, and by North Vietnam from 1954 to unification in 1975, are considered in Chapter 17. That chapter explores the reasons why, on independence, those states rejected the capitalist route; examines the strategies they did adopt, towards the agricultural sector, industry, and towards external economic relations; and seeks to understand why those strategies are now widely seen to have failed. Therefore the present section merely needs to sketch in some basic detail on the structure and performance of the economies in that period.

Between 1952 and 1960, Burma's gross domestic product (GDP) grew at a moderately impressive average annual rate of about 5 per cent. Yet the destruction of production capacity and infrastructure during the war and the disruption of the economy by the post-independence insurgencies had both been so severe that at the end of that period, many crucial economic indicators, including real per capita GDP and the volume of rice exports, were still well below pre-war levels. In part because of economic failure but also because of the disintegration of civilian politics, on 2 March 1962 the army removed the government of U Nu, who had, with brief interludes, been prime minister since 1948. While U Nu had sought the construction of a socialist economy tempered by the principles of Buddhism, the new regime, under Ne Win, was far more doctrinaire. Pursuing 'The Burmese Way to Socialism', it plunged into extensive nationalization, bringing all internal trade in essential commodities, imports and exports, banking, and the major part of manufacturing under state control. Over the period 1960–70, the value of Burma's exports fell, on average, 11.6 per cent per annum, the value of imports, 5.7 per cent per annum. Per capita gross national product (GNP) barely grew at all. Indeed it could be argued that the economy functioned in this period only because of the presence of a vigorous black market. In the early 1970s, more pragmatic economic management, that included a major expansion in foreign borrowing and a substantial increase in the government's rice procurement price, secured an average annual growth of GDP of 6.8 per cent between 1974 and 1980. But in the mid-1980s, sluggish exports and acute debt-servicing problems were at the heart of a further economic crisis. As a final comment, it is important to record the main changes which took place in the structure of Burma's economy in this period. Between 1965 and 1986, the share of agriculture in GDP *rose* from 35 per cent to 48 per cent. The contribution of services fell from 52 to 39 per cent. The share of industry remained unchanged, at 13 per cent. (See Tables 5.1 and 5.2 for comparative data on all the major economies of South-East Asia.)

The communist government which took power in northern Vietnam in 1954, after almost eight years of war against the French, began the socialist transformation of the economy with a major programme of land redistribution, undertaken between 1953 and 1956. This substantial reform, which involved over 70 per cent of the rural population, was carried through without, apparently, damaging agricultural production. Indeed the official figures suggest that rice production in North Vietnam rose from 2.6 million tons in 1954 to 4.132 million tons in 1956. Land redistribution was followed in late 1958 by the collectivization of agriculture, the first level being largely completed by the end of 1960. In contrast to the earlier expansion, over the period 1958–75 there was no increase in total rice production in North Vietnam, while production per capita fell. The extent to which, at different times, this reflected the failures of collectivization (see Chapter 17), a poor allocation of resources for agriculture, or, from 1965, the impact of American bombing, is difficult to determine. From the early 1960s, the government gave clear priority to the expansion of industry, in particular heavy industry, using a strategy that required substantial aid from the Soviet bloc and China. In broad terms, this met with considerable success. By unification in 1975, industrial output, in real terms, was almost three and a half times the 1960 level, while the contribution of industry to produced national income rose from 18.6 per cent to 27.9 per cent. With the stagnation of agriculture, the growth of the North Vietnamese economy in this period, an average annual increase in social product of 5.6 per cent between 1960 and 1975, must be explained largely in terms of the expansion of industry. But at the same time, capacity utilization in the industrial sector was commonly extremely low, as the state-commanded economy failed to secure an efficient allocation of industrial inputs. Chronic imbalances both within industry and between the industrial and agricultural sectors manifested themselves in a huge dependence on imports for essential industrial raw materials, food, and for consumer manufactures, that led by the late 1960s to an escalating trade deficit. In 1975, North Vietnam's trade deficit was five times the value of its exports. This was accompanied by an increase in the dependence of government finances on external assistance. Foreign loans and grants, from the communist bloc, accounted for 22.4 per cent of total budgetary revenues in 1960, 68.9 per cent in 1968, and 54.9 per cent in 1975. This was an extraordinary degree of external dependence.

The Capitalist Economies

Economic change in the capitalist states of South-East Asia in the three decades or so from the end of the Second World War was dominated by a marked decline in the relative importance of agriculture and an increase in that of modern industry. This fundamental transformation, very pronounced from the mid-1960s, is captured in Tables 5.1 and 5.2.

The declining contribution of agriculture to GDP in this period was particularly marked in Indonesia and Thailand, down to 26 per cent and 17 per cent respectively, although it is important to add that in the mid-1980s, agriculture remained quite clearly the

TABLE 5.1

South-East Asia: Structural Change in the Economies by
Percentage Share of GDP, 1965–1986

	Agriculture		Industry		Services	
	1965	1986	1965	1986	1965	1986
Indonesia	56	26	13	32	31	42
Malaysia	28	20	25	35	47	45
Philippines	26	26	28	32	46	42
Singapore	3	1	24	38	73	62
Thailand	35	17	23	30	42	53
Burma	35	48	13	13	52	39
Vietnam	–	45	26	–	–	–

Source: Chris Dixon (1991), *South East Asia in the World-Economy*, Cambridge:
Cambridge University Press, p. 25.

TABLE 5.2

South-East Asia: Structural Change in the Economies by
Percentage Share of the Official Labour Force, 1965–1986

	Agriculture		Industry		Services	
	1965	1986	1965	1986	1965	1986
Indonesia	71	57	9	13	21	30
Malaysia	59	42	13	19	29	39
Philippines	58	52	16	16	26	33
Singapore	6	2	27	38	68	61
Thailand	82	71	5	10	13	19
Burma	64	53	14	19	23	28
Vietnam	79	68	6	12	15	21

Source: As for Table 5.1.

main source of employment in both countries. The increase in
the contribution of industry to GDP was greatest in Indonesia,
Malaysia, and Singapore, although in the first two countries, industry still accounted for only a relatively modest part of total
employment in 1986. The increased contribution of services to
GDP in Indonesia and Thailand between 1965 and 1986 should
also be noted. The Philippines stands as the exception in this
group, with no change in the share of agriculture in GDP and only

a very modest increase in the contribution of industry. This last point will be touched on later.

The industrialization of capitalist South-East Asia in the post-war decades involved one important shift in strategy, adopted at different times and absorbed to different degrees in each country. In the 1950s, as in the pre-war period, industry in South-East Asia mainly involved the initial processing of primary commodities for export and, of particular interest here, the manufacture of simple finished articles for local consumption, replacing imports. Import-substitution industrialization (ISI) was particularly pronounced in this decade in the Philippines, where, behind a range of barriers, including high tariffs on selected imports, discriminatory foreign exchange allocations, and multiple exchange rates, the production of, notably, textiles, beverages, paper, and basic metal goods, grew very substantially. Between 1950 and 1956, value added in Philippine manufacturing rose, in real terms, at an average annual rate of 12.3 per cent. But the limitations of ISI soon became evident. Most importantly, the expansion of local manufacturing for domestic consumption was clearly limited by the size of the local market. In addition, by drawing in imports of industrial machinery and raw materials to sustain the expansion of domestic manufacturing, almost inevitably the strategy would flounder on balance of payments crises. Finally, the local manufacturer, shielded from foreign competition, was under little pressure to lower prices and improve quality, to the disadvantage of the local consumer.

The new industrialization strategy, to manufacture not for domestic consumption but for export, was first adopted in South-East Asia by Singapore, in the mid-1960s. In an important sense, export-oriented industrialization (EOI) was forced upon Singapore, for its expulsion from the Federation of Malaysia in 1965 severely reduced the size of its internal market, fatally undermining the ISI strategy which had been pursued from the beginning of the decade. Singapore's export-driven industrial expansion was built principally upon heavy inward investment by foreign multinationals, the creation of a tightly disciplined and skilled labour force, and strong government intervention and direction. In terms of employment, the leading elements in Singapore's manufacturing sector from the mid-1960s were the construction of drilling rigs and ancillary vessels for off-shore oil extraction, together with tanker construction and repair; textiles and garments; and electrical and electronic goods, notably semi-conductors, integrated circuits, and, at a later stage, disk drives. The expansion of industry was truly spectacular. Value added in manufacturing rose from S$348.4 million in 1965 to S$8,521.9 million in 1980, employment from 47,334 to 285,250. The value of Singapore's manufactured exports, in 1985 market prices, grew from S$933.3 million in 1966 to S$12,368.0 million in 1979. It was largely as a result of this expansion that Singapore's GDP grew, in real terms, at an average annual rate of 13.6 per cent between 1966 and 1969, and at 8.3 per cent between 1970 and 1979, among the highest rates in the world.

In Thailand, Malaysia, and the Philippines, the new industrialization strategy came in at the end of the 1960s and the beginning of the 1970s. For Thailand, the share of manufactures in total exports rose from 3.8 per cent in 1966 to 26.0 per cent in 1976, and to 54.9 per cent in 1986, now far exceeding the share of agricultural commodities. The principal manufactures were processed foods, including canned fruits and vegetables, textiles, garments, electrical and electronic goods, mainly integrated circuits, and jewellery. Together they accounted for virtually 70 per cent of total manufactured exports in 1986. In Malaysia, the share of manufactures in total exports rose from 12 per cent in 1970 to 32 per cent in 1985, their value increasing from M$612 million to M$12,111 million. The principal manufactured exports were electrical and electronic goods, which rose from 3 per cent of manufactured exports in 1970 to 50 per cent in 1985, textiles, clothing, and footwear, and processed primary resources, including wood products.

In Thailand and Malaysia, the new commitment to export-oriented industrialization did not mean the abandonment of the import-substitution strategy. Rather, EOI was superimposed on ISI. Indeed, in the 1980s Malaysia embarked on a second programme of import-substitution industrialization, this time focusing on heavy industry, and including petrochemicals, iron and steel, cement, cars, and motor-cycle engines. The commitment to ISI implied, of course, the maintenance of high tariff protection of domestic markets. As an example, perhaps an extreme one, in 1978, the effective level of protection for consumer durables in Thailand was 495.6 per cent. The importance of this observation is that, in time, continued heavy protection of the domestic market was likely to weaken the expansion of manufactured exports. With profit margins on export sales, in competitive markets, almost certainly smaller than the margins on sales in the protected domestic market, industrial enterprise would naturally be attracted towards the more rewarding, and less demanding, internal market.

A potent variant of the tension between import-substitution and export-oriented industrialization was strongly present in the Philippines and in Indonesia in this period. The regional pioneer in ISI in the 1950s, the Philippines ran into perhaps the principal limitation of the strategy at the beginning of the 1960s, the saturation of the domestic market. There was a modest increase in manufactured exports in the first half of the decade, their share in total export earnings rising from 4 per cent in 1960 to 12 per cent in 1965. Then, in the late 1960s, the Philippine authorities professed a firm commitment to export-driven industrialization. Indeed, the 1970s saw a considerable expansion in the share of manufactures in total export value, to 50 per cent in 1980. Yet, as is evident from Tables 5.1 and 5.2, this failed to translate into a major increase in the share of industry in GDP, while there was *no* increase in the share of industry in employment, comparing 1965 with 1986. The fact was that the earlier phase of import-substitution industrialization had created powerful business interests within the Philippines that were able, through their manipulation of political and bureaucratic alliances, to defend their protected position, to the extent of undermining the implementation of an export-directed industrialization strategy. As a clear example of the power of those interests, despite considerable pressure from the World Bank to loosen its protectionist position, in the mid-1980s the Philippines still had the highest tariff protection of all the capitalist economies in South-East Asia. That the Philippines was able, none the less, to achieve an average annual increase in GDP of 6.3 per cent between 1974 and 1980 was due principally to dangerously heavy international borrowing. The crisis came in the early 1980s.

In Indonesia, following the political and economic stabilization of the mid-1960s, the manufacturing sector grew at a most impressive rate, an annual average of 9.6 per cent between 1967 and 1973, 14.2 per cent between 1973 and 1981. However, while other economies in the region were committing themselves to EOI, Indonesian industry in the 1970s was concerned almost solely with the domestic market. This strategy was strongly bolstered by the huge oil revenues which accrued to Indonesia following the price-hikes of 1973–4. First, those revenues generated rapid growth in the domestic economy, which induced a powerful rise in local demand for manufactures. In any event, the Indonesian domestic market was an extremely large one. Second, they enabled the state to undertake a number of large-scale, capital-intensive industrial projects, directed at the protected domestic market. Finally,

Indonesia's vast oil reserves provided the country with strong primary export growth during the 1970s, so obviating the need to develop non-commodity exports. During that decade, manufactures never exceeded 3 per cent of total merchandise exports. But then, in the early 1980s, the oil boom broke, leaving Indonesia with increasingly severe balance of payments difficulties. From this emerged, towards the end of the 1980s, some two decades after its neighbours, the change in strategy towards an export-oriented industrialization, led by the private sector. It is important to add, however, that the interests of the most powerful political–military–bureaucratic–business alliances in Indonesia remained firmly tied to the strategy of a state-driven, import-substitution industrialization, established in the late 1960s.

(The broad outlines of the post-war, post-independence industrialization of capitalist South-East Asia now having been established, Chapter 18 will return to the subject, to consider three central issues. What principal factors explain the expansion in manufacturing industry in the region in this period? Is that growth leading to the transformation of the capitalist economies into advanced industrial economies? The final question arises from the first two: what has been the nature of modern capitalist South-East Asia's industrialization?)

Even after three decades of rapid industrial growth, in the mid-1980s the largest sector in each of the capitalist economies of South-East Asia, in terms of contribution to GDP, was the service sector. This embraced a vast range of activities, including retail and wholesale distribution, construction, financial and professional services, transportation, tourism, health care, and education. However, more important than the size of the sector, indeed the contribution of services to GDP *fell* in Malaysia, the Philippines, and Singapore between 1965 and 1986 (see Table 5.1), were the changes which took place within it. There is space here to note just two. The first was an extraordinary growth of tourism in Thailand. The number of tourist arrivals rose from around 100,000 a year at the beginning of the 1960s to well over 2 million a year in the early 1980s, the annual revenue from tourism rising from around 250 million to over 75,000 million baht. Towards the end of the 1980s, the industry directly employed around 450,000 people, principally in hotels and restaurants, and was by far the most important source of foreign exchange. The emergence of tourism as a major industry in Thailand was due to two main factors. The country's considerable attraction as a tourist destination, in terms of sea and hill resorts, a distinctive archaeological, architectural, and cultural heritage, and, to acknowledge a dark side, Bangkok's fiery nightlife: and the conjunction of rapidly rising disposable incomes in Europe, North America, Japan, and Australia, and the arrival of mass air-transport, particularly from the early 1970s.

The second example was a very considerable expansion in financial and business services in Singapore, which employed 23,071 in 1970 (3.5 per cent of the labour force), 79,412 (7.4 per cent) in 1980, and 167,222 (10.9 per cent) in 1990. This expansion involved a substantial increase in the number of international financial businesses with a presence in Singapore: in the mid-1980s, no less than 116 foreign banks had branches there. Singapore's emergence as a major world financial centre from the early 1970s rested on a number of factors: its location in the time zone gap between the New York/London and Hong Kong/Tokyo markets became a very considerable advantage with the establishment of 24-hour financial trading, to the extent that by the early 1990s, Singapore was the fourth largest foreign exchange market in the world; the strongly developmentalist policies of the government; Singapore's reputation, fiercely policed by the authorities, for efficient, corruption-free trading; and the presence of a well-educated, sophisticated labour force.

The expansion of the industrial and service sectors meant, as noted earlier, that the contribution of agriculture to both GDP and employment, in Indonesia, Malaysia, and Thailand, fell substantially between the mid-1960s and the mid-1980s (see Tables 5.1 and 5.2). It is important to add, however, that a number of major advances took place within agriculture in this period. Undoubtedly, the most important was the introduction from the late 1960s of high-yielding rice varieties and the complementary chemical and mechanical inputs that constitute the Green Revolution. The new seeds and inputs were taken up with particular enthusiasm in the Philippines, Indonesia, and Malaysia, with a dramatic impact on yields and output. For example, in Indonesia, average rice yield per hectare rose from 2.38 metric tons in 1970 to 3.94 metric tons in 1985, total production increasing from 19.3 to 39.0 million metric tons. Perhaps more importantly, the Green Revolution may also have had a major impact on income distribution in the rice-growing districts where it was extensively adopted, although there has been an extremely vigorous debate, among academics, administrators, and policy-makers, over this issue. Some have argued that virtually all classes of cultivator benefited, in different ways, from the introduction of the new inputs and practices, and consequently that no substantial shifts took place in patterns of socio-economic differentiation. In contrast is the view that the gains from the Green Revolution went overwhelmingly to established rural élites, so sharply widening socio-economic inequalities: the poorer, weaker elements in rural society may have made some gains, while losing ground to the rich; or they may have lost absolutely. These crucial and complex issues are explored in Chapter 16. High-yielding varieties also made a major impact in a number of important tree-crops, notably, in Malaysia, rubber, oil palm, and cocoa. Finally, this period saw, principally in Thailand and in the Philippines, a major expansion in agri-business, in which the cultivator no longer operated as an independent individual but under contract to a large company, which determined the nature and extent of cultivation, made provision for the supply of credit and complementary inputs, and organized marketing.

To conclude this brief survey of the economic experience of post-war capitalist South-East Asia, three final structural changes must be noted. First, picking up a central theme of the preceding survey chapters, the period saw the Chinese entrepreneurial class, in a further major evolution of its economic interests, take a crucial role in the expansion of modern industry and finance. This was the case even in Malaysia and Indonesia, where suspicion of Chinese economic power remained pronounced. An important element in the accumulation of Chinese industrial and financial power was the creation of vast business empires with diverse interests, commonly carried across national boundaries. The examples are legion. The largest business concern in Thailand in this period, in terms of asset value, was the Bangkok Bank–Sophonpanit group, in which the dominant figure was Chin Sophonpanit (1913–88). In 1979 the group embraced 72 companies, together with 26 affiliates, and had total assets well in excess of 150,000 million baht. Its core interests were in banking, investment finance, and insurance, and included the Bangkok Bank, the largest commercial bank in South-East Asia by the end of the 1970s, and a crucial source of finance for local trading companies, including rice exporters, manufacturers, notably of textiles, and, from the mid-1970s, agri-business; Bangkok Insurance, the largest non-life insurance company in Thailand; and Asia Credit, Thailand's largest finance company.

In Indonesia, Liem Sioe Liong (Sudono Salim), born in China in 1916 and a migrant to the Indies in the mid-1930s, built a huge

business empire from the modest beginnings of a peanut oil trading concern before the war. In the mid-1940s, Liem was an
important supplier of foodstuffs, clothing, and medicines for the
forces of the Republic in the independence war against the Dutch.
This lay the foundation for a close association with powerful
elements within the Indonesian military which was to be highly
valuable to the advance of his business ambitions. Under Suharto's
New Order, from the mid-1960s, the interests of the Liem group
included: trade in coffee, rubber, and cloves; automobile distribution and assembly; the manufacture of textiles, cement, flour, and
steel; property and construction; and banking. As a final example
of the modern Chinese tycoon, in Malaysia, Kuok Hock Nien,
born in Johor Bahru in 1923, created a business empire from the
late 1940s that came to embrace sugar refining, flour milling,
hotels, property development, plantations, commodity trading,
and shipping. In 1990, the regional business press reported that he
had assets of US$1.5 billion. It is important to emphasize that each
of the above had very substantial foreign interests and connections:
the Bangkok Bank opened its first overseas branch, in Hong Kong,
in 1954, and by the mid-1970s had major offices in Europe, the
United States, and Japan; the industrial projects of the Liem
group, including the cement and steel initiatives, had substantial
foreign partners; in the 1980s, the Kuok group had interests in
Singapore, Hong Kong, Thailand, Indonesia, the Philippines,
Canada, China, and Australia.

Second, in the post-independence decades, Japan emerged as
the principal economic partner of the capitalist economies of
South-East Asia, bringing to fulfilment a development which had
its origins around the time of the First World War. In the
period from the mid-nineteenth to the mid-twentieth century,
South-East Asia's principal economic ties had been with Europe
and North America, as sources of investment capital and manufactures, and as markets for the region's commodity exports. In the
second half of the twentieth century, the economies of South-East
Asia became more closely integrated with Japan, and then with the
newly industrializing economies of East Asia, in a wider Asian
economy. South-East Asia looked East. A few statistics will
demonstrate the point. In the years 1971–5, 27.4 per cent of the
exports of the ASEAN countries—that is, Indonesia, Malaysia, the
Philippines, Singapore, and Thailand—went to Japan, compared
with 18.2 per cent to the United States, and 13.4 per cent to the
countries of the European Community. In the same period, Japan

accounted for 25.4 per cent of ASEAN imports, the United States for 15.9 per cent, and the European Community for 16.6 per cent. In the period 1970–9, 29.78 per cent of foreign direct investment in Thailand came from Japan, 35.56 per cent from the United States, and 15.4 per cent from the European Community: in 1990, Japan accounted for 44.48 per cent.

The final structural change to be considered applied to the region as a whole. This last comment will also mark a return to a central theme, first considered at the beginning of Chapter 3. In the period from 1945, South-East Asia experienced very rapid rates of population growth, regularly in excess of 2 per cent per annum, occasionally 3 per cent. This growth reflected a dramatic decline in mortality, in the absence of a sharp decline in fertility until the 1970s and 1980s, principally the result of major public health campaigns, for example, DDT spraying in the late 1940s and 1950s to reduce the incidence of malaria, and the widening of access to modern medicine, notably penicillin and other antibiotics. Falling mortality rates implied, of course, increased life expectancy. Here the figures are truly remarkable. Between 1950–5 and 1975–80, life expectancy at birth rose from 48.5 to 65.3 years in Malaysia, 37.5 to 52.8 years in Indonesia, and from 40.4 to 55.8 years in Vietnam. Table 5.3 provides population figures for the 1970s. It might usefully be compared with the population estimates for 1830 and for the early twentieth century, in Tables 3.1 and 3.2 in Chapter 3.

TABLE 5.3
South-East Asia: Population in the 1970s (million)

Country	Population
Indonesia[a] (1971)	119.2
Philippines (1970)	36.7
Thailand (1970)	34.4
Vietnam (1979)	52.7
Cambodia (1970)	7.1
Malaysia (1970)	10.4
Singapore (1970)	2.1
Burma (1973)	28.9
Total	291.5

Source: Charles Hirschman (1994), 'Population and Society in Twentieth-century Southeast Asia', *Journal of Southeast Asian Studies*, 25(2): 387–8.
[a]Java = 76.1 million; Outer Islands = 43.1 million.

In broad terms, in the 70 years from 1830 to 1900, the population of South-East Asia had grown from about 25 million to around 80 million. In the following 70 years, 1900–70, it had increased to around 290 million. In the process, the socio-economic, as well as the physical landscape of South-East Asia had been fundamentally altered. Through the nineteenth century and well into the inter-war period, the region as a whole had had a markedly low population relative to the extent of its cultivable land, and the rapid growth in primary production and trade had been sustained only through large-scale immigration of Chinese and Indians. In the second half of the twentieth century, across South-East Asia, labour shortage had been replaced by labour surplus. Indeed a number of countries, Indonesia, Thailand, and the Philippines, came to export labour on a substantial scale. In the 1980s, more than 100,000 Thais went overseas each year to work, mainly the unskilled or semi-skilled, and most to the Middle East. That labour surplus, the presence of a vast pool of cheap workers, was of course a crucial condition for the rapid industrialization which has been the dominant feature of South-East Asia's most recent economic experience.

SUGGESTED READING

Valuable surveys of economic change in post-war South-East Asia include Chris Dixon (1991), *South East Asia in the World-Economy*, Cambridge: Cambridge University Press, Chapter 5, 'Development Strategies and the International Economy', pp. 149–216; the chapter by Norman G. Owen (1992), 'Economic and Social Change', in Nicholas Tarling (ed.), *The Cambridge History of Southeast Asia*, Vol. 2, *The Nineteenth and Twentieth Centuries*, Cambridge: Cambridge University Press, pp. 467–527; Hal Hill (1993), *Southeast Asian Economic Development: An Analytical Survey*, Research School of Pacific Studies, Economics Division, Working Paper, Canberra: Australian National University; Jonathan Rigg (1991), *Southeast Asia: A Region in Transition: A Thematic Human Geography of the ASEAN Region*, London: Unwin Hyman; John Wong (1979), *ASEAN Economies in Perspective: A Comparative Study of Indonesia, Malaysia, the Philippines, Singapore and Thailand*, London: Macmillan; and, for a longer perspective, Anne Booth (1991a), 'The Economic Development of Southeast Asia: 1870–1985', *Australian Economic History Review*, 31(1): 20–52.

A guide to the literature on the state-commanded economies of Burma and North Vietnam appears at the end of Chapter 17; to the literature on the region's modern industrialization, at the end of Chapter 18; and to the literature on the Green Revolution in South-East Asia, at the end of Chapter 16.

There are a number of lengthy references to Chin Sophonpanit and the Bangkok Bank group in Suehiro Akira (1989), *Capital Accumulation in Thailand, 1855–1985*, Tokyo: Centre for East Asian Cultural Studies; and to Liem Sioe Liong in Richard Robison (1986), *Indonesia: The Rise of Capital*, Southeast Asia Publication Series No. 13, Sydney: Allen & Unwin/Asian Studies Association of Australia, in particular pp. 296–315, and Andrew MacIntyre (1991), *Business and Politics in Indonesia*, Southeast Asia Publication Series No. 21, Sydney: Allen & Unwin/Asian Studies Association of Australia.

For a fine survey of demographic change in this period, see Charles Hirschman (1994), 'Population and Society in Twentieth-century Southeast Asia', *Journal of Southeast Asian Studies*, 25(2): 381–416.

PART II

6
Demographic Change in the Nineteenth Century

THERE are strong reasons for beginning the series of deeper explorations of South-East Asia's economic past which comprise the heart of this book with an essay on demography. Demographic change in South-East Asia, as elsewhere, was intimately related to economic change—to levels of material welfare, nutrition, and diet, to the stability and security of agricultural production, to patterns of occupation and labour burden—although in ways which are difficult to disentangle. In addition, South-East Asia's demographic history is quite distinctive. In the seventeenth and eighteenth centuries the region experienced low population growth in comparison with, for example, China and India, and had a markedly low population density, again compared to China and India. In contrast, the nineteenth century saw a marked acceleration in population growth in South-East Asia. The rates achieved and the length of time over which they were sustained were historically remarkable.

But there might also be good reasons why an essay on demography would make for an uncertain beginning to this part of the book. Most importantly, the study of South-East Asia's historical demography, despite some notable recent advances, remains in its infancy. Certainly, scholarly consensus is far from being achieved. In addition, the vital demographic data for the region for the nineteenth century are poor, considerably worse for the seventeenth and eighteenth centuries—in the words of one writer in this field, 'execrable enough to make an original scholar out of anyone'.

Population Growth in the Seventeenth
and Eighteenth Centuries

The average annual growth of population in South-East Asia over the seventeenth and eighteenth centuries, suggests one brave scholar (Reid, 1987: 35), did not exceed 0.2 per cent, and in many parts of the region was even lower. But that average figure represents not an even growth, with mortality and fertility levels in a constant rough balance. Rather, periods of considerable population growth were followed by periods of low growth or of population loss. Marked population growth was achieved at those times and in those areas where the conditions of life were reasonably stable, and was secured by a combination of early marriage, abundant food, and the people's comparatively good health. In these circumstances, a relatively high birth rate was allied with a moderate level of mortality. Low growth or population loss (with the death rate rising sharply above the birth rate) occurred when and where the conditions of life were severely unstable—an instability occasioned most strikingly by warfare.

South-East Asian warfare in this period resulted in comparatively few battle casualties. The weapons employed were incapable of inflicting death on a large scale. Moreover, in this region of low population density, the prime aim in combat was not to kill the enemy but to seize populations as slaves and captives. The demographic importance of warfare lay, rather, in its destruction of agricultural production. The passage of a large force of men and their transport and combat animals across an agricultural district inevitably laid waste crops and destroyed vital irrigation and drainage structures. The restoration of a prosperous agriculture after such destruction would take a considerable time. Perhaps more important was the sudden loss of manpower, particularly if it occurred at a point of peak labour demand in the agricultural cycle. Men were conscripted for war; communities abandoned their fields, fleeing in advance of invading forces; or, if they failed to escape, were captured and deported. The result in all cases was a collapse of food production. Even where this did not lead to famine and actual starvation, it did leave the population seriously malnourished and thus considerably more vulnerable to diseases which threatened life. Thus there was a general decline in population on Java over the period from the last quarter of the seventeenth century to the mid-eighteenth century, a period of almost constant warfare between rival Javanese rulers. Almost certainly,

Siam lost considerable population in the mid-sixteenth century and again in the mid-eighteenth century as the kingdom was laid waste by the invading Burmese.

However, lying behind this argument are a number of far broader issues. Why was political instability so severe in South-East Asia in this period; was it notably more severe there than in either India or China, which achieved more rapid population growth in the seventeenth and eighteenth centuries; indeed, was food production in South-East Asia distinctly more vulnerable to the dislocating impact of war than food production in either India or China? Zelinsky (1950) attempted an initial exploration of the first of those questions with respect to mainland South-East Asia, adding comparisons with India and China. His principal propositions were that from earliest times mainland South-East Asia had received an almost constant influx of new peoples, channelled along the mountain ridges and valley floors leading from Inner Asia, with each wave creating new tensions and disturbances; and that this geographically fragmented region contained no single core area of sufficient size to impose a lasting peace on the whole. Here these ideas can merely be noted.

Accelerated Population Growth in the Nineteenth Century

The transition to sustained high population growth took place at different times in the different parts of South-East Asia. In the Philippines it occurred at some point in the eighteenth century, in Java in the third quarter of the century. Siam experienced modest population growth in the second half of the nineteenth century, followed by a sharp acceleration around 1900. In the Philippines, population grew at a nominal rate of 1 per cent per annum between 1736 and 1800, and at 1.65 per cent between 1800 and 1876: a series of mortality crises in the last quarter of the nine-teenth century reduced the rate of growth to 0.9 per cent per annum. The rate of population growth achieved on Java in the nineteenth century has long been the subject of considerable schol-arly debate. An early consensus put it at around 2.2 per cent per annum but this is now accepted as being far too high, the result of serious, although difficult to quantify, underenumeration in the population counts of the early nineteenth century. A recent recon-struction (Boomgaard, 1989: 171) produces a rate of 1.25 per cent for the period 1800–50, 1.6 per cent for the period 1850–1900: for the nineteenth century as a whole, the average annual rate of population growth is put at 1.4 per cent. This compares with growth rates for Europe and Asia over the nineteenth century of no more than 0.7 per cent and 0.4 per cent respectively.

Analyses of South-East Asia's accelerated population growth in the nineteenth century have focused principally on an alleged decline in mortality. Four arguments will be considered here, illustrated mainly by material on Java—for the simple reason that Java has attracted far more attention from historical demographers than any other part of the region. The first argument is that the imposition of European rule brought to an end the near constant indigenous warfare which, in the indirect manner outlined above, had severely suppressed population growth in the seventeenth and eighteenth centuries. The end of recurrent war-induced mortality crises allowed fertility to flourish almost unchecked. This argument takes strength from the fact that Java's transition to sustained high population growth, in the third quarter of the eighteenth century, followed the imposition in 1755 of a Dutch-guaranteed peace on the warring Javanese states, and more generally from the fact that the transition occurred first in those parts of South-East Asia (Java and the Philippines) where the *pax imperica*, the imperial peace, was first imposed. But the argument is also undermined, fatally so according to some writers (for example, Peper, 1970), by the fact that the imposition of European rule in itself frequently provoked wars which, because of the technical superiority of Western arms, were considerably more destructive than the indigenous wars of earlier centuries. The principal example here is the Java War of 1825–30, in which the Dutch faced a major, princely-led uprising and where, it is said, one-third of the population was caught up in the hostilities, one-quarter of the cultivated area sustained damage, and an estimated 200,000 Javanese lost their lives. The 'pacification' of Upper Burma by British–Indian forces in the second half of the 1880s, and the Philippine–American War of 1899–1902 may have been comparably destructive. But perhaps the crucial consideration here is that the colonial wars of the nineteenth century occurred with much less frequency and generally were of much shorter duration than the indigenous conflicts of the seventeenth and eighteenth centuries. Over the long term, therefore, the disruptive impact of the latter, their demographic consequences, would have been by far the more serious.

The second argument concerns the possible impact of medical intervention (specifically of preventive medicine) and of public health measures (improvements in sanitation, drainage, and water supply) in reducing mortality. In fact the firm consensus among modern scholars is that, possibly with one exception, medical intervention and public health programmes were of little or no importance in this period. Quite simply, throughout the nineteenth century, only an extremely small proportion of the population of Java, and of the region as a whole, enjoyed modern sanitation, a treated water supply, or had access to Western medicine. Moreover, in many circumstances Western medical science was simply ineffective in this period: against dysentery, cholera, and typhoid— major killers at the time—it could offer only palliatives. In Java, demographically significant medical or public health intervention did not occur before about 1920. The one possible exception was smallpox vaccination. Indeed Boomgaard (1989) regards that intervention as a major cause of the reduction in mortality, and thus the acceleration of population growth, in nineteenth century Java.

This is a controversial argument. Peper (1970) suggests that in this period effective vaccination reached far too few Javanese to be medically significant. There were insufficient vaccinators for a major programme; in general they had inadequate or even no training; the government's vaccination services were poorly organized, at least in the first half of the nineteenth century; and commonly the vaccine administered had lost its potency, for it was difficult to preserve smallpox vaccine in Java's tropical climate. Peper argues that the eradication of smallpox did not become possible until around 1930. Boomgaard's (1989) response is that the vaccinators reached more Javanese than is alleged by Peper; that vaccination campaigns can be successful even if a large proportion of the population has not been covered, it being necessary to vaccinate only the children and to isolate new outbreaks rigorously; and that in nineteenth century Java smallpox vaccine was normally kept alive by human carriers. Boomgaard argues that smallpox had largely disappeared from Java by 1880, at least as an epidemic disease. But even if Boomgaard's views on the effectiveness of the Dutch vaccination campaigns are accepted, there remain two criticisms of his broader argument. As smallpox was but one of the many fatal diseases prevalent in Java in this period, even a dramatic decline in smallpox deaths could have only a limited impact on the mortality rate: and the transition to high population growth in Java took place before the arrival of smallpox vaccine in the island, in 1804.

A contrary observation must be added here. Even if, as Boomgaard argues, smallpox largely disappeared from Java, at least as an epidemic disease, during the course of the nineteenth century, the incidence of other diseases increased, and indeed one major killer made its first appearance. The new killer was cholera, which first arrived in Java in 1821 and reappeared regularly thereafter. Epidemic cholera was always reintroduced from overseas. Here it is important to make the general point that during the nineteenth century, the transmission of disease, both its arrival from overseas as well as its movement through the local population, became considerably more rapid and extensive, as the expansion of commodity production and trade made people more mobile. One major disease which increased in incidence in the second half of the nineteenth century was malaria. This too can be broadly linked to the major economic changes then taking place in Java. The link is that the large-scale construction of irrigation channels and waterways, and the clearing of extensive upland areas to accommodate the expansion of *sawah* cultivation, created the water environment within which the mosquito flourished. Again, the increased mobility of people and animals led to considerably more rapid and extensive transmission of the disease. Reference might also be made to an increased incidence of beri-beri, not specifically in Java but throughout much of South-East Asia. This disease is the result of vitamin B deficiency, and is widely associated with a declining consumption of hand-pounded rice, in which much of the vitamin-rich husk is retained, and a rising consumption of the polished rice produced by modern steam-powered mills, where the husk is removed. A crucial point arises from this discussion: an explanation of the region's accelerated population growth in the nineteenth century that focuses on a declining mortality must reconcile that decline with the increased incidence of the diseases outlined here.

The third argument concerns a possible improvement in nutritional levels, sufficient to increase substantially resistance to major infectious disease: after all this period saw an impressive expansion in per capita food production throughout the region. Unfortunately the precise measurement of nutritional levels in nineteenth century South-East Asia presents a number of formidable problems. Some are methodological: food production statistics are rarely reliable, even where they exist; calculations of average levels of food consumption almost certainly obscure substantial inequalities in distribution; and, perhaps most importantly, throughout rural South-East Asia, a major part of the food consumed was drawn from non-market production, that is from the consumers' own cultivation, from their gathering of forest produce, from fishing, which, precisely because it did not enter the market, could never be statistically recorded. But there are also major problems of definition, arising from the fact that nutritional conditions reflect a combination of the quantity of food consumed and its quality. It would be quite possible for a population to enjoy an increase in the quantity of food it ate but, because that increase had been accompanied by a shift towards inferior foods, to suffer a deterioration in diet. Boomgaard (1989: 96–101), wrestling with these problems in the context of nineteenth-century Java, concludes that the quantity of food consumed per capita, expressed in terms of calories available per hour worked, was slightly lower in 1880 than it had been in 1815; while the quality of food consumed (protein and vitamin content), per hour of work, was substantially lower in 1880 than it had been in 1815. He also suggests that both the quantity and quality of food consumed per capita, adjusted for days worked, were much reduced in 1840: in other words, the 1880 figures represent major recoveries from a mid-century trough. Certainly, there was no marked improvement in nutritional levels in Java across the nineteenth century, according to Boomgaard. Per capita food production had clearly increased substantially, but that increase had been directed towards the export sector, leaving domestic consumption per capita to stagnate. (The reader might refer here to the discussion in Chapter 9 on material welfare in nineteenth-century rural South-East Asia.)

The final argument proposes that the improvements in internal transportation achieved by colonial administrations in the nineteenth century—notably the construction of roads and cart-tracks—substantially reduced the impact of local crop failure. The threat of famine, and thus of high mortality, in a particular district could now be met by bringing in grain from surplus areas. But improvements in transportation, in themselves, do not end local famine. It is not sufficient for grain to be made available in a striken area: the threatened population must have the cash resources, or access to credit through moneylenders, landlords, or relatives, to be able to purchase it. However, in almost all cases the failure of subsistence food cultivation will be accompanied by a failure of market production. In other words, at precisely the time local food production collapses, and for exactly the same reason, the cash income with which food from outside might be purchased also collapses. It might be possible for a colonial administration to relieve that position either by distributing grain without charge or by creating work, usually by means of public construction projects, to enable a distressed population to obtain cash. Enough has been said to show that the relief of local famine in nineteenth-century South-East Asia, in fact in any locality at any time, was a far from simple matter. Indeed there were serious famines in parts of Java in the 1840s, despite the substantial improvements that had been made to the island's road network under Dutch administration. Two alternative arguments on the impact of improvements in transportation may be of interest here. Such improvements—by greatly expanding the market for agricultural production—could encourage a settlement to switch to the cultivation of non-food crops or to sell a major part of its food reserves, in either case dangerously worsening its food position. And, as noted earlier, improvements in transportation may well have an adverse impact on mortality, by making the transmission of infectious disease more rapid and extensive.

In view of the discussion above, it is not surprising that a number of writers in this field are unwilling to accept a decline in mortality as the central explanation for Java's accelerated population growth in the nineteenth century. Their position, however, rests not simply on the particular counter-arguments and counter-evidence noted above but also, at least for one writer, on a broader consideration. White (1973) observes that all the declining mortality arguments cast the Javanese in a passive role: mortality declined, the pace of population growth accelerated, not because of initiatives taken by the Javanese but as a result of external (colonial) interventions. He also suggests that sustained high population growth was economically disastrous for the Javanese, in that it wiped out any increase in per capita output. Thus, for White, the declining mortality explanation leaves an important question unanswered. In the nineteenth century, why did the Javanese not respond to an externally induced fall in mortality by regulating fertility; why did they tolerate such high, economically disastrous population growth over such a long period? White, and others, are therefore led to propose an alternative approach—one in which the focus shifts from an alleged decline in mortality to the prospect of a rise in fertility, and where the Javanese are cast not as passive recipients of external intervention and its consequences but as positive actors.

The starting point for the argument that a substantial rise in fertility took place in nineteenth-century Java is the observation that the Cultivation System, inaugurated in 1830, imposed greatly increased labour demands on the large majority of rural families which came within its administration. Specifically, the Cultivation System forced the withdrawal of male labour from subsistence food production, and directed it into export-crop cultivation and into those related activities (the processing and transport of government crops, the construction of roads, dikes, and warehouses) that together constituted the expanding export sector. But that substantial labour force, removed from the subsistence sector, still had to be supported by it: and this was achieved, in part, by a reallocation of female labour away from domestic tasks, notably spinning and weaving, and into those positions in subsistence wet-rice cultivation now vacated by the men. For both men and women, workloads increased substantially. This argument, although developed for Java, might well be applied to any part of South-East Asia: for throughout the region, the expansion in commodity production which occurred in the nineteenth century clearly implied sharply increased labour burdens for rural families, whether forcibly imposed (as under the Cultivation System) or freely entered into (as, for example, in the rice deltas of Burma and Siam).

According to White (1973) and to an earlier study by Boomgaard (1981), the response of the Javanese family to the increased labour burdens being imposed on it was to produce more children. The central point is that by the age of around seven, children in rural Java—assisting in the labour-intensive tasks of planting, tending, and harvesting the rice crop, or undertaking simple household chores in order to free the women to work the land—have become productive members of the family, adding more to its production than they consume. In White's terminology (1973), the cost of the production of labour power, that is, the cost of supporting a child to the age when it becomes a net producer, was low. At the same time, the benefit that would accrue to the hard-pressed Javanese family from the increased production of labour power (more children) was, for the reasons given, high. There were several measures which a nineteenth-century Javanese couple may have taken to increase the size of their family. White (1973) suggests that in Java both abortion and infanticide were employed to control family size. Thus it was open to the Javanese in the nineteenth century to abandon or curb those practices if they wished to have more children. White also notes the possible importance in this context of a family's decisions on the internal allocation of food: when the demand for labour is high and children are regarded as a major economic asset, it is reasonable to assume that they would be given a larger share of the family food in order to guard against undernourishment, and thus secure their survival. That decision would be particularly important in times of food scarcity. (To be technically accurate, food allocation and infanticide should be seen as influences on the level of mortality, not fertility.) A further possible mechanism to regulate fertility might be noted. During the months in which a mother is breast-feeding, her fertility is reduced and thus further conception delayed. It follows that where a woman wishes to increase the final size of her family, she might reduce the period of lactation for each infant in order to accommodate more conceptions within her reproductive years. These three mechanisms clearly operate at the level of the individual. Each couple, frequently the woman alone, would decide the length of lactation, the allocation of the family food, and whether or not to abort a pregnancy, although such decisions must also be influenced by the society's customs and beliefs. But there are also mechanisms which operate primarily at the level of the community. Thus when the demand for labour is high and children are regarded as a valuable asset, it is reasonable to assume that the community will encourage early marriage, have a low tolerance of celibacy, and accept female remarriage on the early death of a partner.

But the demand for labour/increasing fertility argument is open to considerable objections. Owen (1987b) argues that at present there is no clear evidence for a substantial rise in birth rates in nineteenth-century South-East Asia, or for any of the changes in practice, for example a reduction in the age of marriage, a reduced incidence of celibacy, a shortening of the period of breast-feeding, that might produce it. It should also be said that this argument proceeds on the basis of a number of assumptions which may be difficult to sustain. Indeed, commenting on White's paper, Geertz (1973) challenges the prime assumption itself—that the Javanese family would have sought to meet the increased labour burdens imposed by the Cultivation System by increasing its production of children. Geertz suggests that the increased labour burdens were in fact met principally by a reorganization of labour time and a refining of cultivation practices—in essence an interweaving of subsistence and commodity cultivation—that allowed the Javanese family to fulfil its obligations in the export economy without seriously undermining subsistence food production. (Geertz's views on this subject are considered in Chapter 7.) Note might also be made of the (unproven) assumptions which underlie the abortion argument. The view that the acceleration of population growth in the nineteenth century can be partly explained by the abandon-ment or curbing of abortion rests upon the propositions that the abortifacients then employed were highly effective, that prior to the nineteenth century abortion was practiced on a demographically significant scale, and that a demographically significant reduction in the incidence of abortion actually took place in the nineteenth century. The last two points would also be pertinent to the infanti-cide argument. Finally, the demand for labour/rising fertility school miss some important counter-considerations. Although the presence of additional children may indeed have helped the rural family to meet the increased labour burdens which export expan-sion imposed on it in the nineteenth century, the very act of rearing those children was in itself a major burden; and to the extent that in the final stages of pregnancy and for a short time after delivery, the woman must withdraw from demanding agricultural work, the production of children actually reduces the family's labour power.

A variant of the demand for labour/rising fertility argument advanced by Alexander (1984) avoids some, but by no means all, those criticisms. It avoids them in the sense that, although it too identifies a mechanism to regulate fertility that operates at the level of the individual, it does not involve individuals making economic-ally related decisions about family size. The starting point for Alexander's argument is the observation that in contemporary Central Java there is a firm relationship between breast-feeding and abstinence from sexual relations; in other words, a couple do not resume intercourse after birth until the woman has finished breast-feeding and the child is fully weaned. Breast-feeding, and thus sexual abstinence, may continue for two years or more. The effect of the sharply increased labour burdens imposed by the Cultivation System in the nineteenth century was, following White, to draw Javanese women into sustained work in subsistence cultivation, away from the home and from child-caring tasks. The result was a decline in the intensity and duration of breast-feeding. It follows that the duration of abstinence also declined, and thus fertility rose. But Alexander's argument too misses important counter-considerations. Although an earlier resumption of inter-course would clearly act to raise fertility, the more arduous nature of women's work would act to depress it. Fertility would also be depressed by the increased incidence of separation, as the men left their families for extended periods to labour in distant sugar mills or on government construction projects. It is therefore difficult to accept Alexander's claim (1984: 370) that this single mechanism—increased labour demands/reduced duration of breast-feeding/reduced duration of abstinence—provides the most likely explanation for Java's accelerated population growth in the nineteenth century.

Conclusion

Indeed it is unlikely that *any* single mechanism can explain the transition to rapid population growth in Java, in South-East Asia as a whole, in the eighteenth and nineteenth centuries. Rather, accelerated growth is to be explained in terms of a convergence of many, if not most, of the influences which have been outlined in this chapter, although, and this is the crucial point, their relative importance undoubtedly changed over time. Thus Boomgaard's (1989) study of population growth in nineteenth-century Java brings a number of mechanisms into play and charts their changing strengths through that period. The following passage, concerned with declining mortality, captures this well:

a structural decline of the death rate due to vaccination, improved communications and 'de-urbanization' was partly counter-balanced between 1820 and 1850 by temporary setbacks such as cholera and typhoid fever, lower levels of nutrition, the introduction of the Cultivation System, and the Java War. After 1850, when these factors were no longer present or when their impact had weakened, the effects of this structural decline became more apparent. Between 1850 and 1880 the death rate must have been considerably lower than between 1800 and 1850. (Boomgaard, 1989: 192.)

There is an important related point. The particular influences which determined demographic change in one part of South-East Asia would almost certainly not have been precisely the same influences, or would not have been combined in the same way, as those which determined demographic change in another part of the region. Smallpox vaccination may have been important in one area, less important in another: improved famine relief may have been a major consideration in one district, of no importance in another. Indeed, the fundamental components of demographic change themselves might well have been sharply different in one part of the region from another. In one district, accelerated population growth may have reflected a decline in mortality, in another, a rise in fertility. An even more basic point remains unresolved. While it appears clear that Java and the Philippines experienced rapid population growth in the nineteenth century, it has yet to be established that the Javanese and Philippine rates were matched across the region. In fact, the rate of natural increase in Siam at the close of the nineteenth century, according to Sternstein (1984), was comparatively modest.

To explore effectively this complex, shifting pattern of demographic influences across South-East Asia requires a far more substantial body of statistical data than is at present available. It is simply not possible to build a persuasive analysis while, for most of the region, rates of population growth, levels of mortality and fertility, and the incidence of the major life-threatening diseases, decade-by-decade, have yet to be established. The construction of that statistical base, necessarily involving an extensive reworking of the frequently fragmented crude data from the colonial period, has proceeded furthest with respect to Java, although it is in the Philippines, where from the earlier decades of Spanish rule the Catholic Church, in attempting to count souls, recorded baptisms, marriages, and burials, that the most finely detailed construction may in time be accomplished. In truth, it is only as that process of statistical construction advances that it will be possible to explore confidently South-East Asia's modern demographic history and, of central importance, determine whether, or to what extent, there was in fact a common demographic experience across the region in the nineteenth century.

SUGGESTED READING

An excellent introduction to the historical demography of South-East Asia is provided by Norman G. Owen (1987c), 'The Paradox of Nineteenth-century Population Growth in Southeast Asia: Evidence from Java and the Philippines', *Journal of Southeast Asian Studies*, 18(1): 45–57; and the opening essay, 'Toward a History of Health in Southeast Asia', in Norman G. Owen (ed.) (1987a), *Death and Disease in Southeast Asia: Explorations in Social, Medical and Demographic History*, Southeast Asia Publication Series No. 14, Singapore: Oxford University Press/Asian Studies Association of Australia, pp. 3–30. The latter also includes valuable papers by Anthony Reid (1987), 'Low Population Growth and Its Causes in

Pre-Colonial Southeast Asia', pp. 33–47; Peter Boomgaard (1987), 'Morbidity and Mortality in Java, 1820–1880: Changing Patterns of Disease and Death', pp. 48–69; Peter Gardiner and Oey Mayling (1987), 'Morbidity and Mortality in Java, 1880–1940: The Evidence of the Colonial Reports', pp. 70–90; Norman G. Owen (1987b), 'Measuring Mortality in the Nineteenth Century Philippines', pp. 91–114.

The most substantial modern contribution to the historical demography of Java is Peter Boomgaard (1989), *Children of the Colonial State: Population Growth and Economic Development in Java, 1795–1880*, Centre for Asian Studies Amsterdam, Monograph No. 1, Amsterdam: Free University Press, which, as its title indicates, sets the acceleration of population growth in nineteenth-century Java in the context of the economic changes then taking place in the island. See also *Changing Economy in Indonesia: A Selection of Statistical Source Material from the Early 19th Century up to 1940* (General Editor, P. Boomgaard), Vol. 11, 1991, *Population Trends, 1795–1942*, edited by P. Boomgaard and A. J. Gooszen, Amsterdam: Royal Tropical Institute. Note should also be made of an earlier study, Widjojo Nitisastro (1970), *Population Trends in Indonesia*, Ithaca: Cornell University Press, which covers not only the nineteenth century but the twentieth century to the census of 1961. Graeme J. Hugo, Terence H. Hull, Valerie J. Hull, and Gavin W. Jones (1987), *The Demographic Dimension in Indonesian Development*, Singapore: Oxford University Press, is primarily a study of the contemporary position, but there are brief, valuable sections of historical discussion. Bram Peper (1970), 'Population Growth in Java in the 19th Century: A New Interpretation', *Population Studies*, 24(1): 71–84, included an important early attempt to revise Java's population estimates for the nineteenth century, although Peper's calculations and methods have been superseded by more recent scholarship, notably the work of Boomgaard (1989). The demand for labour/rising fertility argument is developed by Benjamin White (1973), 'Demand for Labor and Population Growth in Colonial Java', *Human Ecology*, 1(3): 217–36 (the same issue includes critical comments on the White article by Clifford Geertz, pp. 237–9; and by Etienne van de Walle, pp. 241–4); Peter Boomgaard (1981), 'Female Labour and Population Growth on Nineteenth-century Java', *Review of Indonesian and Malayan Affairs*, 15(2): 1–31; Paul Alexander (1984), 'Women, Labour and Fertility: Population Growth in Nineteenth Century Java', *Mankind*, 14(5): 361–72. An important attempt to construct population estimates for Java for a period prior to the nineteenth century is undertaken in M. C. Ricklefs (1986), 'Some Statistical Evidence on Javanese Social, Economic and Demographic History in the Later Seventeenth and Eighteenth Centuries', *Modern Asian Studies*, 20(1): 1–32.

For South-East Asia outside Java, the literature in historical demography is shamefully thin. For the Philippines, see the essay by Norman G. Owen (1987b), noted above, and P. C. Smith and Ng Shui-Meng (1982), 'The Components of Population Change in Nineteenth-century South-east Asia: Village Data from the Philippines', *Population Studies*, 36(2): 237–55. For Thailand, see Larry Sternstein (1984), 'The Growth of the Population of the World's Pre-eminent "Primate City": Bangkok at Its Bicentenary', *Journal of Southeast Asian Studies*, 15(1): 43–68; despite its title, this paper includes a substantial discussion of demographic change in the kingdom as a whole.

Finally, note should be made of two early general studies which have retained their value: Wilbur Zelinsky (1950), 'The Indochinese Peninsula: A Demographic Anomaly', *Far Eastern Quarterly*, 9(2): 115–45; Charles A. Fisher (1964), 'Some Comments on Population Growth in South-East Asia, with Special Reference to the Period since 1830', in C. D. Cowan (ed.), *The Economic Development of South-East Asia: Studies in Economic History and Political Economy*, London: George Allen & Unwin, pp. 48–71.

7

The Cultivation System

THE Cultivation System (in Dutch, *Kultuurstelsel*) was a series of government principles and administrative arrangements introduced from 1830, by which the Dutch colonial state forced the Javanese to cultivate selected crops for export on a major scale. It has long been the focus of fierce scholarly controversy. Writing in 1904, an American academic, Clive Day (1966: 311) argued that the Cultivation System had imposed 'incalculable exertions and hardships on ... the subject people'. Yet a Dutch scholar, Gerretson, writing in 1938, declared it to be 'the greatest benefit ever conferred by the Dutch on their East Indian possessions'. As the following pages will demonstrate, modern scholarship has been no less sharply divided.

Foundations for the Cultivation System

To establish the essential background, brief consideration must be given to two earlier instruments employed by European rulers to extract agricultural commodities for export from Java, for both, in different ways, laid the foundations for the Cultivation System. The first was the forced deliveries of the Dutch East India Company (*Vereenigde Oostindische Compagnie* or VOC). In essence, through its treaties with the indigenous rulers brought within its control during the course of the seventeenth and eighteenth centuries, the Company demanded regular delivery of specified commodities (rice, pepper, indigo, cotton, coffee, and sugar), for which it either made no payment or paid a price substantially below the market level. The Javanese rulers then used their traditional authority over their people to secure those commodities for delivery to the Company. In other words, the Dutch East India Company utilized the indigenous structure of authority and deference to extract, by command, commodities for trade. The second instrument was the land tax (here called the landrent) introduced by Thomas Stamford Raffles during the British occupation of Java between 1811 and 1816. Raffles sought, in an early formulation of the landrent, to tax individually each cultivator possessing land. But in the absence of detailed land and soil surveys this was simply impractical, and the returning Dutch administration, which retained Raffles's fiscal innovation, established the village as the unit of assessment and collection, leaving the distribution of the tax burden within the village to its own élite. At first the landrent could be paid either in money or in kind, but within a short time the emphasis was on money payment. Assessment was based upon the type of land, whether irrigated field or dry field, and its estimated production in its main crop, usually rice. The average assessment was set at two-fifths of estimated production.

The landrent reflected Raffles's commitment to liberal ideas of economic freedom, his strong condemnation of the compulsion and monopoly which had been practised by the Company. He anticipated that once the Javanese cultivator was free to cultivate whichever crop was most profitable, and was obliged to pay a land tax in cash, he would greatly increase his production. But Raffles's expectations were not fulfilled. Indeed, during the 1820s the value, quantity, and quality of cultivation for export declined. A number of considerations were at work here. With the abolition of forced deliveries, the Javanese simply withdrew from the cultivation of those crops which, either because they demanded a particularly heavy labour input or were seriously disruptive to cropping arrangements, had been strongly resented under that earlier regime. Or again, many villages, perhaps unfamiliar with or confused by the new arrangements, placed themselves under the authority of a Javanese notable or, less commonly, a Chinese or European entrepreneur. The latter paid the village's landrent, in return for which the village delivered to him part of its crop or made available to him part of its land and labour, which were then usually committed to export cultivations. It might be noted that this was, in effect if not in intention, a forced labour regime, in that here the village was committing its resources to the cultivation of market crops not as a free response to market opportunities but within the structures of traditional obligation and deference. Some villages, however, did seek to pay their own landrent, taking the initiative in organizing production and selling the surplus. But commonly these settlements chose to cultivate for the market not export crops, as the Dutch administration would have wished, but rice, in part because in the 1820s rice prices in local markets were relatively high.

The failure to stimulate export production in this period left the Dutch colonial administration in serious financial difficulties. These were made considerably worse by soaring expenditures, as the administration sought to finance improvements in the colony's infrastructure and, more seriously, struggled to meet the costs of putting down a major revolt against Dutch rule (the Java War, 1825–30). The treasury in the Netherlands, itself under strain, could not carry the burden of an unprofitable Java indefinitely. Indeed, quite the reverse, it looked to the colony to provide it with a substantial income. Thus it was that the Dutch King, William I, began a search for new instruments that would release Java's productive potential and make the colony pay. For example, Du Bus de Gisignies, Commissioner-General between 1826 and 1830, proposed that uncultivated lands on Java be sold or leased to private European planters who would work them with Javanese wage labour. But before these proposals could proceed very far, the King was drawn to alternative ideas being formed by Johannes van den Bosch, Commissioner-General in the Dutch West Indian colonies in 1827–8. Governor-General, then Commissioner-General in Java between 1830 and 1834, and Minister of Colonies in 1834–9, van den Bosch was the architect of the Cultivation System.

Principles and Practice

The broad principles of the Cultivation System were as follows. The rural Javanese were directed to set aside a part of their cultivable land (nominally one-fifth) and commit a part of their labour (again nominally one-fifth or, for each cultivator, 66 days a year) for the cultivation of a crop or crops designated by the administration. The crops included tobacco, tea, pepper, cinnamon, and cloves, but the important ones were coffee, sugar, and, in the early years, indigo. In the case of sugar, the labour for the preparation of the fields and the planting and tending of the crop was organized by the village head and local Javanese officials, supervised by Dutch administrators. The labour for harvesting, transporting, and processing the cane also came from within the village, but was commonly supplemented by recruitment from pools of migratory workers. The village was paid for the crops delivered. Although the crop payment was substantially below the market value of the delivery, indeed, where the village had been cultivating an export crop under the free disposition of land and labour in the 1820s, substantially below the payments it had then received, it was intended to be sufficient, according to the calculations of van den Bosch, to cover the landrent assessment of the village on all its lands. As the landrent was calculated, on average, at two-fifths of the estimated production of the village's main crop (usually rice), and as van den Bosch declared that the government crop would require no more labour than rice, it followed that under the Cultivation System the Javanese village would be required to commit only half the resources of land and labour (one-fifth instead of two-fifths) that it previously had to set aside to meet its obligations to the state. It would have more of its land and labour for its own use, for its own benefit. One further point on the crop payment must be made. Although an 1837 regulation stated that crop payments should be made individually to each cultivator engaged in the cultivation of the government crop, in fact they were commonly paid out in a single sum to the village as a whole, for internal distribution by the village élite. (A further regulation in 1851, insisting on individual payment under official supervision, appears to have been more closely followed.) As was noted earlier, the village was also the basis for the assessment and collection of the landrent, with the internal allocation of that charge again in the hands of the village élite. The economic position of that class was greatly strengthened by these arrangements.

Where the crops delivered from Java's fields required substantial local processing before shipment, this was usually undertaken by private European and Chinese contractors. With respect to sugar, the 1830s and 1840s in particular saw the construction of a considerable number of modern sugar factories, located directly in the island's sugar districts. Until the late 1840s, most were constructed and equipped with the assistance of interest-free loans from the government. These loans were repaid in the form of manufactured sugar. The factories paid for the cane which was delivered to them in the same way, the value of manufactured sugar produced, in respect to both loans and cane deliveries, being specified in the contract between the government and each factory owner. Labour for the sugar factories formed part of the government's compulsory labour demands, local administrators requiring village élites to provide the factory in their district with workers as specified. Those workers received a wage from the factory. It is important to note that compulsory labour services outside the actual cultivation of crops, involving not only work in the sugar factories but the cutting of cane, the hauling of crops for processing or shipment, the cutting of wood as fuel for the sugar factories, and the construction of irrigation works, roads, harbours, factories, and warehouses, were also an important element in the Cultivation System. Moreover, labour was still requisitioned on a large scale by Javanese notables and European officials for personal projects and service.

The central mechanism driving the Cultivation System was the structure of deference and obligation which permeated rural Java, the deeply embedded acceptance by village communities of the commands of supra-village authorities. Working through that mechanism, the Dutch colonial state could force a major expansion of commodity production from rural Java, could coerce villages into extending the area of their land under export crops, and could deliver labour into processing factories, hauling arrangements, and construction work, on a quite unprecedented scale. But it was not the only mechanism. On occasions, the Dutch used physical force. It was known for village headmen to be whipped for their failure to promote the government's cultivations, and for recalcitrant cultivators to be arrested, whipped, or stripped and exposed to the harsh sun. More importantly, the Dutch inserted material incentives to secure compliance. Reference has been made above to the cash payments for crop deliveries and for factory work. But in addition, the village headman received a percentage of the landrent collected in his village and the right to an increased share in the village's cultivated lands, while the supra-village authorities—the Javanese aristocratic intermediaries who delivered the cultivation instructions of the Dutch colonial administration down to the village—took a percentage of the value of the government crops produced in their district and (a Dutch measure to enhance their prestige) were permitted to have special guard units and an enlarged personal entourage.

One further observation will complete this outline of the broad features of the Cultivation System. The actual export of the vastly expanded volume of agricultural production from Java was undertaken in part by private merchants, indeed increasingly so by the middle of the nineteenth century, but principally by the government Netherlands Trading Company (*Nederlandsche Handel Maatschappij* or NHM), which had been established in 1824. Those commodities were then sold on world markets (the NHM was again the principal instrument), usually at prices which were considerably above the payments which had been made to the cultivators in Java.

It is important to emphasize that within this broad framework, there was considerable variation in local practice, that the Cultivation System was not a uniform structure, inflexibly implemented, but rather, in the words of one writer, 'an interlocking set of local accommodations' (Van Niel, 1972: 93). In the first place, the detailed arrangements for each government crop had to be different, for they all had quite distinct cultivation conditions and processing requirements. Sugar was grown, over a cycle of 12–18 months, on irrigated fields which could alternately accommodate rice cultivation. Coffee, a perennial, was grown in upland areas not otherwise cultivated, in forests, and in hedgerows. Thus the arrangements for these contrasting cultivations had to be separately evolved. But even with the same crop, the precise organizational structure could vary from district to district, reflecting local conditions. For example, in Pasuruan Residency, in East Java, the development of a specialized group of free carters by the mid-1830s enabled the local administration to withdraw from organizing the transportation of the sugar-cane, which became a matter of free agreement between the sugar factories and the carters. But in Probolinggo Regency such a group did not emerge in this period, and the transportation of cane remained a compulsory labour service, organized by the local administration, although paid for by the sugar factories. Finally, for obvious practical reasons, specific government cultivations were normally concentrated in particular areas. Sugar cultivation was inevitably concentrated in those districts which had the greatest extent of prime irrigated fields and the most abundant labour; and it was most densely concentrated within a close radius of the district's modern sugar factory, to facilitate the organizing of labour and the transportation of the cane. As a result, in many districts far more than one-fifth of a village's land was given over to the government crop, perhaps as high as two-thirds; but in others, far less.

The Cultivation System was not imposed throughout all Java. The residencies of Batavia, Buitenzorg, Yogyakarta, and Surakarta were never included. Moreover, only some 6 per cent at most of the recorded extent of irrigated fields was ever committed to the government cultivations. The imposition on labour was much more extensive: in 1840 more than 70 per cent of all recorded agricultural households in the residencies where the Cultivation System had been imposed were engaged in forced cultivations, although that proportion then began to decline, to around 40 per cent in 1870. It is also important to note that most of the crops grown under coercion were a source of loss for the Dutch administration or, at best, produced only a very modest profit. The forced cultivation of tea, tobacco, indigo, pepper, cinnamon was abandoned in the early 1860s. Success lay essentially with just two crops, coffee and sugar. They accounted for no less than 96 per cent of the profits of the Cultivation System between 1850 and 1860.

And those profits were enormous, far exceeding initial Dutch expectations. In the years 1831–50, the financial surplus from the colony, paid into the Netherlands treasury, accounted for 19 per cent of the Dutch public revenue: from 1851 to 1870 it accounted for 31.5 per cent. Under the Cultivation System, Java became, in the words of Van den Bosch's successor as Governor-General, J. C. Baud, 'the cork on which the Netherlands floats'. Java also became a source of great private wealth for a few individuals: for the Dutch, and Chinese, sugar manufacturers in the colony, there were fortunes to be made.

The Cultivation System was gradually dismantled over the final decades of the nineteenth century. The abandonment of minor forced cultivations in the early 1860s has already been noted. But the decisive measure was the 1870 Sugar Law, which provided for the phasing out of the forced cultivation of sugar from 1879, to be completed in 1890. As the colonial administration withdrew from direct involvement in sugar cultivation, the private contractors who had processed the government's cane under the Cultivation System assumed a commanding position in the industry. Under the 1870 Agrarian Law, those contractors now took long-term leases on, and thus gained control over, large expanses of sugar land. The most profitable of the government's cultivations, coffee, had the greatest longevity. The 1890s saw some contraction but it was not until 1918–19 that this last of the forced cultivations finally disappeared. The wider range of compulsory labour services—for the construction and repair of public works, for cane cutting, for carting, for factory work—were also dismantled. Thus it was in the 1860s that the colonial administration sharply reduced the conscription of coerced labour for the sugar factories. By 1872 every sugar factory in Java had abandoned the use of labour delivered by the government.

It will be evident from an earlier comment that the Cultivation System was not dismantled because its financial success had begun to falter. Indeed, its sustained contribution to the Netherlands treasury over many decades in large part explains why its abolition caused so much political conflict in the Netherlands and why its actual liquidation was so drawn out. Rather, the demise of the Cultivation System arose mainly from changing attitudes in the Netherlands, closely associated with the political changes of 1848—a growing reaction against the narrow favouritism which corrupted the administration of the System (the fact that lucrative sugar contracts often went to former colonial civil servants or to relatives of senior members of the government), a reaction against its wastefulness and arbitrariness, against the abuses it engendered. This was accompanied by the belief that to release Javanese labour from government coercion would now lead to a more efficient and benevolent exploitation of Java's agricultural resources.

'Agricultural Involution'

Considerable scholarly controversy surrounds the impact of the Cultivation System on the material welfare—for example, on nutritional levels and on patterns of personal consumption—of the rural Javanese. This subject will be explored in Chapter 9, as part of a broader examination of material welfare in rural South-East Asia during the decades of export expansion in the nineteenth century. Greater controversy has surrounded the way in which the rural Javanese are said to have responded to the labour burdens imposed on them by the Cultivation System: essentially, whether they were driven into a process of economic and social levelling and ultimately into economic stagnation or whether, on the contrary, there occurred increasing socio-economic inequality, within which certain individuals demonstrated pronounced acquisitiveness and economic initiative. It is this controversy which is the focus here.

The starting point is Clifford Geertz's *Agricultural Involution: The Processes of Ecological Change in Indonesia*, which appeared in 1963. Before Geertz's analysis is outlined, it must be said that more recent scholarship has been highly critical: 'almost no element in the Geertzian view of Javanese agrarian change is supported by available evidence', suggests one writer (White, 1983: 29). In these circumstances it may be necessary to explain why considerable space is being given to Geertz. It is partly because *Agricultural Involution*, widely acclaimed when it first appeared, has had a major influence on the study of agrarian change not only in Indonesia but far beyond. In addition, it was a book which, if only because it stimulated so much critical comment from specialists, established the agenda for virtually all subsequent research on nineteenth-century rural Java. And finally, to explore how a once well-established orthodoxy comes under attack, arguably is over-thrown, is in itself superbly instructive.

In its analysis of the impact of the Cultivation System on the rural communities of nineteenth-century Java, *Agricultural Involution* focuses on the centrally important sugar cultivation. In broad outline, it argues that the Cultivation System put great pressure on the land resources of the Javanese, in circumstances where, Java even then being densely populated, the availability of new cul-tivable land was already sharply decreasing. That pressure came in two ways. First, the Cultivation System is said by Geertz to have 'detonated', directly and indirectly, a population 'explosion' (Geertz, 1963: 70), although he appears unwilling to identify the precise demographic mechanisms that were at work. (On this point the reader might refer to the discussion in Chapter 6 on population growth in nineteenth-century Java.) Second, the forced cultivation of sugar removed very extensive areas of *sawah* (irrigated fields) from rice cultivation. A remarkable characteristic of such irrigated fields, Geertz argues, was their capacity to absorb increasing num-bers of cultivators per unit of land while maintaining per capita output at a constant, or only slowly declining, level, implying, of course, an increasing output per unit of land. Therefore as Java's population grew and as the demands of forced sugar cultivation sharply increased, more and more labour was packed into the ter-raced rice fields.

To be specific, the practices employed in the cultivation of rice became increasingly finely detailed. Instead of being roughly broadcast, increasingly rice seeds were sown in nursery beds and then carefully transplanted to the main fields; on occasions, seeds were pregerminated in the cultivator's dwelling. The rice fields were more carefully prepared—more thoroughly ploughed, raked, and levelled—before receiving the young plants. More plants were accommodated in a given area by planting them in exactly spaced rows. Weeding was undertaken more frequently and thoroughly; the irrigated terraces were now periodically drained during the growing season to expose the plants briefly to the air. Harvesting of the mature crop was increasingly performed with a razor-like hand blade, cutting each rice stalk individually. Double-cropping, in some areas triple-cropping, was instituted. Local irrigation sys-tems, each a complex of small water channels, hollowed bamboo pipes, and narrow embankments, were extended and refined; the flooding and draining of the terraces were regulated with greater precision. The core methods of wet-rice cultivation remained unchanged. But every stage in the cultivation process, from the preparation of the seeds to the harvesting of the mature crop, became more and more refined. And it is that process of internal elaboration of a basic pattern which Geertz characterizes as 'involution'.

Across the rice-terraced districts of nineteenth-century Java, that elaboration absorbed an astonishing amount of labour, as indeed it was intended to do. But each labour-absorbing elaboration—careful transplanting, fastidious weeding, razor-blade harvesting—produced at least some increase in output per field, and thus sustained the level of production per cultivator. Of central importance in raising the productivity of the rice terraces was what Geertz sees as the 'mutualistic' relationship between wet rice and sugar, in that they demanded, he suggests, an almost identical physical environment (soil and climatic conditions, irrigation flows, labour inputs). In essence, the forced expansion of sugar cultivation, by requiring the creation of new terraces and the extension and refinement of irrigation systems on both existing and new fields, greatly improved conditions for the cultivation of rice. The increased production of rice that resulted from that improvement was secured, of course, by the increased number of cultivators, a larger workforce ready to be committed to the cultivation of sugar at that point in the crop cycle when rice gave way in the fields to the government's cultivation. Thus it was, Geertz argues, that the heavy sugar areas of Java had proportionately more *sawah*, more population, and, even though more of their *sawah* was occupied by sugar, more rice production, than the non-sugar areas. Sugar, wet rice, and population density flourished together.

The pressures imposed on the rural Javanese by rapidly increasing population and the demands of the forced sugar cultivation for *sawah* led not only to an elaboration of cultivation practices but also to an increased intricacy in land-tenure patterns and labour arrangements. There was a strengthening of communal landownership, with the village, as a corporate body, periodically rotating and redividing the fields assigned to individuals. Land-use rights and labour deployment came to be governed by intricate arrangements for subcontracting, leasing, sharing, exchange, and collective endeavour. The individual cultivator, Geertz suggests, commonly occupied a remarkably complex structure of agreements and understandings. A man might lease his land to another for a cash payment, and then work that land as a tenant, perhaps letting parts of the holding to subtenants. An individual might negotiate the right to plant and weed a particular plot in return for an agreed share of the harvest, and then subcontract the work to another. A cultivator might lease part of his land to tenants, while seeking tenancies on the lands of others. These highly intricate, yet flexible land-working patterns and labour arrangements must be seen, argues Geertz, as an attempt on the part of the rural Javanese to provide access to land and to employment for all, in circumstances where a rapidly growing population was bearing down on increasingly strained land resources. For that access, however small, ensured for the individual some claim, even if slight, on the production of the rice fields. It ensured survival.

It is essential to emphasize that, in Geertz's analysis, that response reflected the unique social–cultural attitudes and values of rural Java. Under the pressure of increasing numbers and limited resources, agrarian communities in many third world countries, he suggests, bifurcated into a small class of powerful landowners, and a mass of oppressed dependant cultivators. But the rural Javanese maintained a comparatively high degree of social and economic homogeneity, by seeking a reasonably equitable distribution of the resources available to the community and of the burdens imposed on it. As the pressures intensified, they sought to share their poverty. In contrast to the disintegration into 'haves' and 'have-nots' found elsewhere, nineteenth-century Java held communities of 'just enoughs' and 'not-quite enoughs'.

But, crucially, the maintenance of social and economic homogeneity was inescapably accompanied by a tightening descent into economic stagnation for the rural Javanese. Shared poverty smothered individualism and acquisitiveness, the emergence of a class of rural capitalists with the resources and ambition to seek a major restructuring of the rural economy. And the rigid, insistent elaboration of agricultural practices, the near obsessive determination to absorb labour rather than raise its productivity, closed off the route to agricultural advance. In Geertz's own words, the most important impact of the Cultivation System was that 'it prevented the effects on Javanese peasantry and gentry alike of an enormously deeper Western penetration into their life from leading to autochthonous agricultural modernization at the point it could most easily have occurred' (Geertz, 1963: 53).

Economic and Social Differentiation in Rural Java

Recent empirical research by, in particular, R. E. Elson, M. R. Fernando, and G. R. Knight, has challenged not only Geertz's description of change in nineteenth-century rural Java but the very core of his analysis—the argument that the communities of rural Java, under the pressures imposed by the Cultivation System, maintained a comparatively high degree of social and economic homogeneity.

On the basis of detailed work on the Pasuruan area of East Java, Elson (1978) rejects Geertz's assertion that there was a simple 'mutualistic' relationship between sugar and wet rice, that the Javanese took advantage of the improved irrigation facilities that accompanied the forced expansion of sugar cultivation, injecting more labour into the *sawah*, to secure increasing rice production per unit of land: that sugar and wet rice flourished together. In his view, the link between sugar cultivation and the level of rice production was more complex and of a different nature from that proposed by Geertz. Elson suggests, in part, that in the early years of the Cultivation System, the construction of new irrigation facilities that accompanied the introduction of forced sugar cultivation did indeed contribute to a substantial rise in rice production per unit of land. But the rise in rice productivity levelled out towards the mid-1840s: in fact production per unit of land fell somewhat, as the demand for labour in, most importantly, forced sugar cultivation led to a decline in the quantity and quality of labour committed to the cultivation of rice. Rice-seeds were carelessly prepared, the *sawah* was not properly worked, the crop was prematurely harvested, irrigation facilities were inadequately maintained. And the more heavily a district was committed to sugar cultivation, the more skimpy was its allocation of labour to the cultivation of rice. Over the longer term, sugar and wet rice did not flourish together. The productivity of the rice terraces did not keep pace with the rise in population: and from the mid-1840s, Elson notes, Pasuruan Residency was often a net importer of rice.

Finally, according to Elson, there is no evidence that the process of labour intensification—the involution of agricultural practices—so important in Geertz's analysis, occurred in Pasuruan in these middle years of the nineteenth century. Indeed the evidence on agricultural techniques, noted above, indicates that they deteriorated in this period: in the 1840s and 1850s there was no rise in rice production per unit of land that would indicate an intensified

commitment of labour. One further observation on the relationship between sugar and rice can be added. White (1983) challenges Geertz's assertion that sugar demands irrigation, drainage,
and a general environment almost identical to that for wet rice—
the implication that the forced cultivation of sugar was smoothly
inserted into the rice regime—by pointing out that sugar-cane
takes 18 months to mature, rice just 4 months, and that the two
crops have markedly different water requirements. The irrigation
of the newly planted cane during the dry season 'played havoc with
village agriculture' (Knight, 1982: 140).

Knight (1982), who has undertaken detailed work on the north-
central residency of Pekalongan, challenges Geertz's assertion that
under the pressures of the Cultivation System there was a strengthening of communal landownership and repeated reallocation of
access to *sawah* within the communities of rural Java in order to
spread, and thus lighten, the cultivation and labour burdens now
being imposed. He argues that as the forced cultivations, and sugar
in particular, brought considerable financial benefits (in the form
of crop payments) to landholders, the latter would have had little
interest in reallocating their *sawah*. Although the ownership of land
also brought with it liability for labour services (on construction
works, in the sugar factories), the cash-swollen landowner would
not spread that liability by a partial reallocation of his *sawah* but
escape from it altogether by paying a landless labourer in the
village, or instructing one of his own labourers, to perform the
services in his place. Knight suggests that the periodic reallocation of *sawah*, which did occur on a major scale in Pekalongan
under the Cultivation System, took place *among* the landholders
(and therefore did not involve a broadening of the landholding
group), and was driven by the demands of the sugar factories for
large, consolidated sugar holdings. It was not a levelling mechanism.

Elson's (1984) work on East Java suggests a slightly different
pattern. In parts of that region, but not all, the immediate response
of landholders to the introduction of forced sugar cultivation was
indeed to equalize their holdings (and thus the burden of labour
services that arose from the ownership of land) and to admit others
within the settlement to the landholding group (reducing the per
capita level of labour and cultivation demands). But this was a
short-term accommodation to sharply imposed burdens, and was
soon discarded. The landholding élite then consolidated their control of the land, paying or instructing the class of excluded, land-

less cultivators to perform on their behalf the cultivation and labour obligations attached to the holding of land—in the manner described above. It is also important to note a comment by White (1983) on Geertz's description of Java's highly intricate land-tenure patterns and labour arrangements. Put bluntly, those patterns and arrangements appear to have been no more complex in Java than elsewhere in Asia. Nor, apparently, did they increase in complexity during the nineteenth century.

But the central thrust of the attack on Geertz's analysis in *Agricultural Involution* is directed against the argument that under the pressures of the Cultivation System, the rural Javanese main-tained a relatively high degree of economic and social homo-geneity. Elson (1978, 1984, 1994), Fernando (1986), and Knight (1982) each argue that there was substantial socio-economic dif-ferentiation in rural Java prior to 1830, and that those cleavages were forced still wider during the period of the Cultivation System. Two principal influences were at work: in both, it will be noted, the central element was the increasing monetization of Javanese rural life under the Cultivation System, as crop payments, factory wages, and cartage fees were pumped into the countryside. First, the structure of the Cultivation System administration—the fact that in general Dutch officials and higher Javanese authorities dealt with the settlement as a single unit rather than with each cultivator individually—greatly enhanced the position of the village élite. It was the village chief and his coterie who determined the allocation of fields for the forced cultivations, received the village's crop pay-ments, and collected together its landrent. And they used that political–administrative power and the monies that flowed through their hands to secure for themselves a larger allocation of the vil-lage *sawah*, to demand labour services and deliveries of rice from weaker elements within the village, to divert crop payments into their own pockets, to reduce their own landrent contribution, and to pay or direct others to carry out their cultivation and labour service obligations. Those who lost ground were the much greater number of smaller landholders, denied their due share of the crop payments, pressured by arbitrary labour demands, and required to bear the burden of the forced cultivations and the landrent.

The second major influence was the marked growth and diver-sification of economic opportunities that resulted directly from the expansion of the forced cultivations. The sugar industry, for example, required a great army of cane cutters, factory labourers, carters, wharf coolies; it needed basket weavers and matters (to produce the packing material for the manufactured sugar) and pot makers; it needed woodmen to cut and deliver firewood to fuel the sugar factories. In addition, the specialization of certain individuals and communities in the government cultivations, and the income it brought them, led others to specialize in the production of local food-crops (rice, but also corn and soya bean) and household handicrafts, and thus to the growth of the internal market, serviced by an increasingly large force of traders, pedlars, and carters. It was the landless, in the main, who took advantage of those opportunities. Probably for the first time, many rural Javanese 'could lead a reasonably stable and secure economic existence without having direct access to land' (Elson, 1984: 95). Here, in Knight's words, was 'revealed a pervasive growth of capitalist relations and purposes' (Knight, 1982: 147), a process of widening socio-economic differentiation and advancing economic diversification far removed from the smothering homogeneity and tightening stagnation depicted in *Agricultural Involution*.

Conclusion

In 1984 Geertz published a substantial reply to the critics of *Agricultural Involution*. The defence was strikingly delivered. His dismissal of the history of the emerging rural capitalists, so important in the work of Elson and Knight, as 'a series of weak, incipient movements, local spasms soon swallowed up in the general immiseration, gradual, diffuse and unrelenting, of Javanese village society' (Geertz, 1984: 519) is a typical Geertzian phrase. But it is unconvincing in the face of the substantial data marshalled by recent scholarship. *Agricultural Involution* remains a brilliant hypothesis brought down by empirical evidence. It would be wise, however, to end with a warning. That empirical, local research has focused on districts heavily committed to sugar. It is important to note, for example, that in 1850 over a third of the crop payments for sugar for the whole of Java went to Pasuruan and Besuki Residencies. This constituted a very substantial injection of cash, specifically directed. But, for that reason, can the changes which occurred in Pasuruan during the period of the Cultivation System be regarded as typical of the changes which occurred throughout Java under that regime? More to the point, given the structure of local accommodations and the variety of local conditions, what was typical?

SUGGESTED READING

There is an extensive literature on this subject. The major modern
study is, undoubtedly, R. E. Elson (1994), *Village Java under the
Cultivation System, 1830–1870*, Southeast Asia Publication Series
No. 25, Sydney: Allen & Unwin/Asian Studies Association of
Australia. For statistical data, see *Changing Economy in Indonesia:
A Selection of Statistical Source Material from the Early 19th Century
up to 1940* (General Editor, P. Boomgaard), Vol. 14, 1993, *The
Cultivation System: Java, 1834–1880*, edited by Frans van
Baardewijk, Amsterdam: Royal Tropical Institute.

Excellent introductions to the Cultivation System are provided
by C. Fasseur (1978), 'Some Remarks on the Cultivation System
in Java', *Acta Historiae Neerlandicae*, 10: 143–62; and Robert Van
Niel (1981), 'The Effect of Export Cultivations in Nineteenth-
century Java', *Modern Asian Studies*, 15(1): 25–58. Also valuable as
an introduction is Part I of Peter Boomgaard (1989), *Children of
the Colonial State: Population Growth and Economic Development in
Java, 1795–1880*, Centre for Asian Studies Amsterdam, Monograph No. 1, Amsterdam: Free University Press; Part II provides a
good introduction to economic and social change in Java under the
Cultivation System and before. Two important, earlier, studies—
of the detailed mechanisms of the Cultivation System and its
impact on the Javanese—are Robert Van Niel (1964), 'The
Function of Landrent under the Cultivation System in Java',
Journal of Asian Studies, 23(3): 357–75; and Robert Van Niel
(1972), 'Measurement of Change under the Cultivation System in
Java, 1837–1851', *Indonesia*, 14: 89–109. R. E. Elson (1989), 'The
Mobilization and Control of Peasant Labour under the Early
Cultivation System in Java', in R. J. May and William J. O'Malley
(eds.), *Observing Change in Asia: Essays in Honour of J. A. C.
Mackie*, Bathurst: Crawford House Press, pp. 73–93, demon-
strates the importance of economic incentives and economic co-
ercion in the mobilization of rural labour in the early years of the
Cultivation System. See also G. R. Knight (1990), 'The Peasantry
and the Cultivation of Sugar Cane in Nineteenth-century Java: A
Study from Pekalongan Residency, 1830–1870', in Anne Booth,
W. J. O'Malley, Anna Weidemann (eds.), *Indonesian Economic
History in the Dutch Colonial Era*, Southeast Asia Studies,
Monograph No. 35, New Haven: Yale University, pp. 49–66. Two
articles consider the emergence of 'free labour', that is, labour not
working within traditional ties of coercion, in the sugar factories in

the middle decades of the nineteenth century: G. R. Knight (1988), 'Peasant Labour and Capitalist Production in Late Colonial Indonesia: The "Campaign" at a North Java Sugar Factory, 1840–70', *Journal of Southeast Asian Studies*, 19(2): 245–65 sees here the establishment of a proletarianized work-force—one obliged to sell its labour to exist; in contrast, R. E . Elson (1986b), 'Sugar Factory Workers and the Emergence of "Free Labour" in Nineteenth-century Java', *Modern Asian Studies*, 20(1): 139–74, sees, after the end of government-ordered conscription of factory labour in the 1860s, the continuation of coerced labour deliveries by village élites, but now at the behest of the private sugar manufacturers. For a longer-term perspective, see Peter Boomgaard (1990), 'Why Work for Wages? Free Labour in Java, 1600–1900', *Economic and Social History in the Netherlands*, 2: 37–56. A valuable analysis of the decline of the Cultivation System, focusing on the political decision-making process in the Netherlands in the 1860s, is provided by C. Fasseur (1991), 'Purse or Principle: Dutch Colonial Policy in the 1860s and the Decline of the Cultivation System', *Modern Asian Studies*, 25(1): 33–52.

The agricultural involution hypothesis was established, of course, by Clifford Geertz (1963), *Agricultural Involution: The Processes of Ecological Change in Indonesia*, Berkeley: University of California Press. Critics of that analysis include Benjamin White (1983), '"Agricultural Involution" and Its Critics: Twenty Years After', *Bulletin of Concerned Asian Scholars*, 15(2): 18–31; R. E. Elson (1978), *The Cultivation System and 'Agricultural Involution'*, Centre of Southeast Asian Studies, Working Paper No. 14, Melbourne: Monash University; R. E. Elson (1984), *Javanese Peasants and the Colonial Sugar Industry: Impact and Change in an East Java Residency, 1830–1940*, Southeast Asia Publication Series No. 9, Singapore: Oxford University Press/Asian Studies Association of Australia; G. R. Knight (1982), 'Capitalism and Commodity Production in Java', in Hamza Alavi et al., *Capitalism and Colonial Production*, London: Croom Helm, pp. 119–58; M. R. Fernando (1986), 'Dynamics of Peasant Economy in Java at Local Levels', in David P. Chandler and M. C. Ricklefs (eds.), *Nineteenth and Twentieth Century Indonesia: Essays in Honour of Professor J. D. Legge*, Centre of Southeast Asian Studies, Clayton: Monash University, pp. 97–121. Geertz replied to his critics in Clifford Geertz (1984), 'Culture and Social Change: The Indonesian Case', *Man*, New Series, 19(4): 511–32; his lengthy analytical footnotes repay attention.

Finally, note should be made of a much earlier, highly critical, account of the Cultivation System: Clive Day (1966), *The Policy and Administration of the Dutch in Java*, originally published in 1904, reprinted Kuala Lumpur: Oxford University Press. J. S. Furnivall (1939), *Netherlands India: A Study of Plural Economy*, Cambridge: Cambridge University Press, is an important early attempt at a more balanced assessment of the Cultivation System.

8
The Cultivator and Export Expansion

THE expansion of cultivation for export on the part of the indigenous populations was arguably the most remarkable feature of
economic change in nineteenth-century South-East Asia. The
basic data on that cultivation—where it was located in the region,
the principal crops grown, and its awesome scale—have been presented in Part I. The aim of the present chapter is to explain why
the region's cultivators became engaged in that immense enterprise: why did hundreds of thousands of cultivating families right
across nineteenth-century South-East Asia become so intensively
committed to large-scale export cultivation? In Java, as was explained in Chapter 7, the cultivators' involvement in export production was, in essence, a response to instruction from above. The
colonial authorities determined the nature, location, and scale of
cultivation, and their demands were transmitted down to the cultivators through traditional mechanisms of compliance and obligation. But in this respect the Javanese experience was unique.
Elsewhere in South-East Asia, rural settlements engaged in the
vast expansion of export cultivation as a result of a complex of
market, environmental, and socio-economic forces, varying with
the circumstances of the individual, and by time and place. This
chapter explores those complex influences, taking as examples the
great rice-growing deltas of mainland South-East Asia (the deltas
of the Irrawaddy, the Chao Phraya, and the Mekong), the central
plain of Luzon, and the Bikol region of south-eastern Luzon.

The Cultivators' Toil

By far the major part of the expansion of production for export in
nineteenth-century South-East Asia was achieved not by a more
intensive working of areas already under cultivation but by bring-

ing new tracts under the plough. In other words, for vast numbers of agriculturalists and their families, the expansion of export production involved migration from areas of established settlement to frontier wildernesses, where the land had first to be torn from nature before it could be planted with crops. Almost invariably the clearing of wild tract was a punishing task, made even more demanding by the hostility of the environment. In the mid-nineteenth century, most of the lower delta of the Irrawaddy, soon to be transformed into a vast expanse of rice, was covered with forest-swamp and coarse grassland. To bring a tract in that frontier wilderness into cultivation, the pioneer agriculturalist commonly had to fell an extensive cluster of trees, some as high as 150 feet, burn off the undergrowth, and remove the network of tough, embedded tree-roots. Either the roots were burnt and then hacked out with a crude axe, or the tract was flooded and then left for several years for the roots to rot away. It would be at least three or four years before such land could be ploughed and put under rice. It was easier to clear grassland. Most of the coarse, thick cover, growing to some 10 feet, was simply burnt off; the debris and remaining roots were then harrowed under. In this initial process of clearing and settlement in the lower Irrawaddy Delta, the cultivator may well, in addition, have had to construct modest embankments around his new holding to protect it from excess flooding once it was under cultivation.

The pioneer cultivator could be hit by disaster. He was vulnerable to malaria, dysentery, and the other debilitating diseases which took hold in areas of new settlement. A severe attack could leave him too weak to continue the punishing task of clearing the wilderness and bringing it into production. He could lose his work animals, his water buffalo or bullock, through attacks of rinderpest, anthrax or foot-and-mouth disease. Tigers and snakes could pose a considerable threat, to the psychological state but also on occasions to the actual lives of new occupants on the frontier. The cultivator's crop was also vulnerable—to excess flooding, as monsoon-swollen rivers and heavy tides broke through embankments and bunds, to the ravages of rats, wild pigs, crabs, birds, and a wide variety of caterpillars, worms, and beetles which devoured young shoots and attacked maturing plants. In the frontier reaches of the Chao Phraya plain or the lower Irrawaddy Delta, a single wild elephant could trample down crops, bulldoze ditches and embankments, and crash through dwellings and stores, destroying in minutes a settlement that may have taken years of toil to establish.

There were also human predators. In the Mekong Delta, a pioneer family could bring into production some distant tract, only to be dispossessed by a powerful land speculator who earlier, in certain anticipation that the area would at some point be settled, had filed with the local administration a provisional claim for possession. The lone cultivator had neither the money, the confidence, or the official connections to challenge the speculator's claim. The colonial administration's land survey and registration procedures were too weak, its judicial processes insufficiently impartial to protect the little man. He lost his land. It was legal theft. Or the pioneer might lose his land through debt. Forced to borrow by the cost of bringing an uncleared tract into production or by later misfortune (illness, a disastrous harvest, the loss of work animals), the harshness of the terms imposed or further ill-fortune could well result in default and foreclosure. Cultivators were also expropriated by intimidation and brute force. Police and courts were thin on the ground in frontier districts. Assault, sabotage, and theft were unchecked.

These last observations must be kept in perspective. By no means all the pioneer agriculturalists seeking to increase production on the frontier fell victim to malaria, wild pigs, or land grabbers. But many did, and for all there was the risk that they might. There was also the certainty for all of back-breaking toil in clearing the wilderness and bringing it into production. Why indeed did they do it?

The Cultivators' Reward

One commonly held explanation is that large-scale market production offered the cultivator the prospect of a substantial improvement in material well-being. Over the second half of the nineteenth century, the prices of export crops across the region showed a substantial rise. The wholesale price of paddy in Rangoon, for example, rose from 45 rupees per one hundred baskets in 1855 to 95 rupees in 1900: in 1912 it stood at 160 rupees per one hundred baskets. A substantial proportion of that price was taken by intermediaries—by exporters, millers, and internal traders. But the strength of international demand for rice in this period suggests that the cultivator too received a considerable return. As the wholesale price rose, and as the size of his holdings expanded, his cash income increased. There were also greatly increased opportunities to spend that income, as cheap, mass-produced Western manufactures flooded into the region. The same transport and trading networks that carried agricultural exports out from interior districts to the region's main ports and across the seas to foreign markets, in return brought manufactures from the industrial economies of the West and directed them back into the deepest recesses of the rural interior. Before the end of the nineteenth century, an impressive range and volume of Western manufactured imports was available to the vast majority of rural settlements. Some were, in the circumstances of the time, minor luxuries—European glassware and crockery, metal safes and chests, clocks. But most were necessities of life—textiles, corrugated iron roofs, soap, kerosene lamps—and replaced locally produced articles.

The central consideration here is that an agricultural family or rural settlement, in directing its labour away from the production of household and personal articles (cooking implements, textiles) and towards the cultivation of a single marketable crop, selling its increased surplus production for a cash income and then buying imported manufactures in place of the household and personal articles it no longer produced itself, secured three important advantages. It increased the quantity of the clothing and household implements it consumed. By specializing in the production of that commodity in which it was most adept, and by buying in those articles which could be more skilfully or cheaply produced elsewhere, the rural family or settlement increased the volume of its consumption. Frequently there would also be an improvement in quality. Machine-produced textiles from the factories of Lancashire were commonly more robust, and certainly more evenly woven, than the hand-produced textiles found in the Siamese or Burmese rural household. Third, by relying on imported manufactures to meet a major part of its needs, the rural family reduced the toil that was commonly involved in household production. The hand-weaving of cloth, to give an obvious example, was arduous and time-consuming. In brief, although the expansion of agricultural production clearly involved the cultivating family in back-breaking toil, the income so earned enabled it to find relief from other forms of drudgery.

The new, expanding patterns of consumption were clearly evident across the vast export-dominated districts of South-East Asia. In the Irrawaddy Delta, corrugated iron roofs replaced traditional thatch, European and Indian textiles replaced local cloth, and cultivators' dwellings were stocked with imported lamps, crockery, furniture, and mirrors. The eagerness with which the Burmese cultivator acquired a taste for foreign manufactures was well caught in a report submitted by a settlement officer at the beginning of the twentieth century, in which he described seeing a Burmese 'smoking a French briar pipe and suckling his motherless babe with an English nursing bottle containing Swiss condensed milk' (Adas, 1974: 76). In Adas's (1974) study of the development of the Burma Delta, it is that material reward which emerges as a key factor in the Burmese cultivators' remarkable commitment to export production over the second half of the nineteenth century.

But two cautionary observations must be added. The first involves drawing attention to the precise character of the argument presented in the preceding paragraph. It is that consumer rewards provided sufficient incentive for the cultivator to endure the tough physical demands imposed in clearing the frontier wilderness and bringing it into production. The cultivator faced that challenge for the prospect of corrugated iron roofs, Swiss condensed milk, Lancashire cottons, and imported crockery. To put the argument in this way is certainly not to dismiss it. Many of the imported manufactures stocked in interior markets or peddled by itinerant traders in rural South-East Asia in this period would have secured for the cultivating family a substantial improvement in its material well-being. The corrugated iron roof gave more secure protection against the monsoon storm than thatch; the kerosene lamp, providing light after sunset with only a minimum of preparation, considerably altered the social and production patterns of the household; mosquito nets offered protection against a too-familiar menace; and imported textiles, as noted earlier, relieved the household of a traditional burden. These simple manufactures thus offered real advantages. The advantages of canned milk, biscuits, and glassware, it must be said, were perhaps less substantial. But the essential point is that even where the advantages were of real substance, they must be set against the costs of securing them. Pitching the challenge of the frontier against the consumer aspirations of the cultivator, just how powerful a force could material incentives be?

The second cautionary observation is that not all cultivators found fortune on the frontier. Many fell victim to disease, to the destruction of their crop by flood or pest, to debt, or to land-grabbers. In certain districts, including the extreme western provinces of the Mekong Delta where land-grabbing appears to have been rife, the rate of failure among pioneer settlers may have been high. It might be argued that this reality was less important than the fact that each pioneer setting off for the frontier was consumed with the hope that, irrespective of the failure of others, he surely would be able to build a secure livelihood. Yet in the extremity of the Mekong Delta at least, it would appear that those hopes of material reward were dashed so frequently that it is difficult to see how they could have remained a powerful incentive. In addition there was a substantial body of cultivators who could not in any circumstances entertain the hope of real material reward on that frontier. These were the seasonal labourers, much in evidence in the western extremity of the Mekong Delta, who would offer their labour for one or two meals plus a fraction of a piaster per day. For them, other, far more powerful forces were clearly at work. For the pioneer Burmese settler too, despite the firmer prospect of consumer reward, material incentive alone was not sufficient. Each, to varying degrees, was also being pushed into the expansion of export cultivation on the frontier.

The Push to the Frontier

A wide range of influences can be identified here. Most importantly, economic conditions in the districts from which the pioneer settlers and labourers migrated were often poor or sharply deteriorating. Some of those districts were inherently insecure, and the opening of the frontier simply provided the clear opportunity for relief which its inhabitants may long have sought. The principal example here is the Dry Zone of Burma, a region of relatively scanty and uncertain rainfall, and thus prone to drought, food shortages, and periodic famine. With the opening and advance of the delta frontier from the mid-nineteenth century, distressed inhabitants of the Dry Zone could migrate south to where the vast tracts of cultivable land and strong demand for labour offered some prospect of temporary or permanent relief. In this period the volume of migration into the delta in any year was firmly correlated with the severity of food shortages in the Dry Zone. Thus when the rains for the 1896–7 cropping season failed, the railways and roads leading south were crowded with cultivators in search of land and work. It might also be noted that those districts in the Dry Zone which were most heavily irrigated, and therefore in which food production was most secure, supplied the fewest migrants to the delta. A further example, although on a considerably more modest scale, is the north-east of Siam, another region of scanty, uncertain rainfall, a region of much poverty and of limited economic opportunity. As the area brought into cultivation in the lower Central Plain expanded in the closing years of the nineteenth century, thousands of north-east labourers poured into the heavily commercialized rice districts in search of seasonal work.

Elsewhere, it was the increasing pressure of population on the land that forced cultivators out onto the frontier. In the central Siamese province of Ayutthaya, population growth had led, by the 1880s, to the occupation of virtually all cultivable land. Now the younger adult cultivators, pushed out of households which had become too large for their holdings, were forced to migrate beyond the frontier of settled agriculture to find unclaimed land to bring into production. In the Philippines, a critical element in the substantial migrations from the Ilocos region of northern Luzon southward into the Central Plain from the early nineteenth century was that region's overpopulation. This was manifested in a deterioration of the agricultural environment, the fragmentation of holdings, and the disappearance of agricultural surpluses. Towards the close of the nineteenth century there was a displacement of individuals from Bangkok, many of whom made their way into the wilderness to the east of the capital. Some of those pioneers appear to have held small plots—market gardens, orchards, and rice fields—within the city limits. Either their holdings had been swallowed up by the increased demand for land in Bangkok for commercial and residential purposes, or they were the victims of particular misfortunes—the death or simple disappearance of an economically important member of the family, a crooked land-deal, a gambling obsession. In the more densely populated eastern and central parts of Cochin-China at the end of the nineteenth century, tenant cultivators who were hopelessly in debt often slipped away in the middle of the night and made their way to new beginnings on the western frontier. The oppression by landlords, exploiting the competition among the landless for access to land and capital, was a powerful force for flight. The streams of migrants making their way to the western frontier also included outcasts—rural bandits, troublemakers expelled from their village, criminals escaping the attention of the colonial police.

Two further forces may have driven the cultivator into an expansion of export production. It is sometimes argued that the demand by colonial administrations that taxes be paid in cash forced cul-

tivators into the market, because hitherto so much of rural production was for subsistence, and those rural transactions which did
take place were largely conducted on the basis of barter. But this
argument may be difficult to sustain. Rural populations were more
involved in cash transactions prior to the major expansion of
export production, and therefore more able to meet the cash tax
demands of the colonial state with existing patterns of production,
than the argument allows. And it is doubtful whether, in the early
decades of colonial rule at least, the authorities had the administrative capacity to identify all potential taxpayers and, crucially, to
enforce tax demands against them. Late nineteenth-century
Cochin-China, according to one writer, 'was a tax evader's para-
dise' (Gran, 1975: 350).

The final coercive factor operated in Siam. In 1874 the Siamese
government began the legal elimination of slavery in the kingdom,
a reform which, implemented gradually, was completed in 1905.
Slavery in Siam was not the harsh institution it was, for example, in
the West Indies or the ante-bellum United States ('servitude'
might therefore be a more accurate term). Indeed the poor commonly sold themselves or a member of their family into servitude
for an agreed period in order to discharge a debt or secure a loan.
There is some dispute over the wider economic implications of
abolition. It has been suggested (Johnston, 1976) that abolition
diminished the ability of major landowners to secure labour to
work their holdings, and therefore, presumably, hindered the
expansion of cultivation. More commonly it is argued that abolition freed and, paradoxically, coerced labour into export expansion. Two possible mechanisms were at work. The individual freed
from servitude, cast out of a secure existence, was forced to establish an independent livelihood: the debtor, who earlier might have
sought relief in servitude, was similarly forced to find an independent living, to work off his debt. Thus both were forced out to
the frontier. It is impossible to say how powerful an influence this
was, to estimate the volume of labour that was forced into independent cultivation in this way, not least because implementation
lagged behind legislation. But one source suggests that 'perhaps
the greatest single stimulus to individual initiative [in the rural
economy of late nineteenth-century Siam] came from the series of
measures that freed the slaves' (Sharp and Hanks, 1978: 84).
Wherever administrations elsewhere in South-East Asia sought to
eliminate forms of debt bondage and servitude, presumably the
same forces were set in motion. Political upheaval may have had

similar consequences. The abolition of the Burmese monarchy in the mid-1880s, on the conclusion of the final Anglo-Burmese War, deprived powerful officials of their offices and therefore of their capacity to command labour. Retainers, now released, were presumably forced to create an independent livelihood. But again, it is impossible to say how powerful that influence would have been.

Markets, Subsistence, and Risk

The discussion above may have encouraged the impression that, for the South-East Asian cultivator, commitment to the expansion of export production in the second half of the nineteenth century marked a sharp break with long-established economic and social structures, that it involved a major leap from the relative security but low material returns provided by traditional village life, focused on subsistence production, to the potentially far higher returns but greater risks of market production on the frontier. Indeed that view is explicitly stated in the following description of export expansion in central Siam:

[The] tillers of the soil, whether small scale owner-operators, landless tenants, or migrant laborers ... showed a willingness to abandon the traditional self-sufficient economy in order to increase their farming profits; to tear themselves away from inherited family lands and set off in search of larger and more productive holdings; and ... even to do without the security of the traditional village structure ... it seems clear that a significant number of Thais concluded that it was in their interest to enter the modern, commercialized economy, and they were willing to sacrifice much of their traditional life in order to do so. (Johnston, 1976: 42–3.)

But that description is seriously overdrawn. This final section will suggest that the expansion of market production was a far less decisive departure for the cultivator than this passage asserts. The point is, of course, that the less sharp the break, the easier it was for the cultivator to commit himself to the expansion of export production—and the easier it is to explain the remarkable expansion which took place in cultivation for export in the second half of the nineteenth century.

It should first be emphasized that in making their way to permanent settlement on the frontier, pioneer cultivators were rarely pushing off into the unknown. Most of the migrant groups from the Ilocos provinces in northern Luzon coming down into the Luzon Central Plain had some prior knowledge of their destination. Itinerant traders among them would have used their earlier wanderings through the Central Plain to pick out desirable places for settlement. An individual or small party might be sent out in advance. And, most important of all, towards the end of the nineteenth century, seasonal labourers coming into the Luzon Central Plain for a few months each year to assist with the harvesting of the rice crop, used the opportunity to seek out a tract for permanent settlement. In Burma too, seasonal migration into the delta often paved the way for permanent settlement.

Nor did pioneer cultivators set off into the frontier wilderness without direction. Almost invariably, in searching out a tract for settlement, the pioneer moved along the delta tributaries or, of great importance in the Mekong Delta and the lower Chao Phraya plain, along newly excavated canals, as these provided the only access to the interior wilderness, and the only means by which surplus production would be brought to the market. Consequently, pioneer cultivators, even when acting as individuals, formed concentrations of population, if not firm communities, on the frontier, as they were directed into particular districts behind the canal dredgers. In the Ilocano migration into the Luzon Central Plain, it was common for groups of perhaps twenty families to migrate under the leadership of a headman, and to co-operate in the clearing of the land, the construction of dwellings and irrigation channels, and in planting and harvesting.

Two final points can be made here. Although some pioneers seeking permanent settlement may have made their way directly to the frontier to establish their possession, many first worked as agricultural labourers or tenants on existing holdings, acquiring capital and local knowledge, perhaps laying preliminary claim to a nearby tract, before finally striking out on their own. And, of crucial importance, virtually all the agriculturalists making their way to the rice frontier were already fully familiar with the techniques and practices of wet-rice cultivation. For all these reasons, the act of migration, of clearing the wilderness and of bringing it into large-scale export production was not, for the pioneer cultivator, a sharp departure into the unknown.

Neither, in important respects, did it involve him in great risk. A central argument here is that the agriculturalists who occupied the deltas of the Irrawaddy, the Chao Phraya, and the Mekong in the second half of the nineteenth century were engaged in the cultivation of a crop which was not only a major export but also their own staple food. Basic food subsistence was therefore secure. If the export demand for rice collapsed, the cultivator and his family still ate; in fact, they would be left with a great surplus for their own consumption. If their crop was damaged by flooding, pests, or wild elephants, they could at least protect their own needs by sacrificing market sales. Indeed because climatic and soil conditions in the deltas were often near ideal for the cultivation of rice, perhaps after the construction of water-control facilities, the basic food requirements of the cultivator were commonly more securely met there than in the districts from which they had migrated. Certainly the export-committed agriculturalist in the Irrawaddy Delta in the late nineteenth century was far less likely to face food shortages and famine than many of the cultivators in the Dry Zone.

But agriculturalists committed to the cultivation of non-food crops could also secure their own food subsistence. In the Bikol provinces occupying the south-east extremity of Luzon, production of the staple crop, rice, and of the export crop, abaca, were, in important respects, complementary. Abaca flourished on the upland slopes while rice was best suited to the lowland plains. The labour demands in rice cultivation were strongly seasonal, with heavy inputs for planting and harvesting but a lengthy off-season after the harvest, while the abaca plant could be stripped at any time of the year, and therefore was harvested mainly in the rice off-season. Thus while abaca production in Bikol soared in the nineteenth century, rice cultivation also increased, although, it must be said, that increase did not keep pace with the growth of population.

In further ways, the possible risks of export crop specialization were diminished. Although the committed rice cultivator may have come to depend on imports for a major part, perhaps all, of his textile requirements, and to provide such articles as kerosene lamps, soap, furniture, crockery, mirrors, and clocks, his basic needs for shelter and food were still largely found from within the non-market economy—from household production or from surrounding forests and streams. Materials for the construction of dwellings were simply taken from the forest; fish could be found in streams, ponds, and flooded fields; wild pigs were hunted in the wilderness; vegetables, ducks, pigs, chickens could be raised on higher ground adjacent to the family home. Moreover, were the rice market to falter and thus the capacity of the cultivator to purchase imports to diminish, it was a relatively simple matter for the family to return to the domestic production of essentials (textiles) and to dispense altogether with imported non-essentials (clocks, mirrors). In brief, the export committed cultivator commonly kept one foot in, and was always capable of returning to, the subsistence sector. Even in the 1960s, the economy of Bikol could still be characterized as 'consisting basically of subsistence-oriented agriculture, with overtones of commercial agriculture' (Owen, 1984: 155). That description might be applied, with only modest exaggeration, to other export regions in South-East Asia in an earlier period. Certainly, in moving to the frontier and becoming strongly involved in export agriculture, the cultivator and his family were not throwing themselves entirely on the mercy of the market.

There is a final observation. It was argued above that the agriculturalist committed to the cultivation of export crops in the second half of the nineteenth century retained an important involvement in the subsistence economy. It must now be said that in the earlier period, prior to the great export expansions, the largely subsistence agriculturalist had maintained some considerable involvement in market-exchange. This point was pursued in the opening chapter, on the pre-modern economy in South-East Asia. There it was argued that, in this period, individuals and settlements commonly practiced a marked degree of occupational and crop specialization, produced surpluses, and exchanged and sold in both local and distant markets. Settlements were not closed and self-sufficient. Of course the degree of specialization and market involvement was much less than that achieved in the nineteenth century. But the essential processes were the same, and agriculturalists were well familiar with them. Therefore, for the cultivator, the later commitment to export production involved a major change of scale rather than a sharp break with existing structures. As pioneer cultivators moved into the frontiers of the Irrawaddy, the Chao Phraya, and the Mekong deltas in the second half of the nineteenth century, cleared land, and put it to export production, they were, in essence, simply seizing the opportunity to serve larger markets on a larger scale, to exploit more thoroughly the advantages of specialization than had ever before been possible.

SUGGESTED READING

There is no work which deals exclusively with the commitment of the cultivator to export production in nineteenth-century South-East Asia. Rather that subject appears as one theme, although frequently a central theme, in texts which have a wider canvas. For Burma, the expansion of rice production in the Irrawaddy Delta is excellently treated in Michael Adas (1974), *The Burma Delta: Economic Development and Social Change on an Asian Rice Frontier, 1852–1941*, Madison: University of Wisconsin Press. Reference should also be made to J. S. Furnivall (1948), *Colonial Policy and Practice: A Comparative Study of Burma and Netherlands India*, Cambridge: Cambridge University Press; and Cheng Siok-Hwa (1968), *The Rice Industry of Burma, 1852–1940*, Kuala Lumpur: University of Malaya Press. For Siam, there is a fine study by David Bruce Johnston (1975), 'Rural Society and the Rice Economy in Thailand, 1880–1930', Ph.D. dissertation, Yale University; see also David B. Johnston (1976), 'Opening a Frontier: The Expansion of Rice Cultivation in Central Thailand in the 1890s', *Contributions to Asian Studies*, 9: 27–44, which draws closely on his doctoral dissertation. Also valuable are Lauriston Sharp and Lucien M. Hanks (1978), *Bang Chan: Social History of a Rural Community in Thailand*, Ithaca: Cornell University Press; and Lucien M. Hanks (1972), *Rice and Man: Agricultural Ecology in Southeast Asia*, Chicago: Aldine; these involve an attempt to construct, primarily from oral evidence, the history of a specific community on the frontier, north-east of Bangkok, during the decades of settlement. The abolition of slavery in Siam, focusing on the domestic and international political motives for the reform, is discussed in David Feeny (1993), 'The Demise of Corvée and Slavery in Thailand, 1782–1913', in Martin A. Klein (ed.), *Breaking the Chains: Slavery, Bondage, and Emancipation in Modern Africa and Asia*, Madison: University of Wisconsin Press, pp. 83–111. For Cochin-China, the expansion of rice cultivation in the Mekong Delta is well covered in Guy Gran (1975), 'Vietnam and the Capitalist Route to Modernity: Village Cochin-china, 1880–1940', Ph.D. dissertation, University of Wisconsin-Madison. Also valuable are Pierre Brocheux (1995), *The Mekong Delta: Ecology, Economy, and Revolution, 1860–1960*, Center for Southeast Asian Studies, Monograph No. 12, Madison: University of Wisconsin-Madison; Martin J. Murray (1980), *The Development of Capitalism in Colonial Indochina (1870–1940)*, Berkeley: University of California Press; Robert L. Sansom (1970), *The Economics of Insurgency in the Mekong Delta of Vietnam*, Cambridge, Mass.: MIT Press, Chapter 2; John Louis Bassford (1984), 'Land Development Policy in Cochin-china under the French (1865–1925)', Ph.D. dissertation, University of Hawaii; A. Terry Rambo (1973), *A Comparison of Peasant Social Systems of Northern and Southern Viet-Nam: A Study of Ecological Adaptation, Social Succession, and*

Cultural Evolution, Center for Vietnamese Studies, Monograph Series No. III, Carbondale: Southern Illinois University at Carbondale.

For central Luzon, there are fine studies by Marshall S. McLennan (1980), *The Central Luzon Plain: Land and Society on the Inland Frontier*, Quezon City: Alemar-Phoenix Publishing House; also Marshall S. McLennan (1982), 'Changing Human Ecology on the Central Luzon Plain: Nueva Ecija, 1705–1939', in Alfred W. McCoy and Ed. C. de Jesus (eds.), *Philippine Social History: Global Trade and Local Transformations*, Quezon City: Ateneo de Manila University Press; Sydney: George Allen & Unwin, pp. 57–90; Brian Fegan (1982), 'The Social History of a Central Luzon Barrio', in Alfred W. McCoy and Ed. C. de Jesus (eds.), *Philippine Social History*, pp. 91–129; John A. Larkin (1972), *The Pampangans: Colonial Society in a Philippine Province*, Berkeley: University of California Press; and John A. Larkin (1993), *Sugar and the Origins of Modern Philippine Society*, Berkeley: University of California Press. For abaca production in Bikol, see Norman G. Owen (1984), *Prosperity without Progress: Manila Hemp and Material Life in the Colonial Philippines*, Berkeley: University of California Press; also Norman G. Owen (1982), 'Abaca in Kabikolan: Prosperity without Progress', in Alfred W. McCoy and Ed. C. de Jesus (eds.), *Philippine Social History*, pp. 191–216.

9

Rural Material Welfare in the Decades of Export Expansion

BRIEF references were made in the preceding three chapters to the material condition of the rural populations of South-East Asia in the nineteenth century, in the decades of export expansion. Chapter 6 rejected the argument that an alleged decline in mortality in nineteenth-century Java may have been related to a possible improvement in nutrition. Chapter 7 noted that scholarly controversy has long surrounded the impact of the Cultivation System on the material circumstances of the rural Javanese. Chapter 8 considered the possibility that the prospect of substantial material gain was a key element in the remarkable commitment of the Burmese cultivator to export production over the second half of the nineteenth century. Clearly this is a subject which requires close attention.

It is a subject, however, that easily traps the investigator in a thicket of conceptual and methodological problems. One presents itself immediately: how is material welfare to be defined? In the opening paragraphs of an article on the condition of the rural Javanese under the Cultivation System, an article which will be discussed at length below, R. E. Elson explains:

> The notions of prosperity and poverty are notoriously cloudy ones; often floating within them are clusters of sometimes distantly related ideas: contentment, affluence, leisure, cultural achievement; alienation, want, physical hardship, spiritual misery.... I wish ... to limit the discussion purely to the physical conditions of existence, involving consideration of such things as income, expenditure, taxation, food, clothing, shelter, and possessions. (Elson, 1990: 25–6.)

But that apparently clear statement does not dispose of the matter entirely. It may well be that the psychological condition of a rural population—its sense of alienation, its spiritual state—lie beyond the reach of the historian. Even so there are some 'cloudy' aspects of the cultivator's existence which, even if the historian cannot firmly measure, he can at least comment upon. These would include the harshness of his labour regime and the extent of his economic security. These are not peripheral elements in rural life that can safely be ignored. They may be central. Thus, in considering the strong commitment of the Burmese cultivator to rice production for export in the second half of the nineteenth century, it is insufficient to examine only the physical conditions of his existence, to seek only to measure changes in his consumption of food and clothing, or changes in his disposable real income. Something should also be said about changes in the cultivator's patterns of work and leisure, and in the extent of his economic security or vulnerability, for these, perhaps as much as the attractiveness of imported textiles, kerosene lamps, and corrugated iron roofs, could shape the cultivator's response to widening market opportunities.

Turning to the measurement of the physical circumstances of the nineteenth-century cultivator, two conceptual or methodological problems should be noted. First, changes in the quantity of consumption are commonly accompanied by changes in its quality. As was noted in Chapter 6, it would be quite possible for a rural population to enjoy an increase in the quantity of food it consumed but, because that increase was accompanied by a shift towards less nutritious items, to suffer a deterioration in diet. Or again, a rural community might experience an increase in its consumption of textiles, largely through a growth in its purchase of cheap imports, but suffer a decline in quality—in resilience or durability—were those imports inferior to the local article.

The second problem is more basic. The statistical data needed to measure changes in consumption in nineteenth-century rural South-East Asia are either treacherously flimsy or non-existent. An important point here is that, while colonial authorities largely ignored production for subsistence consumption, even in those parts of rural South-East Asia where the population had developed an acute specialization in cultivation for export, basic needs for food and shelter were still substantially met from the non-market economy—from household production, perhaps supplemented by local barter, and from surrounding forests and streams. In his study of the abaca-producing Bikol region of south-eastern Luzon,

Owen (1984: 145) suggests that throughout the late colonial period the rural population obtained most of its animal protein, fruits, vegetables, and minor staples either from the subsistence sector or from a local market economy closely linked to it. Building materials for shelter—timber, bamboo, nipa palm, rattan—were simply taken from the forest. If, therefore, a major, but indeterminate and possibly changing part of household consumption in nineteenth-century rural South-East Asia lay beyond measurement, is it possible to speak with confidence about the whole?

One final problem must be noted. While it is possible, despite the problems noted above, to calculate, even if roughly, consumption of particular articles in terms of a per capita or per household average, it is rarely possible to say anything about the distribution of consumption within a population. As the discussion in Chapter 7 on the Cultivation System will have made clear, it is precisely the disparities in distribution, and their possible growth, which may be the central issue in the physical circumstances of a rural population in nineteenth-century South-East Asia.

This introduction has not exhausted the conceptual and methodological problems in this field. Further ones will be noted below. But it would be valuable now to move to specific cases. The main body of this chapter examines the material condition of the rural Javanese under the Cultivation System, as noted earlier, a subject which has long attracted scholarly controversy. It concludes with a brief consideration of material circumstances in Lower Burma and in Bikol during the decades of rapid export growth in the second half of the nineteenth century.

Java

During the past century the Netherlands has succeeded in reducing to complete poverty a very diligent and cultured people, which is endowed with a great capacity for development, in a land that may be called an ideal example of tropical fertility. The poverty of the Javanese is so abject that it deserves to become proverbial. It does not matter how much one tries to imagine the greatest possible poverty, that of the Javanese will always be greater (quoted in Penders, 1977: 60).

This was the view of a senior Dutch official in the Indies, writing in 1900. In the middle of the nineteenth century, critics of the Cultivation System had insisted that the rural Javanese were being impoverished. This view was now accepted at the highest levels of the colonial administration. Indeed in 1901 the poverty of the

Javanese was formally acknowledged by the Dutch crown. The Indies government then embarked on a new approach to colonial administration, the 'Ethical Policy', the central aim of which was to raise the native population from its depressed and deteriorating condition.

In its broadest terms, the argument that the Cultivation System impoverished the rural Javanese had two elements. The first was that the government's forced export cultivations disrupted domestic cropping, mainly the cultivation of rice, by drawing away land, labour, water, and draft animals. The heavy demands for labour to plant, tend, harvest, transport, and process export crops, as well as to construct the irrigation channels, roads, port facilities, factories, and warehouses which were essential to the creation of a major export economy, made severe inroads into the amount of time which cultivators could devote to their own crops. Sugar and indigo, produced for export, occupied large tracts of the most valuable rice land for anything up to eighteen months. Sugar mills, powered by water-wheels, and government cane in the fields had privileged access to water courses ahead of the demands of rice cultivation. Heavy demands were made on the cultivator's work animals, in the cultivation of export crops and in their transportation from field to mill, warehouse, or port. But the forced cultivations disrupted domestic cropping in more immediate ways. The need to clear rice lands for the cultivation of an export crop by a specified date often compelled cultivators to abandon a second crop of rice, corn, or vegetables, or forced them to plant quicker maturing, but lower yield, varieties. Whenever rice land was turned over to sugar or indigo, the existing complex of water channels and elevations had to be dismantled: and when the land was returned to rice, they had to be reconstructed. Rice planted on land returned from the cultivation of sugar or indigo may commonly have yielded lower returns. For all these reasons, per capita domestic food production almost certainly fell.

The second broad element in the impoverishment argument claimed that the cash payments which the Javanese received for their labours were far below the market value of the export crops they had been forced to cultivate, and much less than they might have expected if the land had been given over to domestic cropping. Moreover, a major part of the cultivators' crop and wage payments was promptly reclaimed by the government through increased landrent assessments. Even then, the lowly Javanese cultivator rarely received the full payment that was his due, for village and local élites, through whom crop and wage payments were made, commonly siphoned off a substantial share.

The harsh impoverishment of the rural Javanese under the Cultivation System, according to this view, was most starkly illustrated by the series of crop failures and epidemics which visited the north central Java littoral in the 1840s, and which resulted in the death of thousands. The inordinate demands placed on land and labour by the forced cultivations, the severe disruption of domestic cropping, combined with miserably low payment and high taxation, left the population in that part of rural Java in no position to feed itself.

The impoverishment argument, fiercely propounded by critics of the Cultivation System in the mid-nineteenth century and long maintained, has recently been challenged, most comprehensively by R. E. Elson (1990). Elson suggests, first, that the argument has serious logical and structural deficiencies. All too frequently it rests merely on circumstantial reasoning. This can be seen in the assertion that as the Javanese were forced to commit an inordinate amount of time to the government cultivations, then inevitably domestic cropping must have suffered. In fact this outcome was not inevitable. It is possible that the Javanese were able to accommodate the labour demands of the forced cultivations without damage to domestic cropping. Only empirical investigation could settle the issue. Second, in Elson's view, the impoverishment case lacks an historical context. If it is to be argued that the material circumstances of the rural Javanese deteriorated during the decades of the Cultivation System, then it is essential to assess their material condition in the immediately preceding period, to establish a bench-mark against which the subsequent decline can be measured. In fact little or no attention had been paid in the impoverishment case to material conditions immediately before 1830. Finally, Elson criticizes the impoverishment argument for portraying the rural Javanese as passive victims, helpless objects in an expropriating colonial order, without the resources, the opportunity, or the ingenuity to adapt to, or take advantage of, the new circumstances created by the demands of the colonial state for export cultivations.

In constructing his revisionist interpretation, Elson employs three categories of evidence. First, he refers to a substantial body of contemporary descriptions which indicate improvements in the material circumstances of the rural population in various parts of Java under the Cultivation System. For example, W. R. van

Hoevell, a strong opponent of many aspects of the Cultivation System, reported that in Pasuruan in East Java in 1847 he had found 'nothing but prosperity and welfare ... nothing but activity and industriousness, nothing but contentment and happiness' (Elson, 1990: 34). Second, Elson draws attention to the expansion of the Javanese rural economy under the direct and indirect stimulus of the Cultivation System. Some districts, less involved in the government cultivations, emerged as important producers of rice, selling their surplus production to neighbouring areas where heavy commitment to export agriculture had caused local rice-shortages to develop. Elsewhere the improvements in irrigation and transport apparently encouraged the voluntary cultivation of tobacco and coffee. The forced cultivations directly created new economic opportunities in the transport of export crops from field to factory, warehouse, or port, into which Javanese labour and entrepreneurship poured. There were then substantial multiplier effects through the rural economy, generating still further expansion in domestic food production and trade, in household craft production, in local retailing. In summary, directly and indirectly, the Cultivation System brought about a marked growth in the income-generating capacity of the rural Javanese.

Finally, Elson employs statistical evidence. This part of his argument demands more extended consideration, partly because other scholars working on this subject have also relied on statistics, but principally because, in the last analysis, firm conclusions as to the material circumstances of the rural Javanese in the nineteenth century must rest primarily on attempts at numerical measurement rather than on contemporary impressions and logical deduction.

First, in a set of three tables, Elson presents data on crop payments and landrent for the major forced cultivations (sugar, indigo, and coffee) for the period 1837–51 (to 1860 in the case of coffee). The crop payment was the principal income received by the rural Javanese from the system of forced cultivations: the landrent was the major tax imposition placed upon them. In the case of sugar, in a clear majority of residencies the crop payment substantially exceeded the landrent throughout this period. With indigo, crop payments again exceeded the landrent, although by a smaller margin and, taking the period as a whole, in a smaller proportion of the relevant residencies. With respect to coffee, in some residencies (Pasuruan and Kedu), crop payments soared above the landrent assessment. The excess of crop payment over landrent implied, of course, a heavy injection of cash for those Javanese settlements directly involved in the government's cultivations.

Second, Elson offers a set of statistics which indicate a marked increase in per capita expenditure and consumption in Java–Madura in the period 1830–60. That data divides into three categories. There are figures for the government's revenues from the monopoly sale of certain articles of consumption or the monopoly provision of certain services: the revenues from the opium farms, the salt monopoly, the slaughter-tax farms (for cattle, for pigs), the pawn shop farms. There are figures for imports of cloth and cotton goods, and for total imports; and there are figures for the number of domestic animals—buffaloes, cattle, and horses. All show a substantial increase.

Elson accepts that there were times and places where the rural population of Java suffered great deprivation under the Cultivation System. But in exposing the deficiencies of the impoverishment argument, he had denied that deprivation had been general. Now, using contemporary accounts, noting the expansion which had taken place in the rural economy of Java in that period, and laying out his statistical evidence on expenditure and consumption, Elson could be firmly optimistic:

In the final analysis the [Cultivation] System does seem to have provided, both directly and indirectly and at least in the short term, opportunities for a more secure management of domestic economic life and possibilities for economic growth for a peasant society whose options, up to that time, had been severely limited [Elson, 1990: 45] ... it seems difficult to avoid the conclusion that the spending power of the peasantry had grown rapidly from the time of the introduction of the Cultivation System in the early 1830s (Elson, 1990: 40).

But in seeking a major historiographical revision, has Elson overstated his case? Certainly there are criticisms to be made of his arguments and evidence. Looking first at the statistical series which are said to indicate increases in expenditure and consumption in Java–Madura in the period 1830–60, three main criticisms can be advanced. The series showing increased government revenue from the pig-slaughter tax farms can hardly indicate a rise in the consumption of pork by the great mass of the population, who were, of course, Muslims. Pork was mainly consumed by the Chinese minority. Second, two other series, government revenue from the pawn shop farms and the import of cloth and cotton goods, might indicate the very reverse of the argument being advanced—as indeed Elson admits. Increased business for pawn shops might be a sign not of growing prosperity but of increasing hardship in a rapidly monetizing economy. Increased textile imports might indicate not rising consumption but declining household production: to put the point in general terms, given evidence of increasing imports of a major article of consumption, it is safe to conclude only that the population had become more dependent on the world market to meet its needs, not, necessarily, that there had been an increase in consumption. Third, even where there is firm evidence of an increase in total or per capita consumption, this obviously provides no insight into its distribution. Again, this is acknowledged by Elson. It is quite possible that increased imports of cloth and cotton goods, increased sales of opium, an increase in the slaughter of cattle for meat, reflected a sharp rise in the purchasing power of local élites, and that the mass of the population was left impoverished. Indeed, given the apparent ability of Java's rural élites to manipulate crop payments and the collection of landrent to their own advantage (see the discussion in Chapter 7), that outcome seems very likely. There is a further observation. An increase in government income from a revenue farm might reflect not a rise in consumption but the increased ability of the revenue farmer to enrich himself (and the government), perhaps indeed at the *expense* of the population.

There are also criticisms to be made of Elson's argument that as crop payments for the major forced cultivations commonly ran ahead of the landrent, substantial volumes of cash were injected into those districts involved in the government crops. One criticism, that the aggregate figures ignore the crucial issue of distribution, was noted above. As crop payments and landrent assessments were, in the majority of cases, made on a village basis, rural élites had every opportunity to manipulate those transactions to their own advantage, against the interests of the less powerful majority. Second, although on Elson's evidence crop payments commonly exceeded landrent demands in this period, it is important to add that landrent assessments were raised in almost all years, to keep in touch with the rising crop payments. In other words, a major part of the increased payments to the Javanese cultivators was immediately returned to the colonial treasury through higher landrent demands. Anne Booth (1988b: 313) asserts that 'in most year ... usually more than 70 per cent ... of the cash injected into the peasant economy for crop payment was syphoned off again through taxation'. Third, in some cases, settlements engaged in forced cultivations found themselves incurring substantial cash expenditures, the effect of which was to reduce the value of the crop payment they received. Knight (1990: 59) notes that cultivators in a sugar area in Pekalongan Residency had to provide fencing materials (to protect the cane fields against the depredations of cattle and wild boar) as well as ploughing animals, which effectively reduced crop payments by 15 to 20 per cent. And finally, it is important to note a disagreement over the extent to which landrent assessments could be covered from crop payments. Elson (1990: 35) firmly states that, in the case of sugar, crop payments commonly exceeded the landrent due on *all* the land of those engaged in that cultivation, not just the land under the government crop. Van Niel (1972: 105) insists that only exceptionally did crop payments exceed the total landrent assessment, as distinct from the landrent due on land under forced cultivation. Of course, it was only when the crop payment exceeded the total landrent that the substantial injection of cash emphasized by Elson took place.

It may be necessary to qualify Elson's assertion that the Cultivation System directly and indirectly stimulated a major expansion of the rural economy of Java, a substantial growth in the income-generating capacity of the rural Javanese. This may well have occurred in the highly fertile east Java residency of Pasuruan, the focus of Elson's research. But it has yet to be established, through comparable regional studies, that this experience was repeated across the island.

An important part of the impoverishment argument was, as noted above, the fact that in the 1840s a series of food crises ravaged the north central Java littoral, the result, it was alleged, of the inordinate demands placed on land and labour by the forced cultivations. It is perhaps surprising that in his (1990) attempt to refute the impoverishment interpretation, Elson does not confront that important evidence, particularly as recent scholarship has sought to establish that the food crises were in fact unconnected with the Cultivation System. In a study of the famine in Cirebon Residency in the second half of the 1840s, Fernando (1980) notes that it took place in an area, Indramayu Regency, where forced cultivation had not been imposed: and furthermore, that other parts of the Residency, which had borne the burden of forced cultivation, appear not to have been visited by famine. The principal cause of the disaster, in Fernando's view, was the establishment in Cirebon in 1843 of a major rice milling enterprise, a private Dutch concern under the patronage of the colonial administration, the effect of which was to break down long-established local arrangements for the provision of rice for consumption and seed.

In one of his later writings, but published earlier, Elson (1985) too looked closely at a famine in this period, that in Demak and Grobogan in 1849–50. His account of its causes is of particular interest in the light of his earlier work. Elson draws attention to the extremely poor weather that afflicted Demak and Grobogan in the late 1840s, but argues that this simply brought to a head a long-evolving food production crisis which had its origins, it is important to note, in the tax and labour demands of the Dutch colonial state. The crippling burden of landrent had forced many small landholders to sell their plough-animals to raise cash. Without those animals, fewer fields could be put under rice, and those fields which were planted were often cultivated less intensively. Inordinate demands for labour left many cultivators with insufficient time to plant domestic food crops adequately, or indeed at all. There was also, Elson argues, a distribution crisis of long origin, as local élites, shorn up by the Dutch colonial administration, advanced their economic position at the expense of the vulnerable majority. As inequalities grew, the prospect that a food production crisis would degenerate into outright famine sharply increased. But does not Elson's (1985) analysis, in particular his observation that the demands imposed on labour by the forced cultivations dangerously eroded domestic food production capacity in Demak and Grobogan, fit uneasily with the prosperity argument considered earlier? There the forced cultivations were seen to have stimulated a rapid growth in the rural economy of Java, pumped large cash payments into the rural districts, and created substantial employment opportunities for the rural Javanese. Interestingly, in his most recent and substantial work on the Cultivation System, Elson (1994: 114) argues that 'the key to explaining the disastrous effects of the crop failure of the 1840s is not to be sought in an overextension of the Cultivation System, in the sense either of removing too much land or other material resources from peasant food production or imposing an increasingly intolerable labour burden upon peasant food producers'.

There is a further measure of material welfare in Java in the decades of the Cultivation System which challenges Elson's optimism. Using detailed, if commonly fragile, statistical data on the agricultural economy of nineteenth-century Java, including series for the total area of arable land and cropping ratio, distribution of crops, yields, prices, and labour-time per crop, Boomgaard (1989) has estimated per capita food availability, expressed in calories per day. His figures are 1808 calories in 1815; 1457 in 1840; and 1919 calories in 1880 (Boomgaard, 1989: 97–9). If adjusted for changes in per capita workload over this period, the last two figures are substantially reduced, to 1256 in 1840, to 1698 in 1880. In other words, per capita food availability, expressed in calories per day and adjusted for days worked, was slightly lower in 1880 than it had been in 1815: in 1840 it was far lower than it had been in 1815. Further calculations from that data indicate an even sharper decline in the per capita *quality* of food (protein and vitamin levels) available in 1840 compared with 1815, and a clear failure to recover the 1815 figure by 1880. Booth (1988b: 315) confirms that from 1830 to 1870 'food consumption per worker hour almost certainly declined in calorie terms . . . while at the same time less preferred staples assumed a greater role in the native diet'. There is no evidence here of the improvement in per capita food availability that must surely be an essential component of increasing prosperity. Indeed there is the clear suggestion that food availability declined very sharply in the first decade of the Cultivation System, and that the modest recovery achieved after 1840 had, by 1880, still failed to restore the levels found in 1815.

Lower Burma and Bikol

The material condition of the rural populations in the other major export districts of South-East Asia during the decades of export expansion has not received from historians the same rigorous attention that has been given to conditions in rural Java. Certainly the statistical and descriptive records of those other districts have not been picked over to anything like the same degree.

Perhaps the strongest impression left by that limited work is that, like the writing on Java, it offers the most sharply contrasting views. There is a notable clash over material conditions in the rice delta of Lower Burma. Writing in the closing years of colonial rule, the official-scholar J. S. Furnivall argued that 'it is difficult to resist the conclusion that over Lower Burma as a whole [in the period 1870–1923] the great mass of the people were steadily growing poorer' (Furnivall, 1948: 103). Furnivall believed that the economic position of the cultivator and the agricultural labourer in the rapidly expanding rice economy of the delta was highly unstable and insecure. From around 1880, he argued, Chettiar moneylenders, fanning out through the delta, lent the Burmese cultivator so much money, far more than his needs, that at the first reversal—a failure of the crop, illness, a loss of work animals, a downturn in the rice market—he lost his land. The Chettiar would then sell the holding, often with the advance of a further loan, to another cultivator, for the process to be repeated within two or three years. In this way, Furnivall argued, the Burmese cultivator was continually being driven from tract to tract. For the agricultural labourer, insecurity came with the establishment of what Furnivall termed 'industrial agriculture', in which wage labour was engaged not on an annual or seasonal basis, to see a crop through from planting to harvesting, but for just a few weeks, perhaps a few days, to carry out a single task—the building of earthworks, ploughing, planting, or reaping. These arrangements frequently left the labourer unemployed for half the year or more. Furnivall further suggested that with the advance of the commercialized rice economy, cultivators and labourers were disadvantaged by the need to buy essential articles which previously they had obtained free from nature. As virgin land was brought into production, cultivators had fewer opportunities to take thatching material and firewood from the forest. As fisheries were declared the property of the state, fish could no longer be taken freely from local pools and streams. As home weaving withered in the face of foreign competition, clothing had to be bought. Furnivall's conclusion is dramatically stated:

The epic of bravery and endurance . . . the greatest achievement in the history of Burma, the reclamation by Burmese enterprise of ten million acres of swamp and jungle, ends with a picture of imposing Government offices and business houses in Rangoon, and gilded *chettyar* temples in Tanjore, while in the rice districts, the source of almost all this wealth, nearly half the land is owned by foreigners, and a landless people can show little for their labour but their debts, and, for about half the year, most of them are unable to find work or wages. (Furnivall, 1948: 116.)

Writing on the same subject over twenty years later, Adas (1974: 74–6) painted an entirely different picture:

In the early phase of economic growth those . . . cultivator-owners who. overcame the difficulties involved in clearing and cultivating new lands in the Delta were well rewarded for their years of assiduous toil. . . . In most areas of the Delta during the first phase of development tenants enjoyed a standard of living which was roughly comparable to that of cultivator-owners.

As a concluding statement, he noted that 'in its early stages the making of a modern, market economy in Lower Burma was impressive not only in terms of paddy exported and the number of rice mills constructed, but also in terms of the benefits derived by agriculturists who constituted the great majority of Burma's population.' (Adas, 1974: 82.)

Adas marshalled some statistical data—on wage rates for agricultural labourers, on the cultivator's cash income and expenditure—to support his position. But he relied mainly on contemporary observations laced with deduction, as indeed, it is important to note, had Furnivall to opposite purpose. Thus Furnivall quotes from a Settlement Report of the early 1880s to the effect that in parts of the delta the cultivator 'is in a state of chronic indebtedness and as miserable as a Burman can be' (Furnivall, 1948: 91); also using Settlement Reports, Adas notes that attractive foreign consumer goods were found in households all over the delta in the decades of export expansion. Furnivall attributed the high turnover in land occupancy to the cycle of debt, default, and foreclosure; Adas argues that it reflected the ability of tenants to find landlords offering more favourable terms or their ability to buy land of their own. Adas reports the great influx of foreign consumer goods throughout the delta; Furnivall deduced that among those imports, petty luxuries such as European footwear, cigarettes, and provisions were destined for urban markets, while articles of common consumption such as textiles, crockery, and salt largely replaced devastated local production.

A more circumspect treatment of this subject is offered in Owen's (1984) study of abaca production in nineteenth- and early twentieth-century Bikol. It is more circumspect in three ways. Owen is very sensitive to the fragmentary and fragile nature of his evidence, emphasizing that his data on relative crop prices, government revenues, migration, and imports, are indicative rather than decisive. Second, although he concludes that there was indeed a net growth in the purchasing power of the ordinary Bikol abaca-stripper in the decades of export expansion, he stresses that it was rather modest. Finally, Owen emphasizes that in the decades of vigorous export expansion, the rural population of Bikol continued to draw a major part of its consumption, certainly its food requirements, from the subsistence sector or from a local market economy closely linked to it. That consumption was unregarded, and therefore unrecorded, by the colonial authorities. As a result, argues Owen, from this distance 'it is impossible to estimate the economic significance of crops grown primarily for local consumption, though it is clear that they were very much a part of normal Bikol life and livelihood' (Owen, 1984: 139–41). Perhaps more importantly, it is impossible to estimate the degree to which, even the direction in which, their economic significance changed under the impact of export expansion. For the abaca-stripper in Bikol, consumption through the market may well have increased in this period. But of consumption from the subsistence economy, and thus the abaca-stripper's material condition as a whole, what can be said?

Conclusion

Is it not possible, in a final paragraph, to move this subject towards a firmer conclusion? As the descriptive and statistical evidence is so fragmentary and unreliable, it must be doubtful whether, no matter how thoroughly it is picked over, a confidently defendable position could be constructed on the basis of it. If that is the case, it may be more valuable simply to lay out the implications of the alternative interpretations. If it were to be concluded that during the decades of export expansion, the material condition of the cultivating populations in South-East Asia had worsened, the implication must be that cultivators had been coerced, in some way, into large-scale market production. But then it seems inherently improbable that coercion alone—the coercion of the state (in the case of the Cultivation System) or the coercion of environmental and economic circumstance (for example, population pressure in areas of established settlement)—could have produced the vast expansion of export cultivation which took place throughout South-East Asia in these decades. Given the sheer scale of the expansion, the huge numbers of cultivators involved, and the back-breaking nature of this work, it may be more realistic to argue that the agriculturalist, pushing the frontier of cultivation outwards, was motivated principally by a reasonable prospect that he and his family would thereby profit.

SUGGESTED READING

The most substantial consideration of material conditions in nineteenth-century rural Java is provided by R. E. Elson (1990), 'Peasant Poverty and Prosperity under the Cultivation System in Java', in Anne Booth, W. J. O'Malley, and Anna Weidemann (eds.), *Indonesian Economic History in the Dutch Colonial Era*,

Southeast Asia Studies, Monograph No. 35, New Haven: Yale University, pp. 24–48. Support for Elson's generally optimistic view can be found in C. Fasseur (1978), 'Some Remarks on the Cultivation System in Java', *Acta Historiae Neerlandicae*, 10: 143–62; and C. Fasseur (1986), 'The Cultivation System and Its Impact on the Dutch Colonial Economy and the Indigenous Society in Nineteenth-century Java', in C. A. Bayly and D. H. A. Kolff (eds.), *Two Colonial Empires: Comparative Essays on the History of India and Indonesia in the Nineteenth Century*, Dordrecht: Martinus Nijhoff, pp. 137–54. Among modern scholars who, in contrast, argue that material conditions in rural Java under the Cultivation System deteriorated or, at best, stagnated, are G. R. Knight (1990), 'The Peasantry and the Cultivation of Sugar Cane in Nineteenth-century Java: A Study from Pekalongan Residency, 1830–1870', in Anne Booth, W. J. O'Malley, Anna Weidemann (eds.), *Indonesian Economic History in the Dutch Colonial Era*, Southeast Asia Studies, Monograph No. 35, New Haven: Yale University, pp. 49–66; Peter Boomgaard (1989), *Children of the Colonial State: Population Growth and Economic Development in Java, 1795–1880*, Centre for Asian Studies Amsterdam, Monograph No. 1, Amsterdam: Free University Press; Anne Booth (1988b), 'Living Standards and the Distribution of Income in Colonial Indonesia: A Review of the Evidence', *Journal of Southeast Asian Studies*, 19(2): 310–34.

The course and causes of the famines which hit north-central Java in the 1840s are considered in R. E. Elson (1985), 'The Famine in Demak and Grobogan in 1849–50: Its Causes and Circumstances', *Review of Indonesian and Malaysian Affairs*, 19(1): 39–85; Radin Fernando (1980), *Famine in Cirebon Residency in Java, 1844–1850: A New Perspective on the Cultivation System*, Centre of Southeast Asian Studies, Working Paper No. 21, Clayton: Monash University. Elson's most recent views can be found in R. E. Elson (1994), *Village Java under the Cultivation System, 1830–1870*, Southeast Asia Publication Series No. 25, Sydney: Allen & Unwin/Asian Studies Association of Australia, Chapter 4.

For measurement and analysis of crop payment and landrent under the Cultivation System, to suggest a substantial injection of cash into Java's rural districts in that period, see Robert Van Niel (1972), 'Measurement of Change under the Cultivation System in Java, 1837–1851', *Indonesia*, 14: 89–109. The views of a senior Dutch official in 1900 on the impoverishment of the Javanese is taken from Chr. L. M. Penders (1977), *Indonesia: Selected Docu-*

ments on Colonialism and Nationalism, 1830–1942, St. Lucia: University of Queensland Press.

Material conditions in the Burma Delta during the decades of export expansion are considered by Michael Adas (1974), *The Burma Delta: Economic Development and Social Change on an Asian Rice Frontier, 1852–1941,* Madison: University of Wisconsin Press; J. S. Furnivall (1948), *Colonial Policy and Practice: A Comparative Study of Burma and Netherlands India,* Cambridge: Cambridge University Press. Material circumstances in rural Bikol in the same period are considered in Norman G. Owen (1984), *Prosperity without Progress: Manila Hemp and Material Life in the Colonial Philippines,* Berkeley: University of California Press.

For material conditions in rural Vietnam, not considered in the text, see Ngô Viñh Long (1973), *Before the Revolution: The Vietnamese Peasants under the French,* Cambridge, Mass.: MIT Press. This presents a dramatically pessimistic view, arguing in its conclusion that French rule brought 'hunger, misery, and starvation to the peasants' (p. 141).

10
Asian and European
Agricultural Enterprise

CHAPTER 8 sought an understanding of the powerful commitment of rural populations in nineteenth-century South-East Asia to cultivation for export. It concentrated on rice production, an industry in which cultivation was entirely a matter of Asian enterprise and initiative. The present chapter is concerned with the expansion of rubber production in the Malay States and tobacco production in East Sumatra, industries in which Asian producers directly faced European enterprise. That different context provides a second theme for the chapter: the attitudes of Western colonial administrations towards the commonly clashing ambitions of Asian and European agricultural initiative.

Rubber in Malaya

In the mid-1870s, mainly at the prompting of the India Office in London, a number of shipments of *Hevea brasiliensis* were procured from South America for the Royal Botanic Gardens at Kew. There the seeds were germinated. Consignments of plants were then dispatched to botanic gardens in the eastern colonial territories. The bulk of the *Hevea* plants were sent to the Botanic Gardens at Peradeniya in Ceylon, but a small number were sent to the Botanic Gardens in Singapore, the first consignment arriving in 1876. Modest stands were established from these shipments at the botanic station in Singapore and in the garden of the British Resident at Kuala Kangsar in Perak. Clearly, in taking this initiative, it was the ambition of the authorities in London to see the establishment of a profitable new industry in the eastern possessions. However, it would be a considerable number of years before that ambition was realized. The local administration in

Malaya did comparatively little at first to promote the crop. Moreover, planters in Malaya were preoccupied at that time with other crops—coffee, pepper, gambier, tapioca, and sugar—in part because the market potential of cultivated rubber had yet to be clearly established.

Those circumstances began to change towards the end of the 1880s. The year 1888 saw the appointment of H. N. Ridley as Director of the Botanic Gardens in Singapore. With almost manic enthusiasm, Ridley sought to convert official and planting opinion to rubber, in the process earning for himself the popular titles of 'mad Ridley' or, more kindly, 'rubber Ridley'. The common story is that on his travels in the peninsula, Ridley would thrust handfuls of rubber seeds into the pockets of startled planters, urging them to give the crop a try. The first commercial plantings of rubber in the Malay States, in the mid-1890s, were the result of Ridley's advocacy. A modest expansion of the area under rubber in the late 1890s and early 1900s reflected in part the failure of coffee and the poor prospects for other established crops in the Malay States. But principally it was the result of increasingly firm demand for rubber on world markets following the establishment of automobile manufacture in the United States at the close of the nineteenth century and, consequently, the expansion in production of pneumatic tyres.

The explosive increase in the area of land under rubber in the Malay States took place from 1905. Motor vehicle factory sales in the United States, a little over 4,000 units in 1900, stood at 25,000 in 1905 but then climbed to 187,000 units in 1910. The introduction of mass production by Henry Ford in 1907 was of central importance in that growth. There had been 345 acres under rubber in Malaya in 1897. This increased to 25,239 acres in 1904, to 429,406 acres in 1910. Because the newly planted *Hevea* took between five and seven years before it first yielded its latex, Malayan rubber exports remained very modest until the early 1910s. The slow response of supply, at a time when demand was increasing dramatically, pushed rubber prices to very high levels. The maximum price of rubber on the London market in 1900 had been 4/9 per lb. It rose to 6/9 in 1905 and hit 12/9 per lb in 1910. Soaring prices fuelled the rush into rubber cultivation.

The European pioneers responsible for the commercial cultivation of rubber in this initial period were generally proprietary planters, long resident in the Malay States, now turning their hands to rubber. But they were soon overtaken by public companies, floated in London and created specifically to undertake the cultivation of rubber in Malaya. Established local British

merchant firms—Guthrie, Harrisons and Crosfield, Boustead—
played a central role in their flotation, and in providing company
secretarial and management services once they had been established. Between 1903 and 1912, some 260 Malayan rubber companies were registered in the United Kingdom.

Extensive smallholder cultivation of rubber, by Malays, did not
begin until 1909, some four years after the great upswing in European planting. A number of factors explain this slower response.
Many market-oriented cultivators had still to recover from an
earlier disastrous commitment to coffee. The colonial administration was hostile to Malay smallholders cultivating rubber—a central issue, to be considered below. But of major importance, in
these early years the rural Malays chose to engage in the rubber
boom in other, less direct, ways. For example, they worked for the
plantation companies clearing forest cover prior to the planting of
rubber, because this short-contract labouring left village life relatively undisturbed. Joining the plantations' permanent labour force
held virtually no attraction for the rural Malay population, in that
it would have involved a disruptive break with traditional patterns
of activity. (The plantations were therefore obliged to find their
permanent labour from outside Malaya, largely from India: in any
event, immigrant Indians were preferred by European managers
because they were, it was said, a captive and docile work-force.)

But the principal response of the rural Malays to the rubber
boom in its early years was to sell their land to the European estate
companies, who were eager to bring vast areas into cultivation.
Some of that land had been recently acquired, specifically with an
eye to quick resale at a substantial profit. But much was ancestral
village land, long committed to the subsistence cultivation of rice.
Such land sales had a clear, if short-term, economic rationality. It
was impossible to forecast how long the rubber boom would last.
To sell one's land immediately, at a high price, was a certain and
quick way to a large return.

But, as was noted above, from 1909 the rural Malays themselves
decisively took up rubber. Indeed, these years saw a substantial
influx of Malay migrants from the Netherlands East Indies, attracted by the availability of rubber land, notably in north-west
Johor and coastal Selangor. From the available statistics, it is not
possible to quantify the specifically Malay involvement in rubber in
this period. But in 1921, the area of smallholder rubber in Malaya,
with an unquantified, but certainly modest proportion of small-

holdings in Chinese ownership, was just over 823,000 acres, or 37 per cent of the total area under rubber. Drabble (1973: 221) has further calculated that in the same year smallholdings accounted for 25 to 30 per cent of Malayan output. As Malaya supplied one-half of world rubber exports in 1921, this meant that in a little over a decade the Malayan smallholder had come from nowhere to satisfy between 12 and 15 per cent of total world consumption. To return to the central theme of Chapter 8, how is that striking commitment to export cultivation to be explained?

Clearly, rubber offered the rural Malays the prospect of substantial material gain. As the great stands of trees planted by the European companies from around 1905 came into production, the price of rubber on the London market slipped back from the very high levels achieved in 1909 and 1910. Nevertheless, throughout much of the 1910s the crop still fetched very good prices. Certainly in those years the Malay cultivator could obtain a substantially higher cash income from rubber than from any other crop, including rice. That increasing cash income found many outlets. It led to increased consumption of the wide range of imported manufactures—textiles, household implements, corrugated iron roofs—familiar from the discussion in Chapter 8. But a considerable number of Malay cultivators used part of their increased income to undertake the pilgrimage to Mecca. The returns from rubber, material and spiritual, were very considerable.

But the striking commitment of the Malay cultivator to rubber is not to be explained solely in terms of incentives. Also important was the fact that, in a number of respects, the cultivation of rubber imposed no really serious burden. The labour demands of the crop, not simply the amount of labour it required but also its arduousness, were relatively light. The growing and mature *Hevea* tree needed little attention, no more than the occasional light weeding of the surrounding ground. The tapping of the mature tree to secure the latex, which involved making a simple oblique cut in the bark and positioning a small cup near the base of the trunk to collect the liquid, was relatively undemanding work. Some larger smallholdings might employ additional labour for tapping. But tapping on most holdings could be carried out quite easily by the cultivator and his family. Indeed, commonly it took up only half the cultivator's day. The initial processing of the latex on the smallholding involved three modest tasks: adding formic acid to coagulate the latex; passing the coagulum through hand-driven rollers to

produce sheets; and hanging up the sheets to dry. The few simple
implements required—a distinctively shaped knife to incise the
bark, and various containers—were cheap to acquire. Indeed discarded cigarette tins were used to collect the latex, and old
kerosene drums were employed to coagulate it. Cultivation did not
involve the use of work animals. Seeds were easily obtained. In
fact, the only serious burden borne by the Malay rubber cultivator
came with the initial clearing of overgrown tract and the preparation of the land for planting. This was heavy work, commonly
requiring the hiring of additional labour and borrowed money. But
once the crop was planted, labour demands were moderate and
cash requirements extremely low. Indeed Bauer (1948) suggests
that many smallholders were 'no-cost' producers.

The fact that, once established, rubber cultivation imposed such
modest demands on the cultivator's labour was important in
another respect. It meant that the agriculturalist, committed to
rubber, might with ease continue to grow other crops—both cash
crops and subsistence food. Thus rubber was commonly inter-
planted with coconuts, fruit-trees, or vegetables; the rubber smallholder family still found time to raise poultry and to fish; and the
rural settlement, even the individual cultivator, continued to grow
rice for subsistence on other lands. The coexistence of subsistence
and various forms of commercial agriculture within the household
or within the settlement had important implications for the Malay
commitment to rubber. It meant that during the five to seven years
before newly planted *Hevea* first yielded an income, the cultivator
and his family were supported without difficulty by subsistence rice
production and by a modest cash return from, for example,
coconuts. It also meant that, once rubber was being tapped, subsistence food needs were secure, and alternative, if modest, sources
of cash income remained available. In this crucial respect, market
involvement did not imply a dangerous vulnerability in the event of
market collapse. Heavy commitment to rubber held little risk. In
summary, rubber offered the rural Malays the prospect of substantial material gain for modest effort and at little risk to subsistence
security. Little wonder that the 1910s saw a stunning growth in
Malay smallholder cultivation of rubber.

There is, however, one further consideration. The British colonial administration was hostile to Malay smallholder cultivation of
this crop. Official hostility expressed itself in a number of discriminatory measures, some relatively modest, others more serious. In
the alienation of land for cultivation, land with the best location,

with frontage onto a main road, was almost invariably allocated to a European planter. Roads and drainage works served the needs of the plantation sector, the interests of the smallholders being largely ignored. Research into rubber cultivation by the government agricultural stations focused on plantation, not smallholder, cultivation: and the results of that research were freely communicated to the European planters, while local cultivators were left largely in ignorance. The colonial administration's Planters Loan Fund (1904) and the Immigration Fund (1908) provided valuable financial assistance to the plantation sector in its early years: no comparable assistance was extended to the smallholder sector.

More importantly, certainly more directly, the colonial government, through a combination of legislation and administrative action, prohibited the cultivation of rubber on an extensive part of Malay lands. The *mukim* (subdistrict) land registers, introduced from the early 1890s, contained a column which described the nature of cultivation on each plot of land registered, that entry then being duplicated in the land title issued to the applicant. The entry was in part an administrative record of the intended use of the land at the time it was alienated, but it was also meant to direct the cultivator towards those crops regarded as suitable by the authorities. From 1910, however, with the rubber craze at its height, local administrators in a number of districts came to use that entry in the land title in a more interventionist manner, such that it was no longer descriptive or suggestive but forcefully proscriptive. Specifically, land titles were now stamped with a 'no rubber' clause, which meant, obviously, that title was granted on condition that rubber was not cultivated on that land. The immediate initiative for this rigid use of the cultivation condition was the administration's wish to curb the sale of ancestral Malay lands to non-Malay rubber concerns, for clearly land carrying a 'no rubber' clause would be of no interest to the latter. But that rigid use also had the effect, of course, of prohibiting the Malay owner himself from putting the land under rubber.

The 'no rubber' condition became an integral part of land administration in the 1910s. In 1913 the Malay Reservations Enactment gave the authorities the power to gazette selected areas as Malay reserved land, which could not be sold, leased, or otherwise disposed of to a non-Malay. This legislation sought to secure directly that which the rigid use of the 'no rubber' condition had sought indirectly—to curb the dispossession of the Malay of his ancestral land. But then, as an appendage to the legislation, the colonial administration, notably in the state of Selangor, imposed the 'no rubber' condition on much of the Malay reserved land. This was clearly a superfluous reinforcement of the Malay Reservations Enactment, which alone would prevent the alienation of ancestral Malay land. The addition of the 'no rubber' clause was an open attempt to prevent the Malay himself from cultivating rubber on it. In 1917, a meeting of the most senior British administrators agreed that the 'no rubber' clause was to be enforced whenever possible. In the same year, the Rice Lands Enactment laid down that the entry *bendang* (wet-rice field) in the 'nature of cultivation' column of a land register was a binding condition of the title, not merely a description of the land. By law, rubber was not to be cultivated on it. If smallholders violated the cultivation condition of their title and planted rubber, the colonial administration could, as an extreme measure, order the forbidden trees to be uprooted.

Three further discriminatory measures must be noted. In the 1910s land office books were occasionally closed to smallholder land applications, initially because officials were overwhelmed by the volume of applications, but later in order to prevent smallholders from taking advantage of the wartime distraction of British capital to secure prime rubber land. Second, the colonial administration imposed a higher rent on land under rubber, a lower rent on land which carried a 'no rubber' clause. The final measures of discrimination took place in the 1920s. As the post-war boom in the rubber-consuming industrial economies collapsed, and the heavy planting of the mid-1910s came into production, the world price of rubber fell sharply. In November 1922, restriction of exports was introduced in all British territories. The central element in the Stevenson Restriction Scheme was an official assessment of the 'normal output', or Standard Production, of each producer—smallholder, estate, irrespective of size. At intervals of three months, a London Advisory Committee would announce the permitted level of rubber exports for the next period, as a percentage of Standard Production. Each producer's Standard Production was calculated from his actual production in the year November 1919 to October 1920. The Western estates, which kept full records, had little difficulty in establishing their output in 1919–20 to the satisfaction of the authorities. But few, if any, smallholders kept records. So here the authorities imposed Standard Productions, basing their calculations on a scale that declared, for example, that trees aged 6–7 years would yield 180 pounds per acre, while those aged 7–8 years yielded 240 pounds per acre. In these circumstances, discrimination against the smallholder could easily take hold. The most powerful accusation is that the scale used by the authorities substantially understated the capacity of smallholdings. Further discrimination arose through the frequent use of European planters' associations to carry out the inspection and assessment of smallholdings. Drabble (1991: 234, 236, 239) has shown that although the production capacity of a smallholding was on average in the region of 500 pounds per mature acre, the average permitted production for smallholdings over the period 1922–8 (admittedly with considerable variation in assessment by time and by locality) was just 301 pounds per mature acre. In contrast, the average production per mature acre for sterling companies (companies registered in the United Kingdom) in the base year 1919–20 appears to have been 342 pounds: yet the average permitted production for those companies over the period 1922–8 was 370 pounds per mature acre. As a result, for a substantial part of the restriction period, obviously during those quarters when the London Advisory Committee increased the export quota (the permitted level of exports, as a percentage of Standard Production), estate production was not restricted at all. Yet even when the quota was 100 per cent, the position for much of 1926, smallholder production remained sharply suppressed.

It is difficult to identify precisely the complex reasons for the hostility of the colonial administration towards Malay smallholder cultivation of rubber. The dominant view within the British administration was clearly that rubber (perhaps any commercial planting) was not a suitable crop for the Malay population to cultivate. The rural Malay should remain committed to the growing of rice, the subsistence crop which, over long generations, had been at the centre of Malay village life. In other words, rural Malay society was to be shielded from the potentially disruptive impact of the modern commercial world. But what lay behind that view? It is possible to see in this a sentimental attachment on the part of British officials to the idyllic ways of an idealized Malay village, to be contrasted with the brutalizing character of the industrial world from which they came, although if that were the case, it is difficult to understand why European officials across colonial Africa and Asia were not similarly infected by that Arcadian fantasy. It is possible that this view reflected official concern over the level of domestic food production, at a time when, with continuing large-scale immigration of Chinese and Indians to work in the tin mines and on the rubber plantations, Malaya had become a heavy importer of rice. Or it may have been fear of the social and political disorder that could result from severe disruption within the Malay rural economy. A collapse of the rubber market could well bring distress, and British officials pointed with concern to earlier Malay failures with coffee, gambier, pepper, and tapioca. But, and this is a rather more sinister interpretation, even a soaring market might bring disorder. Shifting structures of economic power in the rural districts might provoke a challenge to the traditional sources of authority within Malay society, even to the sultans, upon whom British administration in the Malay states rested. An undisturbed, untraumatized Malay rural population would perpetuate British rule.

A second view widely held among British officials was that Asian smallholdings possessed a number of major technical deficiencies that would in time consign the sector to commercial insignificance. European planters and, through them, colonial officials drew disparaging comparisons between the densely, chaotically planted stands on the Malay smallholdings and the ordered, well-spaced lines of rubber on the plantations. Around 1930 the planting density on smallholdings was on average a little over 200 trees per acre: the average density on the plantations was just 100–120 trees per acre. Officials and planters compared the failure of Malay cultivators to keep their holdings clear of weeds and rough cover, so that their rubber stands often appeared to be neglected and overgrown, with the fanatical zeal with which the plantations removed all rival growth around their trees. They condemned what they saw as the smallholders' excessive, even brutal tapping regimes, which may have raised yields in the immediate term but sharply curtailed the long-run productive capacity of the tree. Holding these views, it was simply inconceivable to most planters and officials in the Malay States that local smallholdings would ever pose a significant threat to estate supremacy.

Reality was far different. An investigation undertaken at the beginning of the 1930s indicated that the Malay smallholder did not, in general, tap his trees indiscriminately. As a significant part, perhaps one-quarter, of the smallholder's stand was left untapped at any one time, adequate opportunity was being provided for the bark renewal—the growth of new bark on that part of the trunk from which the old had been removed by heavy tapping—that would secure the tree's productive life. Furthermore, the 'clean weeding' practised by the plantations was, in fact, ill-advised.

Instead of maximizing the supply of soil nutrients to the trees and reducing the spread of tree diseases, it led to soil erosion, loss of nutrients, and a more rapid spread of disease. The smallholder's overgrown plot, less aesthetically pleasing, represented better practice. Indeed, Barlow (1978: 148–9) suggests that 'clean weeding probably went far to explain the early inferiority of yields on estates to those on smallholdings'. And finally, the greater density of planting on smallholdings may have restricted the growth of individual trees but it resulted in a considerably higher output per acre, as the figures above will have illustrated. In this crucial respect, despite the undisciplined appearance of his plot, the smallholder was clearly the more efficient producer. He was also more efficient by another measure. Once his rubber seeds were planted, the smallholder had very low expenses in cash compared with the recurrent operating costs of the Western estates, which employed a hierarchy of European managers and a large body of immigrant labour. In short, the cash costs of the smallholder were lower and his yields were greater. He was indeed a formidable rival to the estates.

Hence the problem of interpretation. Official opinion in Malaya in the opening decades of the twentieth century held to the superiority of Western enterprise in the rubber industry, and dismissed the local smallholder sector as peripheral. Yet a brief look at the evidence, together with a little straight thinking, would have exposed that position. Is it simply the case that planters and officials were blinded by preconception, and therefore that their views, although in reality untenable, were nevertheless sincerely held? Or is it possible that those views were a cloak, behind which the colonial administration could seek to protect a large Western investment under challenge?

There remains a final point. It is necessary to reconcile the observation that the British colonial administration in the Malay States was hostile to the cultivation of rubber by the rural Malays with the fact that smallholdings accounted for 25–30 per cent of total Malayan output in 1921. There are three ways in which reconciliation might be achieved. They are not mutually exclusive. It can be argued that the Malay smallholders' response to rubber was so strong (after all, it offered the prospect of substantial material gain for modest effort and at little risk to subsistence security) that it simply overwhelmed the administration's opposition. It can be argued that, no matter the strength of feeling within the administration, in practice relatively little could be done to suppress Malay smallholder cultivation of this crop. The 'no rubber' condition entered in Malay land title deeds was widely disregarded. Colonial officials occasionally ordered the removal of offending rubber trees, but far more frequently accepted the planting of rubber as a *fait accompli* when it took place on reserved land. The violation could be punished by the imposition of a higher rent and premium on the holding. But the landowner, cultivating a most profitable market crop, would not be discouraged by that prospect. In any event, the Malay smallholder intent on the cultivation of rubber could avoid official hostility by planting on non-reserved land. Finally, it can be argued that the colonial administration was by no means universally hostile to smallholder cultivation of rubber. Badriyah Haji Salleh (1985: 167) notes the presence of 'a strong body of European civil servants and officials who considered that the economic position of the Malays could best be improved by encouraging them to plant rubber'. Lim Teck Ghee (1977: 78), who in general takes a harsh view of British attitudes and administration, nevertheless reports the public views of James Birch, Resident of Perak, in 1909: if rubber 'makes him [the Malay cultivator] rich and makes him happy, I, as one of his friends look on in perfect compliance'. In matters of day-to-day administration, such attitudes might well have greatly tempered the official discrimination against the Malay smallholder who would take up rubber.

Tobacco in East Sumatra

Certainly, British discrimination against Malay cultivation of rubber in the early twentieth century cannot compare with the Dutch administration's suppression of indigenous cultivation of tobacco in East Sumatra from a few decades earlier. The founding of a major tobacco industry in that region was, in important respects, the achievement of a single Dutch planter, Jacobus Nienhuys, who came to Deli in 1863, drawn by reports that the local population was growing fine quality tobacco. His initial attempts to extract tobacco for sale, directly involving the indigenous populations, met with only limited success. He advanced credit to lowland Malays to plant tobacco for him: but it proved difficult for Nienhuys to keep a secure watch on the holdings, widely scattered across a region of low population density, and too frequently the Malay cultivator simply took Nienhuy's cash but failed to deliver a crop. Nienhuys also attempted to plant tobacco himself, employing

Malays and Bataks from the interior highlands: but the Bataks, occupying a modestly secure, land-rich environment, saw little reason to submit to the harshly regimented life of the plantation labourer. Nienhuys solved his labour problem in 1865 when he went to Penang to recruit a small group of Chinese labourers who knew nothing about tobacco cultivation but who would certainly be determined workers. Four years later, Nienhuys, with two partners, established the Deli Company, which was to become the most important tobacco enterprise in East Sumatra. An explosive expansion in estate production of tobacco followed. In 1889 there were 170 tobacco plantations in the Deli district. Total tobacco production in East Sumatra in that year was almost 185,000 bales, valued at 40.6 million guilders.

Deli tobacco was established on the world market as a distinctive, high quality cigar wrapper leaf. A central concern of the planters was to maintain that quality, to hold on to that distinctive niche in the market. It was for this reason that within the plantation belt of Sumatra's east coast, the cultivation of tobacco was restricted essentially to Deli, Langkat, and Serdang, for only those districts possessed the distinctively rich soils that would produce the finest leaf. It was also for this reason that in the 1870s and 1880s only one crop was taken from each tract, for the planters believed that a second or subsequent crop from the same land would be of a much poorer quality. As a result, the rapidly expanding tobacco industry, constantly clearing, cultivating, and then abandoning each tract, demanded a vast area of land. However, in the late 1880s it was discovered that in fact two or more high-quality tobacco crops could be taken from the same land, provided that the land was left fallow for a period of years between crops. But even with this adjustment, the land requirements of the Western plantations were immense.

In this situation, how were the land requirements of the indigenous population to be accommodated? In 1877 the Dutch colonial administration issued a model contract to be used in the granting of land concessions in East Sumatra. A revision of the model in 1878 required that 4 *bouws* of land, about 2.8 hectares, should be set aside for each household head within a concession. But that allowance was well below the area required by a household to maintain itself, using the traditional form of shifting (swidden or slash-and-burn) cultivation. The Western planters then proposed that if households would forgo that land allocation, the estates would give them access each year to freshly harvested tobacco land for the raising of a subsistence food crop, of rice or corn. The advantage of that arrangement for the planter was, of course, that it gave him command of the full extent of his concession for the cultivation of tobacco, circumventing the requirement that part be set aside permanently for indigenous cultivation. At the same time, to allow the local cultivators brief, strictly controlled access to tobacco land immediately after it had been harvested would not significantly disturb the process by which the land—being left fallow for eight years or so—would regenerate itself in preparation for the next planting with tobacco. The advantages for the local cultivator were that he gained access to a much greater area of land than the 4 *bouws* stipulated in the model contract (in fact three times as much, if $1^1/_2$ *bouws* were cultivated each year and the estate was working an eight-year cycle). Moreover, the cultivator no longer faced the harsh task of clearing wild tract in preparation for cultivation every two or three years, for now he simply took over land recently harvested of tobacco. Developing after about 1890, this arrangement closely intertwined the swidden cultivation practices of the indigenous cultivator with the swidden practices of the European planter. Moving across the concession year by year through an eight- to ten-year cycle, local subsistence food cultivation tightly followed in the steps of tobacco cultivation for export.

But the relationship between planter and cultivator was severely unequal. The indigenous agriculturalist lost all control over where he cultivated, when he cultivated but, above all, what he cultivated. Clearly, the European planters would not allow him to grow a crop whose regime was incompatible with that of tobacco, or whose demands on the soil would undermine the land's regeneration. Cassava, bananas, and pepper were thus forbidden. When rubber appeared at the beginning of the twentieth century, a crop of immense potential for smallholders, the indigenous cultivators in the East Sumatra tobacco districts simply could not take it up. As a perennial that took five years or more to mature, and with a productive life of several decades, rubber could not be integrated into the swidden cycle of tobacco. Tobacco itself was obviously forbidden, for if it was planted on the same land in two consecutive years, first by the estate and then by a local cultivator, the soil would be worked out. Indeed, there were strict regulations in East Sumatra against the planting of tobacco by local people. Officially it was argued that local holdings, poorly cultivated and ill-kept, would be the source of tobacco plant diseases that would swiftly spread to the estates: and that the presence of both a smallholder and estate sector would make tobacco stolen from the estates difficult to identify. But it is also possible that the planters and officials feared that smallholder tobacco, badly grown and inadequately graded, would depress the reputation of East Sumatran tobacco on the world market. If the European estates were to maintain their place at the high-quality end of the world market for cigar wrapper leaf, there could be no smallholder production in East Sumatra. Local cultivators were therefore left with just rice or corn—as subsistence crops. All significant market opportunities were closed to them. Nor could they expand their cultivation of rice or corn to take advantage of the increased local demand for food grains, following the heavy immigration of contract labour to work on the tobacco plantations, for that would have required the adoption of intensive forms of agriculture, which were clearly incompatible with the extensive, swidden practices of tobacco cultivation. In any event, imported rice, from mainland South-East Asia, was cheap.

A common contemporary observation, which has been repeated in modern scholarship (Pelzer, 1978), was that the intertwining of Asian and European, subsistence and export, agriculture in the tobacco districts of East Sumatra dulled the economic drive of the indigenous peoples. It was argued that the local cultivator had grown idle, indeed was heading towards moral ruin, as the estates now undertook the heavy task of clearing and preparing the land for him to cultivate. This is a harsh judgement. There is sufficient evidence to argue that, far from being economically dulled, the local population in East Sumatra responded with vigour whenever there were profits to be made. From the 1870s, settlements near the edge of coastal swamps began planting extensive stands of nipa palm, to produce a roofing material greatly in demand for estate tobacco barns and drying sheds. Opportunities for employment as casual labour—in clearing the forest and constructing barns and sheds—were quickly seized. The economic initiative of the indigenous peoples in the tobacco districts of East Sumatra was not dulled but was vigorously suppressed in the interests of Western agricultural enterprise, to a degree that far exceeded the later hostility of the British administration in Malaya towards Malay cultivation of rubber.

SUGGESTED READING

There is a substantial literature on the Malayan rubber industry. The smallholder sector is the focus of Lim Teck Ghee (1977), *Peasants and Their Agricultural Economy in Colonial Malaya, 1874–1941*, Kuala Lumpur: Oxford University Press; and Badriyah Haji Salleh (1985), 'Malay Rubber Smallholding and British Policy: A Case Study of the Batang Padang District in Perak (1876–1952)', Ph.D. dissertation, Columbia University. Lim is very critical of British policy towards the Malay rubber smallholder; see also Lim Teck Ghee (1984), 'British Colonial Administration and the "Ethnic Division of Labour" in Malaya', *Kajian Malaysia*, 2(2): 28–66. The Malayan industry as a whole in this period is considered in two excellent volumes by John Drabble: J. H. Drabble (1973), *Rubber in Malaya, 1876–1922: The Genesis of the Industry*, Kuala Lumpur: Oxford University Press; John H. Drabble (1991), *Malayan Rubber: The Interwar Years*, London: Macmillan. The first volume pays close attention to the plantation sector, perhaps underplaying the smallholders. The second volume, covering the inter-war decades, provides a thorough examination of both sectors. Drabble offers a less severe view of British policy towards the Malay rubber cultivator. Colin Barlow (1978), *The Natural Rubber Industry: Its Development, Technology, and Economy in Malaysia*, Kuala Lumpur: Oxford University Press, mainly concerned with the modern industry, contains valuable discussion of the technologies and economics of rubber production. The British policy of creating Malay reserved land is discussed in Paul H. Kratoska (1983), '"Ends That We Cannot Foresee": Malay Reservations in British Malaya', *Journal of Southeast Asian Studies*, 14(1): 149–68. Note should also be made of a classic text: P. T. Bauer (1948), *The Rubber Industry: A Study in Competition and Monopoly*, London: Longmans, Green. Concerned mainly with the period from the early 1930s to the mid-1940s, it argues that the restriction schemes of the inter-war decades involved a severe discrimination against the smallholder sector.

The position of indigenous agriculture in the tobacco plantation districts of East Sumatra is considered in Karl J. Pelzer (1978), *Planter and Peasant: Colonial Policy and the Agrarian Struggle in East Sumatra, 1863–1947*, 's-Gravenhage: Martinus Nijhoff; and Thee Kian-wie (1977), *Plantation Agriculture and Export Growth: An Economic History of East Sumatra, 1863–1942*, Jakarta: National Institute of Economic and Social Research (LEKNAS–LIPI).

There is also a brief discussion in Clifford Geertz (1963), *Agricultural Involution: The Processes of Ecological Change in Indonesia*, Berkeley: University of California Press, Chapter 5. For an excellent discussion of plantation labour in East Sumatra, see Ann Laura Stoler (1985), *Capitalism and Confrontation in Sumatra's Plantation Belt, 1870–1979*, New Haven: Yale University Press, Chapters 2 and 3 for the pre-war period. As a point for comparison, the vigorous expansion of smallholder cultivation of rubber in southern Sumatra from the end of the nineteenth century is examined in Bambang Purwanto (1992), 'From Dusun to the Market: Native Rubber Cultivation in Southern Sumatra, 1890–1940', Ph.D. dissertation, University of London.

11

Ethnic Origin and Occupation

A striking feature of the populations which inhabited South-East Asia in this period was the strong correlation between an individual's ethnic origin and occupation. Immigrant Chinese and Indian entrepreneurs filled the occupations of trader, merchant, and moneylender—the intermediary, middleman functions in the economy. Chinese and Indian labourers dominated the urban work-force, toiling in processing mills, on the docks, in warehouses, and on construction projects. Chinese immigrants mined tin in the Malay States, and planted and harvested tobacco on the European plantations in East Sumatra; Indian immigrant labourers tapped rubber on the Western plantations in Malaya, worked in the rice mills, and on the docks of Rangoon. On the other side, the indigenous inhabitants—the great mass of the settled rural population—engaged in household-based cultivation as owner-occupiers, tenants, or labourers. The cultivation of rice for export in the mainland deltas was in the hands of Burmese, Siamese, and Vietnamese households; Malays dominated the smallholder cultivation of rubber in the Malay States.

Often there were strong correlations too between subethnic identities and particular occupations. Indian moneylenders in Burma belonged to the Chettiar caste; Sikh migrants from India to the Malay States and Straits Settlements commonly found employment as watchmen and in the police. Within the Chinese population in late nineteenth-century Siam, Teochiu dominated the rice trade, rice-milling, and revenue farming, constituted a major part of the dock work-force, and formed the labour gangs engaged in the construction of canals and railways: the Cantonese dominated as engineers and mechanics, and as builders: a significant proportion of the tin miners in southern Siam were Hokkiens: Hakka tended to be petty traders: Hainanese were market-gardeners, servants, and waiters. In this schema, the European populations in the region, it is barely necessary to add, occupied the high positions in administration and commerce.

These divisions were by no means rigid. There were in fact considerable numbers of indigenous traders and moneylenders in the region, although each might work on a small scale and perhaps few rose to become major figures in their occupation. Indeed, in early twentieth-century Burma there were far more Burmese moneylenders than Indian Chettiars, although the Chettiars accounted for the bulk of the lending because of the far larger scale of their operations. It is also important to note that occasionally there were differences in ethnic origin/occupation correlations in otherwise similar economies. In late nineteenth-century Burma, immigrant Indian labourers were heavily involved in the cultivation of rice for export, commonly as seasonal workers engaged for planting and harvesting. But in neighbouring Siam, immigrant Chinese avoided labour in the rice fields. However, despite these caveats, the identity between ethnic origin and occupation remains sufficiently pronounced to demand an explanation. There are a number on offer.

Values, Structures, and Experiences

Many of those explanations focus on what are seen as important cultural differences between the indigenes and the immigrants: differences in values, beliefs, aspirations, traditions, and in social organization, which arose, it is argued, as a result of contrasting physical environments and historical experiences.

Perhaps the clearest statement of that approach appears in Skinner (1957), an historical study of the Chinese in Siam. Skinner points out that the south China provinces of Kwangtung (Guangdong) and Fukien (Fujian), which supplied almost all the Chinese migrants who went to Siam, were hilly, infertile, prone to flood and drought, and, by this period, heavily overpopulated. In this 'grimly Malthusian setting', to use Skinner's vivid phrase (1957: 92), 'thrift and industry were essential for survival'. In contrast, the large plain of central Siam was a richly fertile, underpopulated region, in which subsistence was easily secured. The need for hard toil in the south China provinces, simply to survive, and the relative ease of subsistence in central Siam, over the centuries came to shape in their inhabitants two contrasting sets of social values and structures. Thus the qualities perhaps most strongly admired within Chinese society were industriousness and frugality. Those who restrained their present consumption and worked to secure the future were highly regarded. In rural Siam, in contrast, hard toil made little sense and self-denial secured little advantage. Again, Chinese culture stressed the continuity and cohesion of kinship groups. An individual recognized that the application and prudence of his ancestors had given his family what they now possessed, and he, in turn, acknowledged his responsibility to toil and save for the benefit of those who followed. Comparatively distant relatives felt a strong obligation to help one another. The Siamese, in contrast, had no ancestor cult, made little use of family names, and accepted responsibility only for immediate kin. Chinese society emphasized lineage advancement, and placed a high value on material success. Siamese condemned excessive concern with material ambition, emphasized individual salvation, and praised spiritual attainment. The large number of Siamese males who entered the Buddhist order at some point in their life, temporarily renouncing the material world, were held in high esteem.

Skinner points to a further important contrast. For many centuries, the south China provinces had been extensively involved in external trade. Their mountainous terrain made communication by land with the great river valleys of central and north China extremely difficult, and therefore a vigorous coastal trade had developed. From this grew an expansive trade with South-East Asia, long before Western traders came into the region. The merchants who worked from the thriving ports along the south China coast acquired a command of commercial and financial practices probably unrivalled in the eastern seas. The craftsmen, clerks, and labourers drawn into the ports also developed a heightened commercial sophistication. Theirs was a world infused, at all levels, with calculations of return, risk, margin, profit. The involvement of Siam in external trade in that period was far less. Indeed from the late seventeenth century to the middle of the nineteenth, the kingdom largely eschewed trade with Westerners. Consequently, indigenous traders had little opportunity to hone their commercial and financial skills, or to create extensive trading contacts in that direction.

The assertion that physical environment decisively shaped social values, traditions, and aspirations was also employed in a controversial book by Mahathir bin Mohamad (1970), currently the

Prime Minister of Malaysia. From the premise that China's hostile physical environment had forced on its people a continuous struggle for survival, he argues that in this struggle, 'the weak in mind and body lost out to the strong and resourceful' (Mahathir bin Mohamad, 1970: 24). Through generation after generation, only the fittest survived, so producing 'a hardy race'. In contrast, in the richly fertile, thinly populated lowlands of the Malay peninsula, 'even the weakest and the least diligent were able to live in comparative comfort, to marry and procreate' (Mahathir bin Mohamad, 1970: 21). Poor strains were not eliminated, as they were in China. These contrasting processes were reinforced by Chinese society's strong discouragement of marriage between kin, and the Malay 'partiality towards in-breeding' (Mahathir bin Mohamad, 1970: 24).

There are perhaps two distinct, but possibly related, propositions in Skinner's analysis. The first is that the Siamese, in comparison with the Chinese, lacked material ambition and economic aggressiveness. They were an easy-going people who sought pleasure before toil, spiritual repose before material possession. The second proposition is that the social values, societal structures, and historical experience of the Chinese gave them considerable advantages, against the Siamese, in certain fields of economic activity.

In the first proposition, there are resonances of the complaints commonly voiced by European colonialists about native indolence and economic irrationality. A considerable number of such opinions were brought together by Syed Hussein Alatas (1977) in the course of a bluntly titled book, *The Myth of the Lazy Native*. Sir Frank Swettenham, a senior British official in Malaya in the late nineteenth and early twentieth century, could write: 'The leading characteristic of the Malay of every class is a disinclination to work' (p. 44). Sir John Bowring, who visited the Philippines in the 1850s, wrote of the Filipino: 'His master vice is idleness' (p. 59). Clive Day, an American scholar writing at the beginning of the twentieth century, said of the Javanese: 'Nothing less than immediate material enjoyment will stir them from their indolent routine' (p. 62).

Further examples of such views, or of the circumstances which gave rise to them, come easily to mind. In Chapter 10 it was noted that both the Western rubber plantations in the Malay States in the early twentieth century and the Western tobacco plantations in East Sumatra a few decades earlier had found it difficult to recruit labour from among the local population, much to their frustration. In Burma, official reports at the beginning of the twentieth century referred to 'the characteristic thriftlessness of the Burman ... [his] want of foresight and tendency to extravagance and speculation ... squander[ing] his money on unproductive luxuries' (Furnivall, 1948: 115). Some authorities on Burma argued that Buddhism dulled the people's economic initiative by condemning the pursuit of material ambition. That theme, prominent in the colonial period, also surfaces in more recent literature. Swift (1964: 150), in a passage concerned with folk and formal religion in Malay peasant society, suggests that to 'the outside observer [the Malay peasant] seems to be not really concerned with striving for economic success and accumulation of wealth'. Parkinson (1967: 40) argues that Islam has had a regressive impact on the economic behaviour of the rural Malays, because it inculcates in its adherents a fatalistic approach to life, leaving them unlikely 'to strive for their own economic advancement by initiating the changes necessary for it'. Skinner's writings in this vein in the late 1950s have already been noted.

Such views are difficult to sustain. The majority simply collide with the evidence. The extraordinary toil of the populations in the deltas of mainland South-East Asia in bringing the wilderness into cultivation (Chapter 8), the vast commitment of Javanese labour to the production of government crops under the Cultivation System (Chapter 7), must surely dispel the charge of indolence. The explosive expansion in smallholder cultivation of rubber in the Malay States (Chapter 10) surely destroys the proposition that the material ambitions of the rural Malays were weak. Indeed, if there is a single image that runs through the immediately preceding chapters, it is that of rural populations across South-East Asia being sharply responsive to market opportunities, being driven by the prospect of material advance, and, above all, being greatly industrious. There are two further grounds for a challenge to the colonial stereotype. To the extent that the Burmese, to take the example above, are characterized as thriftless and extravagant, with a strong addiction to gambling, this description could also be applied to the allegedly more dynamic immigrant communities. Within the Chinese labouring populations in South-East Asia— among the miners, dock labourers, and estate workers—gambling, drinking, and opium smoking were rife. Yet is it ever argued that the indulgence of those vices—that extravagance—reduced their economic prowess? In fact, it might be argued that those indulgences provided an important stimulus to greater effort, for the individual had to earn to satisfy his cravings.

This leads to some final observations—on the influence of religious belief on economic behaviour. There are two points here. It can be argued that the condemnation of material ambition and the belief that the course of life is divinely determined, the two examples noted earlier, are primarily doctrinal positions which are rarely rigidly observed in daily behaviour. Second, there are certain religious practices which, far from suppressing economic ambition, may stimulate it. In a small town in east-central Java in the early 1950s, Clifford Geertz observed within the Javanese population a close correlation between religious piety and economic standing. The pious Muslims, the *santri*, were traders, store-owners, shoemakers, tailors, barbers: they were 'the vanguard of petty capitalism in Java' (Geertz, 1956: 156). The link, according to Geertz, was the obligation upon all devout Muslims to undertake the pilgrimage to Mecca, the *haj*. This could be a costly undertaking, but in this it provided an important incentive to work hard and live abstemiously over an entire lifetime.

For [the *santri*] it was a source of pride to work hard, dress simply, eat sparingly, and to avoid large ceremonial and festival expenditures. A man who by such means saved enough money to go to Mecca for a year or so at the age of fifty or sixty was immensely respected by the rural Moslem community. (Geertz, 1956: 145.)

In the previous chapter it was suggested that the prospect and cost of undertaking the *haj* may similarly have been an important stimulus to the expansion of rubber cultivation by Malay smallholders in the early twentieth century. A comparable argument might be applied to the Buddhist rice cultivators in the Burma and Siam deltas. The wish to accumulate merit by, for example, building a village temple and supporting its monks, provided a powerful incentive to clearing the wilderness and cultivating for export.

The second proposition embedded in Skinner's analysis—that the social values, societal structures, and historical experience of the Chinese gave them appreciable advantages in certain fields of economic activity—is more plausible. Certainly, the Chinese had an advantage in the conduct of trade. Freedman (1959: 65) draws attention to their pronounced financial skills—their 'shrewdness in handling money' and their striking ability to 'organize men in relation to money'. He suggests that this skill rested principally on three characteristics of Chinese society: the respectability of material ambition, the relative immunity of conspicuous wealth from seizure by political élites, and 'the legitimacy of careful and interested financial dealings between neighbours and even close kinsmen' (Freedman, 1959: 65). Two further points consolidate and extend those observations. Chinese traders commonly worked within extended, kin-based organizations, which facilitated the emergence of bigger firms, pooling capital and enterprise, and sharing commercial risks and opportunities. It gave them a far-flung network of secure trading contacts. Thus a striking feature of the commercial world of South-East Asia in the late nineteenth and early twentieth centuries was the large Chinese firm, based in one of the major ports but with branches, managed by kinsmen, spreading across the region and beyond. A trading firm with that structure was at a very substantial advantage when so much of South-East Asia's trade took place within the wider Asian region. For example, almost all Siam's rice exports were shipped initially to Hong Kong or Singapore. Chinese trading firms, based in Bangkok but with branches or kin contacts in those ports, were virtually invincible in this trade. Siamese traders, small-scale and without external networks, found it almost impossible to break in. The second point, repeating an earlier observation, is that Chinese trading practices, structures, and networks had been embedded and refined during centuries of trade between the South China coast and the southern seas. Indigenous traders in South-East Asia, in general, had not had that crucial experience.

Comparable points could be made about Indian society. Chettiar moneylenders in Burma and Malaya invariably worked as members of kin-based firms. They therefore enjoyed economies of scale—the pooling of financial resources and managerial talent, the sharing of risks and opportunities. Furthermore, the Chettiars were a tightly knit community, with a strong sense of group solidarity.

The main Chettiar temple on Mogul Street in Rangoon ... served as a focal point for the community's activities in Burma.... [There] Chettiars held periodic meetings, determined current interest rates, settled disputes, formed common opinions regarding important political issues ... and exchanged gossip. (Adas, 1974: 117.)

Those tight communal bonds secured considerable commercial advantages. Powerful informal sanctions within the Chettiar community helped to maintain a high standard of business morality, which reduced commercial risk and ensured that Chettiar firms in difficulties received assistance. The domestic life of the Chettiar drove home the values of thrift and industry. 'The wives of even the most wealthy Chettiars dressed simply, performed menial household tasks, and wove baskets or spun thread to help pay household expenses' (Adas, 1974: 115). The upbringing and education of a Chettiar boy concentrated on preparing him for a position in a Chettiar firm. Lastly, the Chettiar caste had had long experience of financial dealing. The caste was engaged in maritime trade as early as the end of the first millenium AD, and had begun to concentrate on banking and money-lending in the sixteenth century. With the advance of British power in India, the Chettiars established close working relationships with Western banks. The result was that Chettiar firms, making their way into Rangoon and then into the furthest reaches of the Irrawaddy Delta in the second half of the nineteenth century, operated with large loans from major banks in India, including the Imperial Bank of India and the Indian Overseas Bank.

Burmese moneylenders had none of those advantages. Most worked as individuals, dependent solely on their own resources, skills, and contacts. Among the Burmese there was little of the strong group solidarity exhibited by the Chettiars. Burmese domestic life did not relentlessly inculcate the virtues of thrift and self-reliance, the upbringing of children was not obsessively focused on success in that field. The Burmese had had no centuries-long experience in maritime trade or in sophisticated financial dealing. They had little familiarity with Western commercial and business practices. Burmese moneylenders had no ready access to the capital resources of the major banks in India. Such were these disadvantages that it is perhaps surprising that there were so many indigenous moneylenders in colonial Burma, although the Chettiars accounted for the bulk of lending. It is possible that the lone Burmese moneylender survived, at least during the decades of boom in the rice economy, principally because, with his detailed knowledge of local conditions and cultivators, he was willing to lend to the less secure borrowers turned down by the more circumspect Chettiar. And it might be added that the small, local Burmese moneylender was himself often supported by Chettiar loans.

The State and the Ethnic Division of Occupation

An alternative interpretation sees the state as the crucial factor in creating, reinforcing, or perpetuating (the choice of verb is extremely important) the ethnic division of labour in colonial

South-East Asia. This is an interpretation applied most forcefully
in studies of Malaya, perhaps inevitably so, for the ethnic divisions
were uniquely sharp there, and indeed have dominated the politics
of independent Malaysia through to the present. An important
writer here is Lim Teck Ghee (1984).

A substantial part of Lim's analysis was considered in Chapter 10.
From around 1910, he has argued, the colonial administration in
the Malay States sought to curb Malay smallholder production of
rubber for export, and to promote Malay cultivation of domestic
food crops, notably rice. The authorities frequently imposed 'no
rubber' conditions on lands alienated to Malays; insisted that
domestic food crops, not rubber, be planted on reserved land; and
imposed discriminatory land rents which favoured the cultivation
of domestic food crops at the expense of rubber. Lim (1984: 41)
argues that these, and other measures, 'acted as an important
brake on . . . Malay rubber development'. Crucially, they amounted
to 'a sustained campaign to confine the Malays to their traditional
agricultural pursuits and to restrict their participation in the
modern economy' (Lim, 1984: 42).

Lim also argues that the British colonial administration sought
to create/reinforce/perpetuate ethnic divisions of occupation through
its education policies. The existence of four separate school
streams—Malay, Tamil, Chinese-language, and English, the last
including the élite Malay College at Kuala Kangsar, attended by
the sons of Malay royalty and aristocracy—strongly enforced
ethnic divisions. Furthermore, the educational provision for
the mass of the Malay population was extremely limited. Malay-
medium schooling was provided only at the primary level. There
were no secondary Malay schools until after the Pacific War. More
importantly, the curriculum followed in the Malay village school
was very narrow. British policy in this area is vividly caught in the
following two quotations. Writing in 1920, the Chief Secretary of
the Federated Malay States declared that the 'aim of the
Government is . . . to make the son of the fisherman or peasant a
more intelligent fisherman or peasant than his father had been, and
a man whose education will enable him to understand how his own
lot in life fits in with the scheme of life around him' (Lim, 1984: 42
n. 31). Addressing the Federal Council in 1919, the High Com-
missioner argued that

it is no real education that qualifies a pupil in reading, writing and arith-
metic and leaves him with a distaste, or perhaps even a contempt, for the

honourable pursuits of husbandry and handicraft. It will not only be a disaster to, but a violation of the whole spirit and traditions of the Malay race if the result of our vernacular education is to lure the whole of the youth from the kampong [village] to the town. (Lim, 1984: 42 n. 31.)

In other words, Lim argues, British education policy sought to hold the Malay in his rural setting, to tie him still more firmly to subsistence cultivation, to isolate him from the modernizing influences found in the now rapidly growing urban centres of the Malay States. It failed to provide him with the skills and ambition to break out of the circumscribed economic role to which he had been assigned. The colonial government's employment practices may have strengthened that restriction. Lower clerical positions in the administration and jobs in the police and on the railways were largely filled with Indians, little or no opportunity being given to the Malays or indeed the Chinese.

As was implied at the beginning of this section, there is in fact a damaging imprecision in Lim Teck Ghee's assessment of the responsibility of the British administration for the ethnic divisions of occupation in colonial Malaya. Did the administration's policies and practices create, or simply reinforce or perpetuate those divisions? Two passages from Lim's article will establish the point. '[The] British played an important, if not overwhelming, role in *creating* and *perpetuating* an ethnic occupational differentiation.' (Lim, 1984: 30, emphasis added.) '[The] British knew that some sort of rough division of labour amongst the races was being structured under their rule and that various policies they pursued *reinforced* or *helped set up* tendencies towards racial separation.' (Lim, 1984: 63–4, emphasis added.) The image in the first quotation is active: the colonial authorities consciously created and then perpetuated ethnic divisions of occupation. The image in the second is essentially passive: the administration was aware that ethnic divisions were being formed, and was aware that its own policies would reinforce the tendencies towards division. This is not an argument about semantics. The imprecision in Lim's position brings the core of the issue into focus.

It is valuable to contrast Lim's assertion of the central responsibility of the colonial state in Malaya with the views of J. S. Furnivall on the state and ethnic occupational divisions in colonial Burma.

It was not the policy of Government to exclude Burmans from [employment in the more advanced sectors of the economy]; on the contrary it wished to help them, but this remained no more than a pious aspiration, because the Government, like the Burman, was the victim of circumstances. (Furnivall, 1948: 122.)

The exclusion of the Burman from modern economic life was not deliberate, was indeed frequently deplored; it just happened. (Furnivall, 1948: 119.)

In other words, the colonial state did not create or perpetuate the problem. Furthermore, despite its good intentions, it could do little about it.

But what then were the circumstances that held the British administration and the Burmese as its victims? In what way did ethnic occupational divisions 'just happen'? Furnivall would argue that the divisions were the inevitable result of the free working out of economic and social forces—the distinct social values, societal structures, and historical experiences of the Indian community which gave it, and Indian and Chinese communities across South-East Asia, considerable advantages in certain fields of economic activity. There are some other factors under this heading, and these will be the focus of the final section.

Mobility and Opportunity

The central point here is that there were important differences in the degree of mobility—geographical and thus commonly occupational—enjoyed by the indigenous populations and the immigrant peoples. Those differences were in part a universal characteristic. Within a settled local population, individuals are likely to be immobilized by family ties and wider social responsibilities, and by a long familiarity that breeds inertia. Immigrants, by the act of migration, have discarded their immediate social bonds and thrown off long familiarity to seek new localities and occupations. But that universal pattern appears to have been reinforced in South-East Asia by a number of distinctive considerations.

Thus commonly, the structures of social and economic obligation and responsibility that are well developed in South-East Asian societies, reinforced by the individual's obligations towards the state, bound the indigenous populations to certain forms of economic activity and often location. In Java, under the Cultivation System, the Dutch colonial administration utilized traditional mechanisms of authority and deference to drive the Javanese into large-scale production for the market. In the middle decades of the

nineteenth century, the great majority of the Siamese rural population were either bound in servitude to a member of the élite, or
were retainers to the élite. They did not have the freedom to move,
physically or occupationally, without the permission of owner or
patron. In addition, the state demanded some four months labour
a year from each adult male, to be employed primarily in the construction of canals, temples, and fortifications. Skilled native
craftsmen were similarly bound in service to a powerful patron or
to the court, and thus denied the opportunity to fix the terms upon
which they worked, or to develop their craft freely. In short, the
mass of the rural Siamese did not possess the personal freedom or
the physical mobility that would have allowed them to move into
the new fields of economic activity that emerged as the kingdom
was opened to international trade in the 1850s.

In contrast, the Siamese state imposed no formal restriction on
the physical or occupational liberty of the immigrant Chinese. The
Chinese paid a capitation tax instead of rendering corvée, and they
were not obliged to attach themselves to an élite patron. Chinese
were not brought to Siam as war-slaves, nor would they sell
themselves into servitude. In other words, the immigrant Chinese
had the freedom to move into the increasingly important non-
agricultural sectors of the expanding Siamese economy—to work
as wage labourers on the wharves, in the rice and saw mills, on the
barges and lighters, and as petty craftsmen and artisans.

There is an important refinement to be added to this argument.
Towards the end of the nineteenth century, the contrasting circumstances of the Siamese and the Chinese—the one bound, the
other unrestricted—were in important respects reversed. In 1874
the Siamese government began the legal elimination of slavery in
the kingdom, a reform which was completed in 1905. But just as
Siamese labour was being released from servitude, the rice-export
economy entered a period of particularly rapid growth. That
growth created ample opportunities in the cultivation of rice for a
rural population in which individuals were increasingly becoming
responsible for their own livelihood. In those circumstances, there
was little pressure on rural Siamese to move out of their long-
established agricultural activities into new sectors—even though
opportunities there were also expanding. It might be added that a
parallel set of circumstances was experienced by the Siamese élite
in this period. Beginning in the late 1880s, King Chulalongkorn
embarked on a major reform of the administration, that involved a
major expansion in the functions of government. This provided the

Siamese élite with more than sufficient opportunities for advancement in government service to discourage them from attempting to make their mark in commerce. In summary, around the turn of the century, the coincidence of rapid economic growth and administrative reform drove the two broad classes of Siamese towards rice cultivation, on the one hand, and government employment on the other, leaving commerce and wage labour outside agriculture largely to the Chinese.

While the mass of the Siamese population acquired a measure of personal freedom, in an important respect the Chinese immigrants had little choice of employment or location in their new land. The secret societies which organized the recruitment of migrants for Siam, directed the labourers on arrival into those sectors of the economy in which they had substantial interests—rice milling, construction work, and dock labour. In other parts of South-East Asia too, the new immigrant was commonly recruited for specific employment to which he was contractually bound. In Burma, most of the immigrant labourers, certainly from the beginning of the twentieth century, were recruited by a *maistry*, an experienced Indian foreman, commonly working for a local employer. The *maistry* not only recruited the men, usually from his home district, but organized their passage and acted as their overseer while they worked on the Rangoon wharves or in the rice mills of the delta. A similar mechanism was used to recruit Tamil labour from south India to work on the rubber plantations in the Malay States. In only a minority of cases did the Indian labouring immigrant land in South-East Asia unburdened by debt or obligation, and thus free, from the outset, to choose his new livelihood.

The broad division of indigene and immigrant into cultivators and non-agricultural wage-workers respectively was further driven by a harsh economic reality. Wage levels in the densely populated districts of India which provided the migrants to Burma were so abysmally low that arrivals in Rangoon accepted conditions of employment that the Burmese, enjoying expanding opportunities in rice cultivation, would immediately reject. Market forces drove the Burmese out of the urban centres—at least until the rapid expansion of the rice economy began to falter around the time of the First World War. Rangoon became an Indian city, by a process which Furnivall (1948: 118) called 'the survival of the cheapest'. Here, as perhaps elsewhere, ethnic divisions of occupation did indeed reflect the free working out of economic forces. 'It just happened', in Furnivall's sharp phrase (1948: 119).

SUGGESTED READING

The argument that the ethnic divisions of occupation between the indigenous and immigrant peoples in South-East Asia derived from cultural differences, which in turn were the result of contrasting physical environments and historical experiences, finds a particularly clear statement in G. William Skinner (1957), *Chinese Society in Thailand: An Analytical History*, Ithaca: Cornell University Press, Chapter 3. The focus on the importance of physical environment, in decisively shaping social values, traditions, and aspirations, can also be found in Mahathir bin Mohamad (1970), *The Malay Dilemma*, Singapore: Donald Moore for Asia Pacific Press. Mahathir's views, in particular his belief in the importance of inherited behavioural traits, has attracted considerable criticism. See Syed Hussein Alatas (1977), *The Myth of the Lazy Native: A Study of the Image of the Malays, Filipinos and Javanese from the 16th to the 20th Century and Its Function in the Ideology of Colonial Capitalism*, London: Frank Cass, which also includes an extensive survey of disparaging views on the abilities of the native peoples, penned by Europeans during the colonial period.

For the argument that religious belief had a regressive impact on the economic behaviour of indigenous peoples, see M. G. Swift (1964), 'Capital, Saving and Credit in a Malay Peasant Economy', in Raymond Firth and B. S. Yamey (eds.), *Capital, Saving and Credit in Peasant Societies*, London: George Allen & Unwin, pp. 133–56; and in particular Brien K. Parkinson (1967), 'Non-economic Factors in the Economic Retardation of the Rural Malays', *Modern Asian Studies*, 1(1): 31–46. Parkinson's article has been reprinted in David Lim (ed.) (1975), *Readings on Malaysian Economic Development*, Kuala Lumpur: Oxford University Press, pp. 332–40. That volume also includes a critical comment by William Wilder (pp. 341–6) and a rejoinder by Parkinson (pp. 346–9), which originally appeared in *Modern Asian Studies*, 2(2), 1968 and 2(3), 1968, respectively. See also Lim Teck Ghee (1977), *Peasants and Their Agricultural Economy in Colonial Malaya, 1874–1941*, Kuala Lumpur: Oxford University Press, pp. 237–8, for the argument that, in a number of ways, religious belief and practice limited the economic drive of the rural Malay.

The contrasting view, that far from suppressing economic initiative, religious practice stimulated it, is forcefully argued, in the context of Java, by Clifford Geertz (1956), 'Religious Belief and Economic Behavior in a Central Javanese Town: Some Preliminary

Considerations', *Economic Development and Cultural Change*, 4: 134–58. All these references focus on Islam. For brief considerations of the economic impact of Buddhism, in Burma, see Aung Tun Thet (1989), *Burmese Entrepreneurship: Creative Response in the Colonial Economy*, Stuttgart: Steiner Verlag Wiesbaden GMBH, pp. 53–5; and Michael Adas (1974), *The Burma Delta: Economic Development and Social Change on an Asian Rice Frontier, 1852–1941*, Madison: University of Wisconsin Press, pp. 111–12.

Maurice Freedman (1959), 'The Handling of Money: A Note on the Background to the Economic Sophistication of Overseas Chinese', *Man*, 59, article 89, pp. 64–5, relates the financial acumen of the overseas Chinese to certain characteristics of Chinese society. A comparable discussion—relating the moneylending success of the Chettiars in part to the community's tight group solidarity—is provided by Michael Adas (1974), *The Burma Delta*, pp. 116–17.

The argument that the state was the crucial actor in creating, reinforcing, or perpetuating the ethnic divisions of occupation, is most forcefully put by Lim Teck Ghee (1984), 'British Colonial Administration and the "Ethnic Division of Labour" in Malaya', *Kajian Malaysia*, 2(2): 28–66. In contrast, J. S. Furnivall (1948), *Colonial Policy and Practice: A Comparative Study of Burma and Netherlands India*, Cambridge: Cambridge University Press, sees those divisions as primarily the result of the working out of economic and social forces beyond the immediate control of government. It is David Johnston (1975), 'Rural Society and the Rice Economy in Thailand, 1880–1930', Ph.D. dissertation, Yale University, Chapter 6, who argues that the coincidence of rapid economic growth and administrative reform in Siam around the turn of the century decisively reinforced occupational divisions between Siamese and Chinese. James C. Ingram (1964), 'Thailand's Rice Trade and the Allocation of Resources', in C. D. Cowan (ed.), *The Economic Development of South-East Asia: Studies in Economic History and Political Economy*, London: George Allen & Unwin, pp. 102–26, also reflects on the Siamese/Chinese divisions of occupation in late nineteenth-century Siam.

12
The State and Economic Change: Élite Interests and Ambitions

THE major economic changes which took place in South-East Asia in the period from the early nineteenth century were inseparable from the actions of the state. On Java, the imposition of Dutch control, bringing to an end near-incessant indigenous warfare, appears to have been a crucial element in the transition to sustained high population growth in the nineteenth century. The Dutch colonial state was the instrument which secured the vast expansion of agricultural production for export on Java under the Cultivation System. In colonial Malaya, the state supposedly created, reinforced, or perpetuated ethnic divisions of occupation.

The state now comes centre stage. The present chapter examines the economic ambitions and policies of the indigenous state in Siam and the colonial state in the Philippines under American rule. The following chapter analyses the relationship between the state and the immigrant Chinese capitalist class in Siam and in Malaya in this period.

Siam

Writing in the mid-1950s, James C. Ingram described the broad experience of the economy of Siam over the previous century in the following terms:

The *Thai* population largely remained in agriculture, and from 1850 to 1950 it neither improved techniques nor increased the proportion of capital to labor. Moreover, in this period most changes in the economy as a whole were in volume rather than in kind. New methods were not used, new products were not developed. No product of any importance (except rubber) was exported in 1950 which was not exported in 1850. (Ingram, 1971: 209; emphasis in original.)

That passage has provided the starting point for much of the more recent writing on the Siamese economy. In the century from 1850 there was a failure to diversify both within and away from agriculture, and a failure to improve agricultural techniques, to raise the productivity of the land. The huge expansion in the cultivation of rice for export had not provided a basis for sustained economic growth, had not initiated the process of economic development. The Siamese economy remained overwhelmingly dependent on the export of a narrow range of primary commodities, the industrial sector remained miniscule, agricultural methods remained very basic. How are these failures to be explained?

One school of thought blames the indigenous rulers of Siam— the royal and noble élites—for an indifference towards fundamental economic change. It is pointed out that in the late nineteenth and early twentieth centuries, the Siamese government committed only a small part of its resources (tax revenues and the proceeds of foreign loans) to projects of a developmental character, concentrating instead on political and administrative initiatives. Its failure to construct large-scale irrigation works in the Central Plain, the great rice-growing region of the kingdom, lies at the heart of the indictment.

In 1902 the Siamese government engaged a Dutch irrigation engineer, J. Homan van der Heide, to prepare proposals for major irrigation works in the Central Plain. Van der Heide's report envisaged the building of a weir across the Chao Phraya River at Chainat on the northern edge of the lower Central Plain, the cutting of two main canals running parallel with the river, and the construction of a network of smaller channels from those main canals to carry water to the different parts of the lower delta. Van der Heide estimated that his scheme would irrigate more than half the land currently under cultivation in Siam, securing the rice crop from failure because of the inadequacy of the monsoon rains. The production capacity of the Central Plain, the security of rice cultivation there, would be greatly enhanced. The region would be transformed.

The Siamese administration showed no strong enthusiasm for these proposals. For some six years it put off a decision, while asking van der Heide to submit more modest schemes. Then, in 1909, it abandoned all proposals for large-scale irrigation works. In the years which followed some small schemes were undertaken—in the Pasak district on the east bank of the Chao Phraya, north of

Bangkok, from 1916, and in the Suphan district, on the west bank, from the mid-1920s. But there was no major irrigation initiative in this period, indeed none until after the Pacific War. Yet in the years in which van der Heide's proposals were being considered, the government committed itself to a substantial programme of railway construction, to tie the northern and southern extremities of the kingdom more firmly to Bangkok. Almost all the £8 million which Siam raised in foreign loans between 1905 and 1909 was used to finance railway construction. The railways were not built for economic reasons. The kingdom's exports did not depend on rail transport. The rice harvests of the Central Plain were brought down to the mills and wharves of Bangkok by barges working their way through an extensive network of canals, rivers, and small channels; teak was floated out of the northern forests and down to Bangkok by the main rivers; while the tin mined in the southern peninsular provinces was taken out by sea, shipped principally to Penang. Nor did the railways open up important new areas to an expansion of production and trade, for the new lines, driving into the extremities of the kingdom, traversed districts with low populations and limited commercial potential. Rather the railways were built for administrative/political reasons. They were to secure the effective government of the whole kingdom, in particular the furthest provinces, by Bangkok, by improving the lines of communication for day-to-day administration and, in times of threatened crisis, by making possible the rapid deployment of troops.

One explanation for the Siamese government's commitment to railways and rejection of irrigation is provided by Feeny (1982). He suggests that in this period, there was frequently a divergence between the interests of the mass of the Siamese population and the interests of the government élite. When those circumstances arose, the élite chose to advance its own interests, against those of the majority. Such was the case with an irrigation initiative. For the reasons given above, irrigation would have secured major advantages for innumerable rice cultivators in the Central Plain. But, Feeny suggests, for its part the government had only limited means by which it could capture a share of the gains that would come from an investment in irrigation. There are two arguments here. Under the terms of the treaties between Siam and the Western powers which opened the kingdom to virtually unrestricted free trade in the middle of the nineteenth century, land taxes and customs duties were frozen at very low levels. This meant that only a small fraction of the increases in land and foreign trade values that would result from the construction of large-scale irrigation works in the Central Plain would come to the government through its tax revenues.

The second argument concerns the private interests of the government élite. In the last years of the nineteenth century, prominent members of the government had acquired substantial landholdings in an area immediately to the north-east of Bangkok, the Rangsit district. The élite had been attracted by the fact that, as a result of the construction of water retention locks and drainage canals by a private company, Rangsit had the most advanced water control facilities in the Central Plain at that time. Cultivators had rushed into the area, seeking land to work. Rents and land values had risen sharply. For the government élite in Bangkok, their Rangsit holdings were therefore a valuable asset. According to Feeny, van der Heide's scheme, in providing large areas of the Central Plain with water control facilities at least equal to those in Rangsit, challenged the private interests of the government élite in two ways. It would have been difficult for the élite to secure ownership of the lands served by the van der Heide scheme, in the way it had earlier secured control of the smaller Rangsit district. The area involved was huge. But also, Feeny suggests, that earlier investment in Rangsit had sapped the financial resources of the élite. In other words, the van der Heide project would have created very substantial opportunities for private accumulation through acquisition of land, but the government élite, in whose hands lay the decision on van der Heide, was not in a position to seize those opportunities.

Second, and more seriously, by creating extensive newly irrigated areas across the Central Plain, the van der Heide project would have drawn large numbers of tenant cultivators away from Rangsit, provoking a sharp fall in rents and land values. In other words, van der Heide threatened the élite's existing investment in Rangsit. The only irrigation initiative pursued by the administration in these years was, as noted above, the relatively small project in Pasak. But as Pasak lay adjacent to Rangsit, that project would have had the effect of improving water conditions in Rangsit itself, leading, it was hoped, to the retention of its tenants and an enhancement of rents and land values. In brief, the government invested in irrigation only when the interests of powerful elements within the élite were thereby served. Where a proposal would create opportunities for private accumulation which the élite could not seize, or threatened their existing interests, it was rejected.

Railways, in contrast, by enhancing the control of the central government over the whole kingdom, clearly served élite interests. Bangkok would have the means to reduce the incidence of local abuses and extinguish crises in distant provinces which, left unchallenged, might provoke foreign intervention. Railways had a central role in averting the imposition of colonial rule, in securing the élite's position, during the age of European territorial aggression.

There are other examples, it is said, of the élite sacrificing the broader interests of the majority to their own interest. Although the government discussed at length a major investment in the development of improved rice-seed varieties and more advanced cultivation practices, little was actually accomplished. An experimental rice farm was established in 1916/17. Significantly (in the eyes of Feeny) it was located in the Rangsit area 'where the Bangkok officials [as landowners] would be among the beneficiaries' (Feeny, 1982: 104). Again, investment in education was very modest. At the beginning of the 1910s, well below 10 per cent of all boys between the ages of 6 and 14 years were attending elementary and primary schools. There was no university in Siam until the establishment of Chulalongkorn University in the mid-1910s. The élite wanted enough educated men to run the administration, but not an educated class that might in time push them aside. The government preferred to invest in the modernization of the armed forces, for the same reason as it invested in railway construction. And substantial resources were committed to maintaining the court. These expenditures would do little to strengthen the economy.

This school of thought can be challenged at two levels. There is the level of detailed argument, at which the fine points of evidence and its interpretation are closely picked over. From a complex literature, two examples must suffice. Feeny's proposition that the Siamese administrative élite, having speculated heavily in Rangsit towards the end of the nineteenth century, was probably not in a financial position to purchase a major part of the large area that would be served by van der Heide's scheme, is simply a hypothesis. There is no evidence that the earlier investment had seriously sapped the élite's financial resources. Moreover, it is difficult to see why the Bangkok administrative élite would not have welcomed the opportunities provided by van der Heide to expand its holdings in further premier rice-cultivating districts, strengthening its *rentier* position, especially as the Rangsit canals, dikes, and embankments were apparently beginning to deteriorate. Similarly, no primary evidence is offered to support the view that the government located its experimental rice farm in Rangsit simply to benefit the élite landowners. There were sound agricultural reasons why Rangsit might have been chosen. It was a district of intensive cultivation and consequently one in which the problem of declining yields was perhaps particularly acute: and it had the most advanced water control facilities in the kingdom.

The second, broader challenge to these views is the argument that whatever the private interests of the administrative élite, Siam's economic policy was shaped by far more powerful influences, largely beyond government control. Those influences arose from the weakness of Siam's geo-political position in mainland South-East Asia from the middle of the nineteenth century, which exposed it to decades of aggressive European pressure. This argument is, in fact, the central element in a second interpretation of the causes of Siam's economic failures in this period.

There was a brief reference to part of this interpretation earlier. Under the treaties between Siam and the major Western powers—the first was the Bowring Treaty, signed with Britain in 1855—land taxes and foreign trade duties were frozen at very low levels. Consequently, in this period the Siamese government could increase its tax revenue only by improving the effectiveness of tax collection (the financial and provincial administrations were reformed from the late 1880s) or by creating new taxes other than on land or foreign trade (the revenues from the consumption of opium and spirits, and on the conduct of gambling, came to account for a major part of the state's income by the early twentieth century). Government revenues also rose as the volume of agricultural production and foreign trade went up, although only moderately, as the rates of land tax and customs duty were frozen. This lack of fiscal autonomy imposed a severe constraint on the capacity of the Siamese administration to finance major internal reform—the construction of large-scale irrigation works, the creation of a modernizing education system.

External circumstances limited the government's ability to secure financial resources in another way. A potent weapon in the scramble by the Western powers for commercial advantage, political influence, and territory across much of Africa and Asia in the imperial age was the large foreign loan, commonly secured on one of the borrower's major assets—a railway line, the customs revenue. Difficulties in repayment, an urgent need for further loans to bolster deteriorating finances, could provoke deeper Western intrusion and then intervention. The Siamese government was thus acutely aware that raising a foreign loan involved far more than a simple commercial calculation. The contemporary experience of China—where a run of foreign loans bearing markedly onerous terms appeared to presage the dismemberment of the country—was a powerful warning. Consequently, although Siam raised a number of loans in Europe in the early twentieth century, the kingdom borrowed far less than the strict conservatism of its financial administration would have entitled it to do.

The external circumstances of the kingdom also had a powerful influence on the way in which the government's resources were deployed. The dominant issue facing Siam in the second half of the nineteenth century was the threat posed to its political independence by the Western powers which had come to occupy the rest of mainland South-East Asia—Britain on Siam's western and southern borders, France to the east. The government's aim, above all else, was to contain that threat, for all other ambitions would become irrelevant if independence were lost. Those circumstances dictated that the government invest heavily in railway construction, a strengthening of provincial administration, and modernization of the armed forces. They implied a relative neglect of education and irrigation. Put bluntly, the railway would assist in securing Siam's political independence, irrigation works would make no such contribution. In any event, even in the absence of a major irrigation initiative, Siam was still to be one of the world's most important producers and exporters of rice.

Both these interpretations—the one seeing the economic policies of the Siamese state as being decisively shaped by the private interests of the government élite, the other seeing the state's economic role being severely constrained by the external circumstances of the kingdom—will be taken up again in the following chapter, which examines the relationship between the state and the immigrant Chinese capitalist class. Here it would be valuable to interpolate two views which, again concerned with Siam, play down the importance of the state as an economic actor.

The first argues that the lack of improvements in cultivation methods (notably the failure to mechanize) and in agricultural inputs (the failure to use higher-yielding seeds, to apply fertilizers) in the main rice export districts of the kingdom from the late nineteenth century can best be explained not in terms of an absence of government commitment to agricultural research but in terms of relative factor endowments. Sompop Manarungsan (1989) asserts that with an abundance of uncleared land, the rational response of a rural population seeking to increase production was to bring that land into cultivation (to extend over a wider area existing agricultural methods and inputs) rather than intensify cultivation (introduce improved seeds and fertilizers) on land already in use. Similarly, with an abundance of work animals in central Siam in the first decades of the twentieth century, and with the high cost of farm machinery and motor fuel, there was little incentive for the rice cultivator to mechanize. In other words, even if the government had committed itself to the development of more advanced cultivation practices and inputs, it is doubtful whether rice cultivators would have taken them up. Ingram (1971) focuses on factor endowments from another perspective. The expansion of Siam's economy from the 1850s, he argues, created a greatly increased demand for urban wage labour. The rural population showed little inclination to respond, principally because the cultivation of rice for export now offered substantial material returns, and consequently those urban positions were filled largely by Chinese immigrants. However, Ingram continues, if large-scale Chinese immigration had not taken place, urban wages may well have risen sufficiently to attract labour from the rural sector. High wages and the loss of manpower in agriculture 'might, in turn, have induced farmers to use more capital and to improve their techniques' (Ingram, 1971: 210). Again, the central consideration was not the government's commitment to agricultural advance but whether there was the incentive for cultivators to take up new methods and use improved inputs.

The second interpolated view asks a fundamental question. Just how important were irrigation and agricultural advance? Feeny's position is that 'explanations of government failure to arrest or reverse the productivity [declines] in the agricultural sector [from the early twentieth century] play a crucial role in understanding Thai underdevelopment' (Feeny, 1979: 118). But Falkus (1991) notes that there is no description here of the precise relationship between improved agricultural productivity and structural change in the economy. The relationship implied, Falkus continues, is that structural change would result from increased domestic demand (higher cultivators' incomes) or from increased imports and capital inflows made possible by a widening trade surplus (higher rice exports). If this is the model, it is an unconvincing one. In almost all nineteenth century primary producing countries, argues Falkus, the rate of growth of the export sector and its size relative to the economy as a whole were simply insufficient to set structural change in train. There is no reason to identify Siam as one of the exceptions. Certainly, if the rice export sector had failed to trigger structural change in the second half of the nineteenth century, when world demand for rice was expanding rapidly, it was unlikely to do so in the decades which followed, when the international rice market faltered.

The Philippines

To provide a comparison with the Philippines in this context may appear somewhat bizarre. Throughout the colonial era Siam retained its political independence, while the Philippines was under foreign rule for longer than any other territory in South-East Asia, first Spain and then, from 1898, the United States. American administration may itself have been distinctive among colonial administrations in South-East Asia. By the time it acquired the Philippines, the United States had emerged as a world economic power. Moreover, it brought to its new responsibilities a firm anti-colonial tradition and, perhaps, a measure of idealism. Yet a brief examination of the flaws in the Philippine economy during the American period, the role of the state in shaping economic change in the Islands, and the economic ambitions and interests of those who controlled the Philippine state, brings out some notable parallels with Siam.

Certainly, the economic weaknesses are strikingly similar. The period of American administration saw a major expansion in agri-cultural production (sugar, abaca, coconuts, and tobacco) for export, particularly following the establishment of free trade between the Philippines and the United States by legislation in 1909 and 1913, but little industrial development. In other words, there was a sharp reinforcement in Philippine dependence on primary export production (indeed, a remarkably high degree of dependence on the American market alone) but a marked failure to diversify towards industry. The dominant agricultural sector was characterized by low productivity, undercapitalization, a high level of tenancy, and acute indebtedness: and little was achieved in alleviating those problems. In the words of one scholar (Owen,

1971a: 105): 'At the end of the American period, the average *tao* lived where his grandfather had lived, was deeper in debt, remained without land title, and grew his crops as inefficiently as anywhere in the world.' The issue here is not whether the state had the capacity, the instruments to confront those weaknesses, although that question is a perfectly legitimate one. It is whether the élite which commanded the state actually had an interest in confronting them.

As an opening point, it must be said that there was little coherence, no cleanly thought-out design, in American economic policy in the Philippines. Indeed frequently there were serious internal contradictions. For example, the establishment of free trade between the Philippines and the United States, which secured for a number of Philippine agricultural exports advantageous entry to the biggest economy in the world, clearly gave considerable encouragement to the expansion of primary production and trade. Yet the large-scale American investment in Philippine commercial agriculture that would have reinforced that expansion was, in effect, blocked. The Philippine organic act, signed into law in 1902, limited the amount of public land which the Philippine government could sell or lease to 16 hectares for an individual and 1024 hectares for a corporation. American companies contemplating investment in the colony needed access to far larger tracts. Also in 1902 the American Congress extended the Chinese exclusion laws, applicable to the American mainland, to the Philippines. This too choked off investor interest, for any major commercial initiative, for example in plantations, was now denied access to cheap labour from China. The core of the matter was that Congress possessed little knowledge of the Philippines, largely because the welfare of the United States, a world economic power, did not depend to any significant degree on the economic fortunes of the Islands. As a result, American economic policy in the Philippines tended to be shaped by domestic interest lobbies pursuing solely domestic issues. There was a clear example immediately above. The Congressional restriction on the sale or lease of public land to corporations reflected pressure from senators from sugar-producing states, determined that the Philippine sugar industry, competing with their constituents, would not be further strengthened by American investment. The American Congress lacked the consistency of interest and moral vision, perhaps even the knowledge, to plot an assault on the weaknesses of the Philippine economy.

There is, however, a more important point. Although the basic legislation on economic matters in the colony was set down by the American Congress, real political power almost invariably lay with the Philippine élite. American rule in the Philippines was characterized by what Stanley (1974: 270) has called 'the politics of attraction'. The installation of the new colonial administration in the Islands in 1899 ignited an insurrection that was not broken by American forces until 1901. The ferocity of that rising, together with the harshness of the measures frequently employed in its suppression, fed into the powerful anti-colonial strand in American domestic politics, exacerbating the unease and ambivalence felt by vast numbers of Americans towards their new acquisition. Those circumstances thus required for the United States that victory over the Philippine insurrectionists 'be complemented by accommodation—that Filipinos be not merely defeated, but converted' (Stanley, 1974: 268). Crucial to the achievement of that last ambition was the presence of a Filipino landed and professional élite which had built its wealth and position largely through the expansion of agricultural production for export from the middle of the nineteenth century. That class had provided much of the opposition to the Spanish regime in its final decades, and indeed many of its members had taken part in the revolt against Spain which had broken out in August 1896 and then in the insurrection against the United States. But once the insurrection was broken, the landed élite eagerly demonstrated its willingness to mediate between the new colonial rulers and the mass of the Filipino people. In this way American unease and Filipino élite ambition came together. From the earliest years of the new regime, but decisively with the creation of the Assembly in 1907, the United States transferred administrative, political, and legislative powers to Filipinos, but in practice to the established élite, and in so doing lost much of its capacity to command events. 'The politics of attraction wed the United States to the class interests of the Philippine élite' (Stanley, 1974: 270), the interests of great landholdings and agricultural exports.

The fortunes of the Filipino élite were thus greatly boosted by the tariff measures of 1909 and 1913 which gave a number of Philippine crops, notably sugar, advantageous access to the American market. The élite's domination of commercial agriculture was protected against American investment by the limitation which Congress had placed on the acquisition of public land by corporations, while existing estates were left essentially untouched. More importantly, the landed Philippine élite could not countenance measures directed against the core problems in agriculture: high rates of tenancy, low productivity and the absence of significant innovation in cultivation methods and inputs, the impoverished condition of tenants and landless labourers. In general, in this period it saw no great advantage, but perhaps a considerable threat, in diversification of the economy away from agriculture. The élite strongly opposed any significant increase in the taxation of agricultural lands or income, an increase that would have provided the state with the resources to promote improvements in agriculture and diversification towards industry. Per capita tax revenue and government expenditure in the Philippines were among the lowest in colonial South-East Asia: as a consequence the Islands' economic infrastructure was among the worst. Throughout the American period, the Philippine élite projected its interests as those of the Philippines as a whole. Frequently, they were not.

All colonial administrations to some degree required the collaboration of an established local élite in order to function: so all were to some degree wedded to the interests of that élite. Bound into the relationship, the colonial state disturbed the indigenous order at its peril. Radical change was thereby precluded. Those considerations also applied in Siam, where, from the final decades of the nineteenth century, the established élite sought to buttress its internal position. The first section of the next chapter will take this theme further.

SUGGESTED READING

Although the main body of the book was first published as long ago as 1955, James C. Ingram (1971), *Economic Change in Thailand, 1850–1970*, Stanford: Stanford University Press, remains a most useful introduction to the modern economic history of that country. More recent research may have added considerably to our knowledge (although it is remarkable how much ground Ingram covers) and yet the major issues he identified have remained central in subsequent writings, while Ingram's own views continue to provide valuable insights. A more recent, strongly statistical, account of economic change in Siam in the modern period is provided by Sompop Manarungsan (1989), *Economic Development of Thailand, 1850–1950: Response to the Challenge of the World Economy*, Institute of Asian Studies, Monograph No. 42, Bangkok:

Chulalongkorn University. Malcolm Falkus (1991), 'The Economic History of Thailand', *Australian Economic History Review*, 31(1): 53–71, a broad analytical essay, contains a number of stimulating observations.

Turning to the more detailed literature, the argument that the failures of government economic policy in the late nineteenth and early twentieth century are to be explained in terms of the Siamese élite's determination to protect or enhance its own interests, even where that conflicted with the interests of the mass of the population, is strongly projected in the following: Chatthip Nartsupha and Suthy Prasartset (1978), *The Political Economy of Siam, 1851–1910*, Bangkok: Social Science Association of Thailand; and Chatthip Nartsupha, Suthy Prasartset, and Montri Chenvidyakarn (1978), *The Political Economy of Siam, 1910–1932*, Bangkok: Social Science Association of Thailand. These are volumes of collected documents, in large part translations from Thai of material held in the National Archives in Bangkok: both volumes have extended analytical introductions. This argument is also projected in David Feeny (1982), *The Political Economy of Productivity: Thai Agricultural Development, 1880–1975*, Vancouver: University of British Columbia Press; David Feeny (1979), 'Competing Hypotheses of Underdevelopment: A Thai Case Study', *Journal of Economic History*, 39(1): 113–27, covers much of the same ground, more briefly. For the contrasting argument, that the limited capacity of the Siamese state to engineer major economic change in this period was the result not of the élite's overriding determination to enhance its own interests but of the baneful influence of the kingdom's vulnerable external circumstances, see Ian Brown (1988), *The Élite and the Economy in Siam, c.1890–1920*, Singapore: Oxford University Press; see also Ian Brown (1992), *The Creation of the Modern Ministry of Finance in Siam, 1885–1910*, London: Macmillan, Chapter 6. The restricting influence of Siam's external circumstances also receives emphasis in Peter F. Bell (1970), *The Historical Determinants of Underdevelopment in Thailand*, Economic Growth Center, Discussion Paper No. 84, New Haven: Yale University.

For the Philippines, Norman G. Owen (1971a), 'Philippine Economic Development and American Policy: A Reappraisal', in Norman G. Owen (ed.), *Compadre Colonialism: Studies on the Philippines under American Rule*, Michigan Papers on South and Southeast Asia No. 3, Ann Arbor: University of Michigan, pp. 103–28, provides concisely and provocatively what the title promises. Similarly with Glenn Anthony May (1980), *Social Engineering in the Philippines: The Aims, Execution, and Impact of American Colonial Policy, 1900–1913*, Contributions in Comparative Colonial Studies No. 2, Westport: Greenwood Press. The origins and implications of 'the politics of attraction' are explored in Peter W. Stanley (1974), *A Nation in the Making: The Philippines and the United States, 1899–1921*, Cambridge, Mass.: Harvard University Press.

13
The State and Economic Change:
Chinese Capitalists

Chinese Capital in Siam

THE argument, outlined in the previous chapter, that explains the failures of government economic policy in Siam in the late nineteenth and early twentieth century in terms of the determination of the Siamese administrative élite to protect or enhance its own interests, has a further important aspect—one that focuses on the relationship between the élite and the Chinese capitalists who occupied such a prominent position in the Siamese economy in this period.

This relationship was the particular concern of a group of Thai scholars that emerged in the mid-1970s, among whom Chatthip Nartsupha was perhaps the most prominent. Its starting point was the assertion that in nineteenth-century Siam, the king controlled the largest part of land, labour, and capital resources. Consequently, the crown received—through tax revenues, interest payments, rents from land, and the command of corvée labour—a severely disproportionate share of the kingdom's surplus production. This implied that the crown alone had the capacity, commanded the resources, to initiate major economic change. No other concentration of economic power, independent of the crown, could emerge. The crown, commanding the surplus product of the kingdom, stood in the way of the development of an independent indigenous bourgeoisie.

At the same time there was the potential of an *implanted* bourgeoisie, in the form of the Chinese merchant community. The Chinese possessed considerable entrepreneurial skill, extensive commercial networks, and easy access to capital from trade. Even so, they failed to develop into an independent bourgeoisie, with the capacity to initiate major economic change. The reason for this failure, according to Chatthip (1978), was that the Chinese merchant class was subordinated to Siamese political authority, serving its interests, and increasingly sharing its perspectives. Because of the Siamese élite's exclusive hold on political and administrative positions, Chinese capitalists were forced to seek powerful élite patrons to secure their commercial interests. The patron, by necessity an important figure within government, provided protection against the exactions of officials, fixed administrative decisions in his favour, and provided access to new capital resources. In return, clients made payments, in many forms, to their élite patrons. These powerful, mutually advantageous alliances were occasionally reinforced through intermarriage.

However, one effect of those bonds, the argument continues, was to drive local Chinese capital and enterprise towards those forms of economic activity which sustained Siamese élite interests. Two examples must suffice. By the end of the nineteenth century, revenue farms were drawing in a quite astonishingly high level of Chinese capital and business commitment. As was last explained in Chapter 4, the revenue farm was an arrangement in which the government granted a private individual or syndicate the monopoly right to collect a specific tax, sell a particular commodity (opium, liquor), or operate a specific service (gambling dens) in a designated area for a fixed period (usually three years). The individual or syndicate, that is, the revenue farmer, paid the government for this right. The sums over and above that payment which the revenue farmer secured from the collection of the tax or from the sale of the commodity was his net profit. That profit could be very considerable. The advantage of this arrangement for the government was that it obtained a substantial income while the costs of revenue collection were borne by the revenue farmer. Indeed, at a time when the government's authority in many areas far from the capital was slight, it was common for Bangkok to transfer to local Chinese capitalists a range of government functions in addition to the collection of revenues, in effect making them responsible for administration in that part of the kingdom. For the Chinese capitalists, the revenue farm was, obviously, an important business venture. But in addition it made it possible for them to exploit related commercial openings, in ways which will be examined in the second part of this chapter. However, and this is the central point here, all such opportunities were set by the Siamese government élite. It determined the principle that the kingdom's revenues would be farmed out: and, in detail, it decided which particular revenues would be contracted to a farmer, which farmer, and when. And in the early twentieth century it decided, after all, to abolish the revenue farms. Chinese capitalists worked within those boundaries.

The second example: in the late nineteenth and early twentieth century, major figures within the Siamese government élite joined with prominent Chinese capitalists in a number of business ventures—rice milling, land development, and, of particular note here, banking. The mid-1900s saw the establishment of the Siam Commercial Bank, the first indigenous modern bank in the kingdom. (It remains a major bank in present-day Thailand.) The founders of the bank included the Minister of Finance (the leading figure), the King (in the form of the Privy Purse Department), and a number of prominent Chinese revenue farmers/merchants/rice millers. The Siamese partners brought to the venture the authority of their government positions (and therefore the implication of official approval and assistance) and capital: the Chinese partners also brought capital, together with extensive connections into the trading community of Bangkok. Once again, this was an important business opportunity for Chinese capitalists: but one set by Siamese political authority. Dependent on the Siamese élite, because they commanded no political or administrative power of their own, the Chinese capitalists were absorbed into it, assuming élite ambitions and faithfully serving élite interests. In this way, the Chinese capitalist class was emasculated, left incapable of effecting fundamental change in the basic structure of the Siamese economy.

This view of the experience of the Chinese capitalist class in Siam can be challenged on a number of grounds. For example, it is possible to construct alternative analyses to explain why Chinese capital was so strongly committed to revenue farms, rice mills, land development, and banks, why, in the early decades of the twentieth century, it did not establish an important interest in modern industry. Bell (1970) explains the lack of Chinese investment in industry, which clearly would have demanded a long-term commitment of capital and enterprise, in terms of the preference of Chinese capitalists, as aliens, for greater liquidity. He also notes the high level of remittances to China in this period, the implication being that substantial funds were drawn away from long-term investment in Siam itself. An alternative, and probably stronger argument is that with the signing of the commercial treaties between Siam and

the Western powers from the 1850s, the kingdom had been open
to a virtually unrestricted influx of inexpensive manufactures mass-
produced in the industrialized West. That influx prevented, at least
as an immediate prospect, a substantial expansion of industrial
production in Siam, for local manufacturing, struggling into existence, would simply be swept aside by far more powerful foreign
competition. In other words, the reason why Chinese capitalists in
Siam failed to diversify into industrial production in the late nineteenth and early twentieth century, failed to lead the Siamese economy towards a major restructuring, was that in an open economy
the opportunity to do so, except in rare circumstances, did not
exist.

The rare exceptions point up a further important argument. As
was noted above, in the first decade of the twentieth century,
Chinese capital in Siam established an important interest in modern banking, in alliance with the Siamese political élite in the case
of the Siam Commercial Bank but also alone, in the Chino-Siam
Bank. Those banks faced strong competition from the local
branches of major Western banks, notably the Hongkong and
Shanghai, and the Chartered. But the advantages possessed by the
Western branches—they were part of long-established banking
networks embracing all the major commercial centres in the East—
were matched by the fact that the new Siamese ventures had very
strong connections within the Bangkok trading community (the
Chinese partners were prominent figures in that community) and,
in the case of the Siam Commercial, the support of government. A
second exception provides a further insight. In 1913 the King (in
the form of the Privy Purse) and one of his senior ministers, in
alliance with a prominent Sino-Siamese entrepreneur and a
Danish businessman long resident in Bangkok, established the
Siam Cement Company. Starting production in May 1915, within
a few years the company dominated the domestic market. Its success rested in part on a substantial and rising local demand for
cement, the presence locally of extensive deposits of limestone and
clay, and the ease with which the promoters, through their Danish
partner, could gain access to the technical expertise and industrial
plant that would ensure the production of cement of a quality at
least equal to that of imported brands. But the central consideration was that imported cement had to bear very high freight
charges, high in relation to the costs of production. Consequently,
it entered the Siamese market at a clear price disadvantage. In
other words, the Siam Cement Company possessed a crucial
measure of non-tariff protection.

The important point to be drawn from the establishment of the Siam Commercial Bank and the Siam Cement Company at the beginning of the twentieth century is that they demonstrate an eager commitment on the part of members of the Siamese political élite and Chinese capitalists to major new commercial ventures. There can be no question here of Chinese capitalists being tightly constrained by a subordinate relationship to Siamese political authority, or of the Siamese political élite being constrained by an inescapable commitment to long-established interests. It should be added that from the mid-1920s, following the renegotiation of the nineteenth-century treaties which had prevented Siam from setting its land tax and duty rates, further opportunities for commercial diversification arose which the Chinese capitalists and the Siamese political élite (in 1932 the absolute monarchy was overthrown in favour of a non-royal, commonly military-dominated, government) moved quickly to exploit. The 1920s and 1930s saw the establishment of modern factory production of cotton textiles (an army venture), matches, cigarettes, and beer. In a still later period, from the 1950s, the alliance between Thai political power (notably senior officers in the armed forces) and Sino-Thai business achieved a remarkable expansion in the industrial and services sectors, a restructuring of the Thai economy that suggests to many that the kingdom is on the edge of becoming a major manufacturing power. (There are important issues here which are taken up in two later chapters: Chapter 14, which examines industrial development in South-East Asia before the Pacific War; and Chapter 18, which considers the rapid industrial expansion which has taken place in many parts of the region since around 1960.)

That alliance had failed to secure a significant diversification of the Siamese economy in the late nineteenth and early twentieth century, to restate the argument, because at that time the external economic circumstances of the kingdom did not permit it. This proposition runs parallel to one outlined in the preceding chapter: the capacity of the Siamese state to raise tax revenues and to secure foreign loans, as well as its freedom of action in deploying the resources which it did command, was severely constrained by the vulnerable external political circumstances of the kingdom in the age of imperialism. In brief, the root causes of the weaknesses of the Siamese economy in this period were to be found outside Siam.

The Malayan Tin Industry: Chinese Capital, Western Capital, and the State

In contrast to the broad sweep of the analysis in the first part of this chapter, the second, concerned with Chinese and Western capital in the Malayan tin industry in the late nineteenth and early twentieth century, focuses on a narrow point, although one which illuminates a number of issues of wide importance. With the establishment of British administration in the west coast states of the peninsula in the mid-1870s, Malayan tin production expanded greatly, increasing almost four-fold in the final two decades of the nineteenth century. In 1900 Malaya was by far the world's most important producer of tin, accounting for 51 per cent of world production. Until towards the close of the nineteenth century, extraction was almost entirely in the hands of the Chinese. With few exceptions, the Western mining companies which sought to establish themselves failed. However, in the first decade of the twentieth century, Western capital made a major advance. By 1910 Western mines accounted for 22 per cent of tin production in the Federated Malay States. By 1920 that figure was 36 per cent: and in 1929 Western mines overtook the Chinese sector. Chinese production fell absolutely, as well as relatively, between 1910 and 1920. By 1930 it had partially recovered in absolute terms, although relative decline had, of course, continued. Therefore the issues are: why did Chinese capital overwhelmingly dominate the Malayan tin industry in the late nineteenth century; and in what circumstances did that domination end?

Two crucial, tightly related factors were the nature of the tin seams at a given time, and the contrasting mining methods of Chinese and Europeans. In the final decades of the nineteenth century, the tin seams being worked were rich and close to the surface. The mining methods of the Chinese were quite simple. Large gangs of labourers, using only the most basic implements, dug out, carried, and washed vast volumes of tin-bearing soil. There was no heavy machinery. These were highly labour-intensive, primitive methods: but they were very effective in working the richly laden, easily exploitable seams. The European mining companies which tried to enter the Malayan industry in this period, in contrast, brought in advanced techniques and elaborate machinery. These proved inappropriate. Chinese mines had the additional advantage of being individual enterprises or small partnerships, which implied that their administrative costs were low. European mining companies were large-scale concerns, with an elaborate, expensively paid management hierarchy.

By the turn of the century, however, the rich and easily worked seams were largely exhausted. In future, marginal seams, swampy areas, and partially mined deposits would have to be worked. This would require the introduction of new mining methods and techniques, involving heavy (and expensive) machinery. Western technology and mining experience now came into their own. The crucial innovation was the steam- or oil-powered bucket-dredge, capable of working out huge volumes of tin-bearing soil. The first bucket-dredge began operation in the Malay States in 1912. Within two years, there were seven dredging companies (with an aggregate nominal capital of £885,000) at work in the Federated Malay States. All were Western companies. Therefore as the bucket-dredge became increasingly important in the extraction of tin in Malaya in the opening decades of the twentieth century, Chinese domination was broken and Western capital advanced.

Two further instruments had secured Chinese domination of the industry in the late nineteenth century: and their removal would thus contribute to the later breaking of Chinese superiority. The first was Chinese control of the supply of labour. Using the powerful regional networks of the secret societies, Chinese mining capitalists organized the recruitment of Chinese labour in south China, the sea passage to the Straits ports of Singapore and Penang, and, crucially, the allocation of migrant labourers to employers in the Malay States. The important mechanism here was the credit ticket. The Chinese mine-owner in Malaya met the cost of the immigrant's passage. On arrival, the labourer was bound to this employer, toiling for no wages but given a pittance to cover his daily expenses, until the mine-owner calculated that the passage had been paid off. That mechanism of labour control was strengthened in the 1880s by the introduction of the discharge ticket system which stopped labourers from securing work unless they produced a ticket from their previous employer to show that they had been legally discharged. Of course an employer would provide a labourer with a discharge ticket only when he had completed his contract and, in the employer's view, settled his debts. In addition it was common for mine labourers to be paid on just two, or indeed only one occasion each year. In the long months between payments, labourers were therefore forced to buy food and other necessities from the mine-store on credit, at high rates of interest, an arrangement that tied the labourer even more tightly to his employer, through a debt which was virtually impossible not to incur and then control. Moreover, the major mine-owners commonly held the opium and gambling farms for the districts in which their mines were located. Chinese labourers were attracted by the easy availability of opium and gambling on site, and this dragged them still further into debt to the mine-owner. In the final decades of the nineteenth century, these mechanisms of labour control were highly effective. Chinese capitalists were thus able to suppress wages, which, given their highly labour-intensive production methods, was essential to the maintenance of profitability. At the same time, the Western mining companies which sought to establish themselves found it extremely difficult to recruit and hold Chinese labour.

The final factor that secured Chinese domination of the mining of tin in Malaya in the late nineteenth century was the profit which the mine-owners, as revenue farmers, made from the opium, spirit, and gambling farms. Indeed it has been argued (Wong, 1965: 81; Yip, 1969: 104) that often Chinese mine-owners/revenue farmers would mine tin at an apparent loss, which was then covered by the huge profits made from the farms. In other words, the principal business of the large Chinese capitalist would have been the revenue farms, and the mining of tin was essentially the mechanism by which he gathered into one district a large Chinese labouring population, with its great capacity for gambling, drinking, and smoking opium, to secure the farms' profits. The newly established British administration in the Malay States, argues Butcher (1983), well understood that relationship. Eager to see a rapid expansion in production and trade, the colonial administration often awarded the major farms to prominent Chinese mining capitalists, knowing that they would then bring in still more Chinese labourers in order to boost the farms' earnings.

Around the turn of the century, the structures which had helped to sustain Chinese domination of the tin industry—control of the labour supply and the profits from revenue farming—either fell away or were removed. From the mid-1890s the colonial administration began the abolition of the major revenue farms in the Federated Malay States, either replacing a farm with government collection or, in the case of gambling, suppressing the activity as a source of public revenue. Abolition proceeded rapidly. The opium duty farms in the protected west coast states had gone by 1901; the spirit farm went in 1910; the gambling farm, the last of the major revenue farms in the Federated Malay States, was terminated in

1912. The colonial government also struck at the Chinese capitalists' control over the supply of labour. Legislation was passed in the Straits Settlements and the Federated Malay States which aimed at the suppression of the Chinese secret societies, whose powerful networks had been crucial in tying labour to the Chinese-owned mines. Further legislation in the mid-1890s abolished the credit ticket and discharge ticket systems. However the disintegration of the Chinese capitalists' control over labour was the result not simply of colonial legislation. Even before it was abolished, the credit ticket system was in sharp decline, partly because the authorities in China had sought to suppress it, particularly from the 1880s, but principally because an increasing number of migrants were now paying their own passage, with the assistance of loans from friends or family, or from savings accumulated during earlier labour contracts in the British territory. For its part, the discharge ticket system had rarely worked effectively, for in periods of labour shortage, employers, including mine-owners, had willingly taken on labourers who did not possess the ticket. Moreover, as other sectors of the economy grew, undermining the dominance of the tin industry as an employer, job opportunities multiplied outside the mines. Miners' wages, long driven down by the credit ticket system, the discharge ticket system, and the near absence of major alternative employment opportunities in the interior of the peninsula, now went up. The profitability of the labour-intensive Chinese mines was seriously damaged.

This first-level explanation of Chinese domination of the Malayan tin industry in the late nineteenth century and of its overthrow early in the twentieth raises deeper questions. First, to what extent was the colonial administration's legislation against the credit ticket system and the discharge ticket system, and then its abolition of the revenue farms, deliberately designed to break the Chinese position in the industry? Perhaps surprisingly, most of the writers on this subject take a rather lenient view of the actions of the colonial administration. 'The available evidence does not point to a coherent or concerted effort to weaken Chinese mining enterprise', argues Wong (1964: 148). 'It may be argued that these changes [the abolition of the revenue farms] were part of an overall social evolution and did not constitute a deliberate policy to weaken the competitive position of the Chinese against the foreign tin mining industry', suggests Yip (1969: 151). Butcher (1983: 408) notes that the records of the official discussions which led to the abolition of the revenue farms contain no reference to the view that the profits from the farms were giving Chinese mine-owners a considerable advantage over European mining concerns. Rather Wong and Yip argue the somewhat different point that 'it was the aim of the British administration to encourage the growth of western, and particularly British, mining enterprise' (Wong, 1964: 148). That ambition could clearly be seen in the Perak Mining Code of 1895, the first comprehensive regulation of the industry and the model for all subsequent mining legislation in the Federated Malay States. The Code demanded the use of less wasteful, technically more advanced methods of mining, a demand which only Western enterprise was in a position to meet. In other words, the British administration did not seek to break Chinese domination *per se*: but it did wish to advantage more advanced (Western) interests.

Two brief, related comments might be made on those arguments. It is frequently difficult to identify with real precision the aims which lie behind a given policy. In introducing a particular measure, an administration rarely has a single objective. Thus it is possible that in abolishing the revenue farms, for example, the colonial authorities in Malaya were prompted primarily by the fact that, with a strong administrative structure now in place in the Malay States, some three decades after the first British intervention, the government was at last in a position to collect these revenues itself. But if abolition also struck at Chinese domination of the tin industry, at a time when Western capital was beginning to make headway, then so much the better.

The second deeper question, growing out of the first, is this: how important was the intervention of the colonial state for the triumph of Western capital? Jomo Kwame Sundaram (1986: 171, 177) sees it as decisive. However, although the balancing of influences is extremely difficult, the evidence presented earlier suggests that the interventions of the colonial administration encouraged, but did not determine, the advance of Western interests. This was true on points of detail: the breaking of the Chinese capitalists' control of labour owed at least as much to the rapid increase in labour demands in other sectors of the economy as to British legislation. And it is true on the central issue: the changing technological requirements for the profitable mining of tin in the Malay States, which shifted the advantage decisively in favour of Western enterprise at the beginning of the twentieth century, owed nothing to government intervention.

This leads to the final, and most intriguing question. If leader-

ship of the Malayan tin industry from the early twentieth century
was to go to those who used the most advanced mining methods,
why did the Chinese not adopt them and maintain their supremacy? Why did Chinese mine-owners not buy the bucket-dredge?
Part of the explanation may lie in the fact that Chinese miners did
not possess, or were unable to acquire, the advanced engineering
skills, the training, or the long experience in the technology that
were essential for the effective use of this sophisticated machinery.
A more common explanation, however, is that the cost of the
bucket-dredge, many tens of thousands of pounds, was beyond the
financial resources of the Chinese capitalists. Butcher (1983: 407)
notes that Chinese 'mining operations were financed in large part
by short-term loans borrowed from Chettiar moneylenders at very
high interest rates, and at times when credit was scarce, as
occurred in 1907–8, even this source was not available'. Wong
(1964: 146–7) sees this as a problem of business organization. By
far the most effective way to raise the large capital sums needed to
purchase the bucket-dredge, he argues, was through the formation
of joint-stock companies. But Chinese mining capitalists 'were
reluctant to change owing to ignorance of the practice of joint-
stock ownership, conservatism, their individualism and clannish-
ness. At the outbreak of World War I, there was not a single
Chinese mining company operating on the limited liability principle.' (Wong, 1964: 147.)

However, it is difficult to reconcile that approach with the reality
of the vast power of Chinese commerce in South-East Asia in this
period—investments in mills, mines, trading houses, revenue
farms, plantations. In building up that position, did the Chinese
have recourse only to short-term, high-interest loans, and never to
long-term borrowing, trading profits, income from the sale of land,
buildings, businesses? Were those alternatives never open to them,
even at the point, to return to the Chinese mining capitalists,
where substantial investment had become essential to defend a
long-held domination?

It is tempting to suggest an alternative view, even if only as a
hypothesis. The major Chinese mining capitalists, after careful calculation, may have decided quite freely not to invest in the new
technology. Their interests lay principally in the revenue farms: the
mining of tin was essentially the mechanism by which a large
Chinese labouring population was brought into a district to boost
the farms' profits. It follows that when the British colonial administration abolished the revenue farms, the central reason for the

involvement of the Chinese in tin mining disappeared. But even if the revenue farms had remained in place, the changing technological requirements of tin mining in the Malay States clearly implied a much reduced recruitment of labour: tin mining would no longer draw together those large, opium-smoking, drinking, gambling Chinese populations that had long sustained the profits of the Chinese capitalists.

At the same time, if the Chinese mine-owners had sought to meet the challenge of the Western mining companies by adopting the new technology, their chances of maintaining a dominant position in the industry would still have been slim. Western firms in Malaya could draw on considerable experience with the bucket-dredge in other parts of the world: moreover, they could anticipate favourable treatment from the colonial authorities in such important matters as the allocation of mining land. With those prospects, expensive investment by the Chinese in the new technology simply carried too high a risk.

An awareness that their long-term prospects in the tin industry were closing coexisted with a realization that new commercial opportunities were opening up—perhaps in banking or manufacturing. In other words, the end of Chinese domination of tin extraction in Malaya may be explained less in terms of intervention on the part of the colonial state in support of Western enterprise, still less in terms of the alleged weaknesses of Chinese business organization in the long-term management of capital, but as the outcome of a calculated decision by Chinese capitalists to restructure their commercial interests. This was probably a South-East Asia-wide phenomenon. This same period saw in Siam a realignment of Chinese capital away from the collapsing revenue farms towards modern banking (the Siam Commercial Bank) and then manufacturing. The following chapter, concerned with early industrial development in South-East Asia, takes up this theme.

SUGGESTED READING

The argument that Chinese capitalists in nineteenth and early twentieth century Siam were drawn into a subordinate relationship with the Siamese administrative élite, which left them serving élite interests, is advanced in the introductions to Chatthip Nartsupha and Suthy Prasartset (1978), *The Political Economy of Siam, 1851–1910*, Bangkok: Social Science Association of Thailand; and Chatthip Nartsupha, Suthy Prasartset, and Montri Chenvidyakarn

(1978), *The Political Economy of Siam, 1910–1932,* Bangkok: Social Science Association of Thailand. The argument which explains the apparent lack of Chinese investment in industry in terms of the community's preference for liquidity and the high level of its remittances to China, can be found in Peter F. Bell (1970), *The Historical Determinants of Underdevelopment in Thailand,* Economic Growth Center, Discussion Paper No. 84, New Haven: Yale University. Ian Brown (1988), *The Élite and the Economy in Siam, c.1890–1920,* Singapore: Oxford University Press, explains the failure of Chinese capitalists to diversify strongly into industrial production in the early twentieth century, to lead the Siamese economy towards a major restructuring, primarily in terms of the openness of Siam to imports of Western manufactures. Considerable detail on the Chinese, Siamese, and European capitalist groups in the kingdom in the period from the middle of the nineteenth century through to the overthrow of the absolute monarchy in 1932, can be found in Chapter 3 of Suehiro Akira (1989), *Capital Accumulation in Thailand, 1855–1985,* Tokyo: Centre for East Asian Cultural Studies. See also Chapter 2 of Kevin Hewison (1989), *Bankers and Bureaucrats: Capital and the Role of the State in Thailand,* Southeast Asia Studies, Monograph No. 34, New Haven: Yale University.

The literature on the tin industry in colonial Malaya has long been dominated by two books: Yip Yat Hoong (1969), *The Development of the Tin Mining Industry of Malaya,* Kuala Lumpur: University of Malaya Press; and Wong Lin Ken (1965), *The Malayan Tin Industry to 1914,* Association for Asian Studies, Monographs and Papers No. 14, Tucson: University of Arizona Press. A brief summary of the principal arguments of the latter can be found in Wong Lin Ken (1964), 'Western Enterprise and the Development of the Malayan Tin Industry to 1914', in C. D. Cowan (ed.), *The Economic Development of South-East Asia: Studies in Economic History and Political Economy,* London: George Allen & Unwin, pp. 127–53. The argument that the intervention of the colonial state was decisive for the advance of Western capital in the tin industry in the early twentieth century is pursued in Jomo Kwame Sundaram (1986), *A Question of Class: Capital, the State, and Uneven Development in Malaya,* Singapore: Oxford University Press, Chapter 6. The relationships between revenue farming and economic change in the Malay States in the late nineteenth and early twentieth century, including broader Chinese business interests, are explored in John G. Butcher (1983), 'The Demise of the

Revenue Farm System in the Federated Malay States', *Modern Asian Studies*, 17(3): 387–412. Those issues are further considered in Howard Dick (1993), 'A Fresh Approach to Southeast Asian History'; and John Butcher (1993), 'Revenue Farming and the Changing State in Southeast Asia', in John Butcher and Howard Dick (eds.), *The Rise and Fall of Revenue Farming: Business Élites and the Emergence of the Modern State in Southeast Asia*, London: Macmillan, pp. 3–18 and pp. 19–44 respectively.

14
Early Industrialization

IT would be unrealistic to look for major industrial growth in South-East Asia during the colonial period. Economic change in the region from the middle of the nineteenth century was built on a dramatic expansion in primary production for export. In that process local production of such articles as textiles and agricultural and household implements commonly withered, as labour, capital, and entrepreneurial endeavour were drawn into commodity production for world markets and as inexpensive manufactures, mass-produced in the factories of the industrial West, flooded in. The same forces discouraged the creation of new manufacturing activities. Indeed, it was common for colonial administrations in South-East Asia actively to bar industrial development in order to reserve the colonial market for metropolitan manufacturers.

None the less, by the early 1940s an extensive range of modern industrial activity had been established in the region. The term 'modern industry' needs to be defined. Here it encompasses the processing of raw materials and the manufacture of finished articles in factories or workshops using mechanical power and employing a labour force that either is engaged full-time or for which that employment represents the major source of cash income. It therefore excludes household production, commonly undertaken in rural areas as a secondary occupation, although in reality the dividing line between this and certain forms of modern industry was frequently blurred.

Although the focus in this chapter is on the range of modern industrial activity in colonial South-East Asia, it is also important to provide some indication of the size of the sector relative to that of the economy as a whole. The imprecisions of definition noted above makes this somewhat difficult, but four examples will establish the broad magnitude. For Siam, in 1938/9 'manufacturing' accounted for 9.9 per cent of gross domestic product. In the Netherlands East Indies, in 1939 'manufacturing' accounted for 14.9 per cent of the total income of the indigenous population: the figure for Java and Madura alone was 17.2 per cent. Also in the Netherlands East Indies, 'factories and workshops employed more than 660,000 workers in 1940, with manufacturing industry employing an estimated 550,000 workers' (Segers, 1987: 28). In French Indo-China in the late 1930s, a maximum of 120,000 workers were employed in 'modern industry (including mining and manufacturing)'. In size, as well as in its range, modern industrial activity in late colonial South-East Asia was surprisingly substantial.

The Range of Industrial Activity

Modern industrial production in colonial South-East Asia can be divided into two broad categories. The first is the initial processing of agricultural and mineral commodities for export. This was the first important form of modern industry to be established in colonial South-East Asia, and it remained, at least in terms of employment, the dominant form throughout the colonial period. Four examples make the point. The first is rice milling, concentrated in the premier ports of the mainland deltas—Rangoon, Bangkok, and Saigon–Cholon. Machine-powered rice milling arrived in South-East Asia as the great expansion in rice cultivation and export got underway. In Siam, the first steam rice mill was built in 1858, by an American firm. The first steam mill in Rangoon was constructed, by an Australian, in 1860. Numbers grew rapidly. There were 47 steam rice mills in Lower Burma in 1898, 59 in Bangkok in 1910. In the late 1930s there were 27 large, mechanized rice mills in Saigon–Cholon. 'The rice mills are ugly buildings several stories high', noted a contemporary observer (Robequain, 1944: 276):

They are built of corrugated iron because masonry walls would soon be cracked by the vibration of machinery. They house very bulky processing equipment, usually imported from Germany or America—ventilators for the preliminary cleaning of the material; huge emery millstones which do the husking ... separators which sort the unpolished rice, the bran and the husks ... cylindrical emery millstones with concentric movements which strip the grain of its last covering and transform unpolished into polished rice.

These large mills each had a capacity of between 100 and 200 tons of *padi* a day, some mills much more than that. They employed a substantial labour force, a major proportion on a seasonal basis, with the milling months running roughly from December to June. A major Chinese company in Bangkok in the 1900s owned four large rice mills which together employed over 1,000 workers. At the end of the 1930s, the Saigon–Cholon mills employed more than 3,000 workers during the milling season, recruited either in the city itself or from surrounding rural districts. In Burma, also at the end of the 1930s, 27 European-owned rice mills employed almost 11,000 workers.

There were substantial differences, between Bangkok, Rangoon, and Saigon–Cholon, in the ethnic ownership of the large mills. In its early expansion, rice milling in Bangkok was the near exclusive preserve of European capital and enterprise. But that domination was quickly challenged by local Chinese capital. In 1898, Europeans owned and operated only 4 of the 42 rice mills in Bangkok, accounting for just 10 per cent of milling capacity. Chinese mills accounted for 83 per cent. By 1920, only one European company, the East Asiatic, was still involved in rice milling in Bangkok. In Rangoon, in contrast, European capital retained its domination for much longer. In 1898 Europeans owned 30 of the 47 rice mills in Lower Burma, including all the largest mills, which were concentrated in Rangoon. In that same year, 81 per cent of the labour force in this sector was employed in European-owned mills. But thereafter the European domination was challenged. The figure in 1929 was 39 per cent. In Saigon–Cholon, European and local Chinese capital each took a major share in the large-scale milling sector. If, in the late 1930s, resident Chinese owned and operated 23 of the 27 large, mechanized rice mills in the port, the two largest mills were French owned.

The second example of a processing industry is sugar milling, located principally in the main sugar-growing areas of Java, and Luzon and Negros, in the Philippines. On Java, the great expansion of the industry began in the 1830s, with the introduction of the government's forced cultivations. By the early 1880s there were just over 200 working sugar mills in the Netherlands East Indies, with a total annual production of around 300 million kilograms. As steam-engines displaced water-wheels, the production capacity of each mill rose. As a result, although the number of working mills fell to about 180 by the 1920s, total annual production approached 3000 million kilograms at the end of that decade.

The Javanese sugar industry was hit hard by the 1930s depression. In 1940 there were only 85 working mills, producing just under 1600 million kilograms. The number of workers employed in the mills, according to one calculation, rose from 74,550 in 1921 to 88,512 in 1929, only to fall to 40,893 in 1940. Roughly three-quarters of mill workers were employed on a seasonal basis. As with the rice mills in mainland South-East Asia, ethnic patterns of ownership varied by time and place. In the middle of the nineteenth century, the period of the Cultivation System, both European and local Chinese capital were heavily involved in sugar milling. But then Chinese commitment decreased, leaving the European interest clearly dominant. In contrast, in the Philippines, at the end of the 1930s approximately 45 per cent of the capital invested in the sugar mills (here called sugar centrals) was held by Filipino planters and cultivators, with Americans holding 30 per cent and Spaniards 25 per cent.

The third example is the smelting of tin, using large-scale, technologically advanced, capital-intensive processes. This was an industry located principally in British Malaya, and established towards the close of the nineteenth century. In earlier decades, the smelting of tin in the Malay peninsula had been carried out in innumerable small furnaces, scattered through the mining districts and operated by the Chinese interests who controlled the mining itself. Although crude, the Chinese furnace was efficient and economical, while refinements in practice and design were common. In 1887 the Straits Trading Company, a European concern, constructed a modern smelter on Pulau Brani, a small island off Singapore. A second smelter was built at Butterworth, on the mainland of the peninsula, opposite Penang, in 1901. Straits Trading quickly took a major part of the smelting business, although it was only from the mid-1890s that the Chinese share began to fall in absolute as well as relative terms, as sharp rises in wages and in the price of charcoal undermined their competitive position. In the period 1911–14, Chinese furnaces took just 15 per cent of the tin output of the Federated Malay States. Straits Trading and the Eastern Smelting Company, the latter originally a Chinese concern but subsequently bought out by British interests, accounted for the rest. Straits Trading dominated, smelting around 70 per cent of the tin output of the Federated Malay States in 1911. The Western smelters took ore not simply from the Malay peninsula but also from southern Siam, Tonkin, and the Netherlands Indies islands of Bangka and Belitung. Indeed, in that same year, 1911, Straits Trading smelted fully one-third of world production of tin ore.

The final example is the petroleum industry, located in the Netherlands East Indies and in Burma. This industry took the processing of its raw input far further than did the tin, rice, and sugar industries, which were concerned merely with the initial processing of commodities into forms convenient for shipping. The petroleum industry in South-East Asia manufactured final products. In the late nineteenth and early twentieth century, the oil companies in the Netherlands East Indies produced mainly kerosene (lamp oil). They then diversified. In 1939, of a total crude oil production in the Indies of almost 8 million metric tons, 91 per cent was treated in local refineries to produce, *inter alia*, petrol, aviation fuel, kerosene, diesel oil, paraffin wax, and asphalt. Production found both export and local markets. Refining was heavily capital-intensive, involving the use of advanced technologies. Ownership was therefore concentrated in a few Western hands. In late colonial Burma, the Burma Oil Company accounted for 75 per cent of the production of crude oil, and 85 per cent of refining. In the Netherlands East Indies, the Royal Dutch–Shell group, an amalgamation formed in 1907, held a virtual monopoly in the period before the First World War. Standard Oil of New Jersey established a local company in 1912. In 1913, there were 12 refineries and paraffin factories in the Dutch colony, together with 6 kerosene tin, sulphuric acid, and candle-making factories, employing a total of 7,366 registered workers.

The presence and scale of these processing industries was a matter of commercial logic. Preliminary processing separated the product from its waste—the rice grain from its husk, the tin from the ore, the sugar content from the cane. Those processes were carried out close to the areas of cultivation and extraction, rather than in the markets of final consumption, to avoid the costs of shipping essentially valueless debris. The same argument applied to petroleum, with the distinction that there the high value forms, in the plural, were final manufactures.

The second broad category of industrial production was the manufacture of finished consumer goods, usually for the domestic market but frequently for export as well. This category can be roughly subdivided into those industries which flourished despite competition from imports, and those which could survive only behind protective barriers.

Prominent in the first was the manufacture, roughly from the late nineteenth century, of a range of building materials, notably bricks, roofing tiles, pipes, tanks, cement. Three factors were important in the growth of this sector. A rising local demand for building materials, as the construction of government and commercial offices, roads, harbours, bridges, railways, irrigation works, and modern housing grew apace; the easy availability from local sources of essential raw materials, notably limestone and clay; and, arguably the crucial factor, the fact that building materials have a low value relative to bulk and weight, which meant that imports had to bear high freight charges relative to production costs, which left them unable to compete on price in local markets. In other words, there was a crucial measure of non-tariff protection for the domestic producer. It was common in this period for metropolitan interests, notably in France, to oppose industrial development in the colonies. But there had to be exceptions. 'Even the most ardent opponent of colonial industrialization', noted one observer in the early 1940s, 'could scarcely argue ... that the [colonial] market for bricks, cement and the like, should be reserved for factories in distant France' (Shepherd, 1941: 21).

The rise of cement production demands particular emphasis. Large-scale cement factories were built in most, if not all the major South-East Asian economies in this period. In French Indo-China, the Société des Ciments Portland Artificiels de l'Indochine built a large plant at Haiphong in 1899. An associated company later constructed another factory at Hué. The Haiphong factory produced 235,000 tons of cement in 1937, of which no less than 53 per cent was exported to markets across the East. In that same year, the industry employed around 4,000 workers. In the Netherlands East Indies, the Nederlandsch-Indische Portland Cement Maatschappij began production at a factory near Padang in West Sumatra in 1912. In 1929, total production in the Indies was 154 million kilograms, virtually all from the West Sumatra plant. This represented just under 40 per cent of domestic consumption in that year. In the Philippines, the manufacture of cement began in 1914, with a company financed by the Recollect friar order in alliance with a group of prominent Manila businessmen. After a troubled early history (the company ceased production in 1918) the concern was acquired in 1928 by a local industrialist. Renamed the Rizal Cement Company, it resumed production and grew rapidly. Meanwhile, in the early 1920s, the National Development Company, a government concern, had established the Cebu Portland Cement Company, with a factory at Naga on the island of Cebu.

In 1936 total cement production in the Philippines was approaching 133 million kilograms, of which the Cebu Portland Cement Company accounted for almost 77 million. Imports were less than 1 million kilograms. In Siam, as noted in the previous chapter, the Siam Cement Company, formed in 1913 by a consortium comprising the King and one of his senior ministers, a prominent Sino-Siamese entrepreneur, and a Danish businessman long resident in Bangkok, soon dominated the domestic market. In Burma, the Burma Cement Company, beginning production in 1935, achieved an annual output of about 60,000 tons on the eve of the Pacific War.

Also prominent in this first category was the manufacture of foodstuffs and beverages, including biscuits, vermicelli and macaroni, margarine, confectionary, aerated waters, ice cream, produced mainly for the European populations concentrated in the urban centres. It is particularly interesting to note the production of beer, partly because modern breweries were built in all the major states of the region, but also because the basic raw materials (malt and hops) were not found in South-East Asia but had to be imported, often from as far as central and eastern Europe. In French Indo-China, breweries were built in Hanoi, Haiphong, Cholon, and Phnom Penh. In the Philippines, the brewers San Miguel was founded in 1890 by a Spanish businessman long resident in Manila. As early as 1908 San Miguel was outselling imported beers by five to one, and in the late 1920s accounted for some 90 per cent of domestic beer consumption. In that decade San Miguel diversified into soft drinks and dairy products, and secured exclusive rights to bottle and distribute Coca-Cola in the Philippines. In the 1930s it began the manufacture of yeast and glass bottles. (San Miguel is now probably the largest agri-food processing conglomerate in South-East Asia.) The early 1930s saw a modest rush to establish breweries elsewhere in South-East Asia, with Malayan Breweries in Singapore (1931), Boon Rawd in Siam (1933), and in the Netherlands East Indies, the Nederlandsch-Indische Bierbrouwerijen (1931) and the Archipelbrouwerij (1933). The Indies breweries received a measure of government protection, against Japanese imports, in their early years. But far more important for the success of this industry was an element of non-tariff protection. Because beer deteriorates within a few weeks of being brewed, once a fine natural local beer became available (most of the breweries in South-East Asia employed experienced European, commonly German brewmasters), discerning drinkers were quick to reject imported beers which contained artificial preservatives to sustain them during the long sea voyage to the East.

The most notable example of an industry which, in this period, could survive only behind import barriers or with some other form of government support was the modern textile industry—notable because of the vast scale and fierce competitive edge of the imports it faced. From the middle of the nineteenth century, huge consignments of cheap, mass-produced textiles flooded into South-East Asia, biting into local handicraft production and inhibiting the establishment of modern factories in the region. The pioneer textile mill in South-East Asia was constructed, by French industrialists, in Hanoi in 1894. Two more mills were then built at Haiphong and Nam Dinh. When these three French concerns were amalgamated in 1913 to form the Société Cotonnière de l'Indochine, they employed 1,800 workers. By 1938 this figure had risen to an estimated 10,000, although a substantial proportion worked on an irregular basis. Together with a second, smaller, French company, the Société Filteries de l'Indochine, the Société Cotonnière de l'Indochine monopolized modern textile production in the colony.

At first sight, the growth of this important industry (the textile mill at Nam Dinh employed more workers than any other factory in French Indo-China) may appear surprising. French colonial thinking held that industrial production should be concentrated in metropolitan France while the colonies provided raw materials and markets. And indeed textiles were among the four most important exports from France to its Indo-China possessions. But on occasions practical constraints deflected theoretical ambitions. In this case there were two such considerations. Once in occupation of northern Vietnam, from the mid-1880s, the French administration found that local household weavers were importing large quantities of low priced cotton yarn from British India, against which expensive French yarns were never likely to be able to compete. The only way in which French interests could break into this lucrative trade was through the establishment of a modern spinning mill in northern Vietnam, which would take advantage of the cheap locally grown cotton and the abundance of cheap local labour. These were the origins of the initial mill built in Hanoi in 1894, and the basis for the subsequent expansion of modern spinning capacity in Haiphong and Nam Dinh. A modern weaving capacity was soon added. This leads to the second constraint on theoretical ambitions. The cloth woven in Indo-China's French-owned mills was of a rather coarse, cheap quality, destined for the lower end of the market, and therefore not in competition with the fine expensive fabrics imported from France, which were purchased by European residents, wealthy Chinese, and prominent members of the indigenous population. In other words, in this case colonial industrialization did not threaten metropolitan manufacturing interests. At the same time, the French colonial tariff structure (the Méline tariff in 1892, the Kircher tariff in 1928) largely kept out the cheap coarse textiles of other industrial nations, notably Britain and Japan. Without that protection, the local textile industry would not have survived.

Modern textile factories came to other parts of South-East Asia rather later, in the 1930s, of course behind substantial import barriers (tariffs or quotas). In some cases the factories were government enterprises. The Siam Cotton Mill, the first modern spinning and weaving factory in the kingdom, was established by the Ministry of Defence in 1935 to supply cloth to the military. The state also took the initiative in the Philippines, where the National Development Company established a modern spinning and weaving mill in Manila, production beginning in mid-1939. In the Netherlands East Indies, mechanized weaving emerged during the 1930s as a leading industry in the colony, employing around 70,000 people in 1940. By that time the Indies was virtually self-sufficient in woven sarongs, the principal article of clothing for the local population. The large-scale weaving industry was dominated by European and Chinese firms.

There was a further category of manufacturing industry in South-East Asia that grew up behind import barriers. With the raising of tariff rates and the imposition of import quotas, principally in the 1930s, a number of major Western manufacturers for whom South-East Asia had long been an important market, began producing goods locally in order to avoid the import restrictions and maintain sales. They jumped over the tariff wall. In Siam, British–American Tobacco began manufacturing cigarettes in 1930. A Japanese-owned cotton textile mill started work in the Philippines in 1938, avoiding the restrictions which had been placed on imports from Japan. In the Netherlands East Indies, the list was particularly long: British-American Tobacco (1923), General Motors (1927), Unilever (1934), Goodyear (1935), National Carbon Company (1935), Java-Textiel-Maatschappij (1937), Philips (1940).

Conclusion

Having established the range and size of modern industry in late colonial South-East Asia, and indicated the circumstances in which it had flourished, this final section digs a little deeper. It offers an observation and poses a question.

The observation relates to an important thesis that will be developed in the following chapter: that in a number of major respects, the inter-war decades, and in particular the 1930s, can be seen as a crucial turning point in the modern economic history of South-East Asia. One of those respects was in the consolidation of a modern industrial sector. There is a further argument, again to be developed in the next chapter. It is tempting to see the changes which took place in the economies of South-East Asia in the 1930s in terms of the shuddering impact of the collapse of world trade and investment, as local repercussions of a huge external crisis. In fact they generally had origins *internal* to South-East Asia, or if external, quite unrelated to the world-wide depression. The growth of modern manufacturing is part of that argument too. There are three points to be made.

The 1930s saw governments across South-East Asia committing themselves to the expansion of modern industry, frequently in open rejection of the long-established view that colonial industrialization should be discouraged in the interests of metropolitan manufacturers. In some cases, this commitment to industrialization was partly a response to the economic distress created by the world depression. In the Netherlands East Indies, the expansion of industry was intended to create new sources of employment for many of those displaced from agriculture and mining by the collapse of commodity markets. But more frequently industrialization was seen as a solution to more deep-seated, long-term economic problems. In the Netherlands Indies, again, it was intended to improve the standard of living of the indigenous population, a prominent concern within the Dutch colonial administration from the beginning of the twentieth century. It was also seen as a possible solution for the dense overpopulation of Java, for it now appeared increasingly unlikely that the agricultural sector could continue to provide the means of subsistence for the rapidly growing numbers. In Siam, the government sought to reduce the extent of foreign, notably local Chinese control over important sectors of the economy. Industrialization was driven by economic nationalism. In the Philippines, industrialization was the response of the indigenous administration, having secured internal self-government in 1935 and the promise of full independence for 1946, to the fear that the country's agricultural exports would be devastated when, on independence, they lost privileged access to the American market. Some, if not most of these concerns may well have been brought into sharp focus by the world depression. Yet each was clearly distinct from it, being of a long-term nature and, commonly, of internal rather than external origin.

One further concern, certainly in the Netherlands East Indies, was the rapid advance of cheap Japanese manufactures in the local market, threatening metropolitan industries. The Dutch administration's response was to raise tariffs sharply and impose import quotas, behind which domestic manufacturing then grew. Again it is possible to see this simply as a reaction to a crisis born of the depression, for the flooding of Japanese manufactures into South-East Asia was driven by the sharp devaluation of the yen in December 1931, part of Japan's strategy for economic recovery. But it is also important to see it in a long-term perspective. For decades Japan's industrial power had been growing. At some point it was bound to challenge Western exporters in the important markets of South-East Asia. The Japanese advance would then be reined back by import restrictions and by the establishment of an industrial capacity in the region itself. These circumstances would arise, with or without the crisis of the world depression.

Finally, it is important to see the industrialization drive of the 1930s in terms of the evolving ambitions and interests of the various capitalist groups in South-East Asia. European capital in the region now saw increasing opportunities in modern manufacturing. Metropolitan industry sought to locate production in the region. Local capital saw and seized the same opportunities. In particular, Chinese capital continued to diversify out of the trade, moneylending, and tax-farming which had been its dominant concerns in the early twentieth century. That diversification may have been further encouraged by the world depression. But it was inevitable, even without it.

The big question promised earlier is as follows. In what ways, and to what extent, did the growth achieved by the early 1940s lay the foundation for the dramatic industrial expansion which took place from the 1960s? This is an extremely difficult question to answer, partly because the phenomena themselves are so complex but also because so little research has been undertaken on the earlier period. A few brief points can be offered here.

The obvious initial line of inquiry would be to determine the extent to which the companies and business families which were prominent in the pre-war years were still prominent in the later period. There was some measure of continuity. The Siam Cement Company, founded in 1913, expanding and diversifying in the pre-war decades, is now a mighty conglomerate. San Miguel's present eminence was noted earlier. But generally there was relatively little continuity in business organization or family, certainly not in the Netherlands East Indies or French Indo-China where the end of colonial rule was accompanied by severe political and economic dislocation, but neither in Siam, Malaya, and the Philippines where transitions were smooth. In other words, South-East Asia's dramatic industrial expansion from the 1960s has been built principally on new money, new men, and new alliances.

In other respects, it is possible to identify important parallels. Both industrialization drives were dependent on state intervention. In the 1930s government intervened by taking on the ownership of industrial concerns (in Siam and the Philippines) or by providing the protection and support without which private capital would not act. In the later period the state was again crucial, perhaps more so. Or again, South-East Asia's most recent industrial growth has been strongly export-oriented, and commonly has involved giant international companies relocating production in the region. Both these features were also present, admittedly to a diminished degree, in the 1930s. Local production of beer and cement often found substantial export markets in that decade: while British-American Tobacco, General Motors, Goodyear, to name the obvious examples, established local production.

SUGGESTED READING

Distressingly little has been written on the growth of modern industry in South-East Asia during the colonial period. For the region as a whole, there is just one slim text, Jack Shepherd (1941), *Industry in Southeast Asia*, New York: Institute of Pacific Relations, although even that focuses strongly on just French Indo-China, Netherlands India, and the Philippines. Although published over half a century ago, it remains a useful introduction: and it does convey vividly the enthusiasm for industrialization in the 1930s. Among the individual countries, the Netherlands East Indies is well served by *Changing Economy in Indonesia: A Selection of Statistical Source Material from the Early 19th Century up to 1940*

EARLY INDUSTRIALIZATION215

(General Editor, P. Boomgaard), Vol. 8, 1987, *Manufacturing Industry, 1870–1942*, edited by W. A. I. M. Segers, Amsterdam: Royal Tropical Institute. This volume contains a wealth of statistical data, as well as a long and valuable introduction.

For the other countries of the region, information on the development of modern industry in the colonial period has to be gleaned from writings whose principal focus commonly lies elsewhere. For Burma, the mechanical milling of rice is discussed in Michael Adas (1974), *The Burma Delta: Economic Development and Social Change on an Asian Rice Frontier, 1852–1941*, Madison: University of Wisconsin Press; and Cheng Siok-Hwa (1968), *The Rice Industry of Burma, 1852–1940*, Kuala Lumpur: University of Malaya Press. The development of modern industry, more broadly, in Burma receives some attention in Aung Tun Thet (1989), *Burmese Entrepreneurship: Creative Response in the Colonial Economy*, Stuttgart: Steiner Verlag Wiesbaden GMBH. For modern tin smelting in Malaya, see Wong Lin Ken (1965), *The Malayan Tin Industry to 1914*, Association for Asian Studies, Monographs and Papers No. 14, Tucson: University of Arizona Press. For French Indo-China, there are two principal sources: Charles Robequain (1944), *The Economic Development of French Indo-China*, London: Oxford University Press; and Martin J. Murray (1980), *The Development of Capitalism in Colonial Indochina (1870–1940)*, Berkeley: University of California Press. There is a valuable discussion of French colonial economic policy, and its implications for the development of modern industry in Indo-China, in Irene Nørlund (1991), 'The French Empire, the Colonial State in Vietnam and Economic Policy: 1885–1940', *Australian Economic History Review*, 31(1): 72–89.

For Siam, see James C. Ingram (1971), *Economic Change in Thailand, 1850–1970*, Stanford: Stanford University Press, particularly Chapter 6; Suehiro Akira (1989), *Capital Accumulation in Thailand, 1855–1985*, Tokyo: Centre for East Asian Cultural Studies, Chapters 3 and 4; Kevin Hewison (1989), *Bankers and Bureaucrats: Capital and the Role of the State in Thailand*, Southeast Asia Studies, Monograph No. 34, New Haven: Yale University, Chapters 2 and 3; Ian Brown (1988), *The Elite and the Economy in Siam, c.1890–1920*, Singapore: Oxford University Press, Chapter 5. For industrial growth in the Philippines, particularly in the interwar period, see Ian Brown (1989), 'Some Comments on Industrialisation in the Philippines during the 1930s', in Ian Brown (ed.), *The Economies of Africa and Asia in the Inter-War Depression*, London: Routledge, pp. 203–20.

15
The Inter-war Crisis

THE inter-war years mark the end of the great period of commodity export expansion in South-East Asia which had begun in the middle decades of the nineteenth century. Of course there had been crises in that period of growth, sharp contractions, and failures that had brought expansion in particular commodities or economies to a temporary halt. But the inter-war crisis was unprecedented in its scale, in its comprehensiveness, and, crucially, in its very nature.

It is tempting to see the origins of the crisis in the fragility and collapse of international commodity markets, to view it as a crisis solely of external provenance. After all, strongly rising world demand for South-East Asia's agricultural and mineral riches had been the driving force behind the nineteenth-century expansion in primary production and trade. With the onset of the deep contraction in the industrial economies from the end of the 1920s, that engine had failed. But to view the inter-war crisis simply in these terms is to miss an internal dynamic of comparable force—a gathering domestic crisis in the region's agricultural economy. The first part of this chapter explores its nature.

The Internal Crisis

Two main elements were at work. In the 1920s a number of South-East Asia's commodity exports were in, or were fast approaching, long-term oversupply. A notable example was rubber, the boom crop of the opening two decades of the twentieth century. In the Malay States, as was noted in Chapter 10, the large-scale planting of rubber by Western interests had begun in 1905, smallholders entering the industry in force some four years later.

Because it took between five and seven years for the newly planted tree to yield its first latex, Malayan rubber exports remained very modest until the early 1910s. The slow response of supply at a time when demand was increasing rapidly pushed rubber prices to record levels. The average price of standard quality rubber on the London market in 1910, the peak year, was 8/9 per pound. Soaring prices fuelled the rush into rubber cultivation.

The first wave of planting came into production in the years immediately before the First World War. Prices fell sharply, to an average on the London market of around 2/3 per pound in 1914. They held up during the war years and into the post-war boom, before falling again at the beginning of the 1920s as the industrial economies were hit by recession. However, prices were still sufficiently firm to secure a further major expansion in capacity. The area planted to rubber in Malaya rose over four times between 1910 and 1922, to over 2.3 million acres.

World consumption of rubber recovered strongly from the post-war recession, rising from a trough of 278,000 tons in 1921 to 804,000 tons in 1929, powered by the American boom. Yet the earlier expansion in rubber acreage now threatened to depress the market severely, pushing prices below profitable levels for the Western estates. In late 1922, therefore, restriction of output was imposed in British territories. Restriction provided immediate respite for Malayan estate producers. But it may, in the longer term, have exacerbated the core problem, for by holding up prices, it encouraged a major planting of rubber in the Netherlands East Indies, where restriction did not apply. That new capacity began to come on to the market towards the close of the 1920s. At that point the end of restriction in the British territories, in 1928, also brought an explosion in Malayan output, exports leaping from 294,446 tons in the last year of restriction to 455,545 tons in 1929. Then, imposed on surging Netherlands Indies and Malayan output, came the sharp contraction in demand, as the industrial economies plunged into depression. The average price of rubber on the London market had been 2/11 per pound in 1925, falling to around 1/6 per pound in 1927. It stood at a fraction below 6 pence per pound in 1930, a little over 2 pence in 1932.

A second example is provided by the Javanese sugar industry, although it is important to note that its circumstances were quite different from those of Malayan rubber. The important consideration here was a substantial increase in sugar yields per hectare, notably in the 1920s, the result of a widespread adoption of high-yielding varieties of cane. Over the period 1914–31, sugar production on Java doubled although the area under cane increased by only one-third. That sharply increased productivity meant that Java improved and then held its share in an increasingly competitive and fragile international market, as world prices fell and stocks rose from the mid-1920s. But increased productivity in the 1920s was also an important reason why, when the crisis struck the Javanese sugar industry in the early 1930s, the collapse was particularly severe.

The second main element in the internal crisis was more funda-mental. The huge expansion in cultivation for export which had taken place across South-East Asia from the middle decades of the nineteenth century had been achieved almost entirely by bringing into production vast tracts of previously uncultivated land. There was, clearly, a physical limit to that process. The land frontier would close. This does not mean that at a precisely identifiable point in time there would be no more waste tract to be brought into cultivation, but rather that over a period of years, gradually if unevenly, it became increasingly difficult to find prime untamed land to bring into production. The result, no matter how gradual or uneven in coming, was a fundamental shift in agrarian struc-tures and conditions.

Most importantly, it led to a substantial decline in average yields per acre, certainly in the rice deltas. As less fertile, more flood-prone marginal land was brought into production, yields were bound to fall. They were already falling on established lands that had been worked year after year without the application of fertilizer or improvement in cultivation methods. In Burma, according to Adas, by 1930 'the average productivity of an acre of paddy land in the Delta was below that recorded in most other rice-growing countries' (1974: 131). Declining yields per acre meant a reduc-tion in the surplus the Burmese cultivator could bring to market and thus a reduction in income. At the same time, again as a con-sequence of the closing frontier, the purchase price of land and land rents rose. Many cultivators, in particular marginal small-holders and tenants, were badly squeezed: a large number were dispossessed. Tenancy increased. In 1906/7, 30 per cent of occu-pied land in the Burma Delta was let to tenants at full rent; in 1929/30 the figure was almost 46 per cent. Over the same period, the proportion of occupied land in Lower Burma controlled by non-agriculturists rose from 18 per cent to 31 per cent. In addi-tion, terms of tenancy became harsher. In many parts of the delta, landlords began to demand 50 per cent of the crop as rent, refused remissions when floods or pests devastated the crop, and imposed single-year contracts on their tenants, opening the way for an annual imposition of still harsher terms. There no longer existed an open frontier to offer escape from oppression. It is clear that there was an agrarian crisis of growing severity in Lower Burma well before the world depression struck.

An important reservation must quickly be added. Adas (1974) sees the rice frontier closing in Lower Burma in the period 1908–30, while Larkin (1982) suggests that the interior frontiers of the Philippines began to close from around 1920. But elsewhere in South-East Asia the land frontier had either long closed (much of Java) or remained largely open (perhaps parts of the Central Plain of Siam or the western extremities of the Mekong Delta). In other words, the crisis engendered by the closing agricultural frontier may well have been a potent element in the depression crisis in Lower Burma, even in the Philippines. Elsewhere, it may have been of little moment. The crisis of overproduction noted earlier was just as patchy: a powerful element in the depression crises for Malayan rubber and Javanese sugar, of less or little import elsewhere. This points to a central theme.

The Early 1930s

It makes little sense to talk in general terms about the impact of the world-wide depression of the early 1930s on the economies of South-East Asia, for there was great diversity across the region. A striking example is provided by the contrasting depression experiences of the Javanese and Philippine sugar industries (Table 15.1).

In both Java and the Philippines, the volume of sugar exports rose very substantially in the late 1920s. But while exports from Java then fell away sharply, in the Philippines expansion continued right through the depression years. As a result, in 1934 the volume of Philippine sugar exports was almost three times greater than their volume in 1926, while in Java sugar exports in 1934 were more than one-third below their 1926 level. To put it another way, in 1926 Java exported almost five times more sugar than the Philippines; by 1934 Java's sugar exports were only fractionally ahead of Philippine exports. Or again, even with a sharp set-back in 1935, the volume and value of Philippine sugar exports in 1936 were twice the levels of 1926. Over the same period, the volume of Java's sugar exports had halved, their value had fallen eight times

TABLE 15.1

The Philippines and Java/Madura: Sugar Exports,
1926–1936 (in millions)

	The Philippines[a]		Java/Madura[b]	
Year	Volume	Value	Volume	Value
1926	411	64	2001	270
1927	553	101	2338	365
1928	570	96	3069	376
1929	695	106	2981	312
1930	744	104	2838	254
1931	753	100	1865	129
1932	1017	120	1888	99
1933	1079	129	1389	62
1934	1153	131	1388	45
1935	516	66	1410	36
1936	900	124	1010	34

Source: Ian Brown (1989), 'Some Comments on Industrialisation in the Philippines
during the 1930s', in Ian Brown (ed.), *The Economies of Africa and Asia in the
Inter-War Depression*, London: Routledge, p. 212.
[a]Volume in millions of kilograms; value in millions of pesos.
[b]Volume in millions of kilograms; value in millions of guilders.

over. Between 1931 and 1935, the area under cane on Java fell a
staggering 86 per cent. In one country, the industry boomed: in a
near neighbour, it collapsed.

The crucial factor was access to markets. From the beginning
of the twentieth century, Java had exported mainly to markets
in Asia. Singapore, China, Japan, India, and Australia took on
average 75 per cent of its exports of sugar up to 1930. With the
onset of the depression, those markets closed, as tariff barriers
were imposed to defend local sugar production. No new markets
of comparable size could be found. In any event, with the
Netherlands East Indies remaining on the gold standard until
1936, Java's sugar was too expensive in the important markets
which from the beginning of the 1930s had abandoned gold.
Severe contraction in production was unavoidable.

In contrast, Philippine sugar had a huge secure market.
Legislation in 1909 and 1913 had given Philippine exports free and
unlimited entry into the United States. In 1929, 96 per cent of
Philippine sugar exports, which had more than doubled in volume
over the decade, were destined for the American market. With the

onset of the depression, that market remained open. Philippine producers were therefore able to increase output and exports through the depression years to compensate for falling prices. But there was a further twist. The early 1930s saw protracted negotiations over Philippine independence, a central element involving consideration of the ways in which, during the transition to independence, the free access of Philippine exports to the American market would be brought to an end. Faced with the prospect that a limit would soon be imposed on the amount of Philippine sugar that could be imported duty free into the United States, each producer sought to increase his output in an attempt to secure the largest possible share of the threatened national quota. The result was the dramatic surge of exports in 1932–4 seen in Table 15.1. The drop in 1935 marks the imposition of the quota, although, with a strong recovery in 1936, Philippine sugar exports were still way ahead of their pre-depression levels.

As a second example, it would appear that during the depression years, economic conditions were substantially worse in the rice-exporting Burma Delta than in comparable districts in the Central Plain of neighbouring Siam. Two pieces of evidence sustain this view. While the early 1930s witnessed a high level of protest and disorder in rural Burma, much of it small-scale, scattered violence but also including, in the Hsaya San rebellion of 1930–2, a major uprising against the colonial regime, there was no serious disorder in rural Siam. Second, Stifel (1976) has shown that in the 1930s, the rate of land alienation as a result of debt foreclosure, surely an effective indicator of economic distress, was substantially higher in Lower Burma than in selected provinces in central Siam. In Lower Burma, between 1930 and 1939 there was an increase in the proportion of total titled area owned by absentee landlords (a proxy measure for land losses due to mortgage foreclosure) of 19.7 per cent. In some districts the figure was substantially higher. In the Siamese province of Nakhon Pathom, perhaps 'representative of conditions in the Central Plain' (Stifel, 1976: 258), the proportion of land losses as a result of mortgage foreclosure to total titled area increased by only 5.7 per cent over the same period, although in other parts of the Central Plain, for example Ayutthaya province and the Rangsit district, the figure was considerably higher.

In the absence of more detailed research, it is difficult to explain these contrasting experiences. It would be tempting to look to the growing internal crisis in the rice economy of Lower Burma, the crisis engendered by the closing land frontier, which had yet to hit

Siam or to hit it with the same severity. But that would explain a higher absolute level of land alienation rather than the faster rate of alienation observed above. A more effective explanation might be built on the observation that on the eve of the depression, the burden of agricultural debt was heavier in Lower Burma than in central Siam. In Burma, Chettiar moneylenders from India had been deeply involved in the expansion of the rice acreage from the last decades of the nineteenth century. In Siam expansion had relied almost entirely on the much smaller capital resources of local moneylenders, family, and friends. Consequently, when rice prices collapsed during the depression, sending the real value of agricultural debt soaring, the scale and pace of default and foreclosure would have been substantially greater in the Burma Delta than in the Central Plain of Siam.

Detailed research would undoubtedly establish further contrasts. It would be valuable, for example, to compare depression conditions in East Sumatra and the Malay States, two major plantation regions heavily dependent on imported labour. *A priori* reasoning suggests that East Sumatra, a major rice-deficit region, was hit relatively hard, partly because the sharp contraction in tobacco cultivation resulted in a corresponding contraction in the access of the local population to plantation land for growing rice or corn (see Chapter 10 for a description of the integration of local food crop production with the cultivation regime of the export crop, tobacco), partly because in 1933 the Dutch administration restricted the import of rice into the colony. In the Malay States, in contrast, when rubber production was cut back in the early 1930s, garden plots were created on the plantations for the cultivation of food crops by and for the plantation labour force.

The general point is that there appears to be no set of principles to explain why the depression years were harsher in one area than in another. There was no predictable pattern. Rather, local circumstances held the key: the access of Philippine sugar to the United States market; the burden of agrarian debt in Lower Burma on the eve of the depression; the ease with which the labour force on Malayan plantations could move into subsistence food production.

There is a further important argument. For the vast rural populations across South-East Asia heavily involved in production for the international market, the economic crisis of the early 1930s may well have brought only a relatively modest deterioration in material conditions, even in those districts where the depression appears to have had a more severe impact. There is no doubt that as primary commodity prices collapsed, those populations experienced a substantial drop in money income, although some may have been able to increase market sales to compensate in part. However, there were a number of ways in which, faced with those circumstances, rural producers could defend their real income and material condition. There were avenues of escape from the full consequences of the drop in money income. There were strategies for survival.

One important strategy involved cultivators and plantation and mining labourers establishing or expanding subsistence production for their own consumption. An example was given immediately above. On the rubber plantations in the Malay States, the Indian labour force, faced with a sharp contraction in tapping and wages, was allowed to establish garden plots on which to cultivate subsistence food crops. Also in the Malay States, Chinese labourers displaced from the tin mines by the depression established vegetable gardens that not only provided a measure of subsistence but also opened up a new opportunity for production for a local market. On Java, the fierce contraction in the cultivation of sugar for export released prime irrigated land for the cultivation of rice for domestic consumption. The area under rice on Java and Madura, having remained roughly constant throughout the 1920s, rose almost 14 per cent in the 1930s.

There is a further important aspect to this argument. As was explained in Chapter 8, for rural populations in nineteenth-century South-East Asia heavily committed to export cultivation, many basic needs, for shelter and food, had still been met largely from household production or through the generosity of nature. Materials for the construction of dwellings were taken from the forest; fish were found in streams, ponds, and flooded fields; wild pigs were hunted in the wilderness; vegetables, ducks, pigs, and chickens could be raised on ground adjacent to the family home. The cultivator had not abandoned the subsistence economy, thrown himself entirely on the mercy of the market. The point should be clear. When external markets disintegrated in the early 1930s, South-East Asia's rural populations were not, in general, disastrously exposed. A long maintained or easily recreated involvement in the subsistence economy did much to protect them from outright collapse.

A second possible escape route was to secure reductions in payments for tax, rent, and debt. This is a controversial proposition, for a strong body of scholarly opinion holds that, far from finding relief in this direction, rural communities in South-East Asia faced sharply increased tax, rent, and debt payment burdens during the depression years. Scott (1976) has argued that during the early 1930s, the colonial administration, facing serious financial difficulties as a result of falling tax revenues, had no choice but to attempt to enforce its tax demands against the local population in full. Moreover, with prices falling and taxes and debts fixed in money terms, the real value of those demands was rising sharply. In Scott's view, their vigorous enforcement drove rural South-East Asians, in anguished protest, into violence and outright rebellion.

The contrary view, favoured here, is that commonly these demands were poorly enforced or effectively resisted. Adas (1979) has pointed out that the colonial administration in Burma granted substantial remissions on land taxes throughout the years of the depression, perhaps out of concern for the cultivator's material condition, perhaps in recognition that in the circumstances it would be near impossible to collect taxes in full, and foolish to try. In addition, rural populations probably had a greater capacity to escape or resist tax demands than Scott allows. In this view, the violence which swept through large parts of South-East Asia in this period was a pre-emptive strike, not the enraged response of communities whose subsistence had been destroyed by the crushing demands of the state. Government offices were attacked less as protest than as an attempt to wipe out administrative records, so weakening the capacity of the state to collect taxes. In a comparable way, attacks on the premises of major landowners and money-lenders served to break their capacity to collect rents and loans, or their will to do so.

The reduction in money income was also mitigated through a fall in the prices of articles of common consumption. As export prices had collapsed, so too had the prices of many manufactures, both imported and locally produced. As well as being part of the general process of deflation, this also reflected the impact of a huge influx of low cost Japanese manufactures into South-East Asia in the early 1930s, which pushed aside long-established and more expensive Western goods. Important here was the large devaluation of the yen in late 1931, sharply reducing the local currency price of Japanese imports. It is interesting to note that in British Malaya at least, many colonial officials and Western commercial houses, while regretting the reverses being suffered by metropolitan manufacturers in local markets, recognized that the cheaper imports from Japan were doing much to protect the material condition of local populations during the crisis. Not only were the prices of staple goods, notably textiles, much reduced: new articles, which earlier had been too expensive to find a large local market, were introduced, an important example being the bicycle.

Two qualifications should be noted. Although the influx of Japanese manufactures clearly helped to protect the material condition of local populations facing a sharp contraction in money income, in the absence of detailed research and calculation it is impossible to say precisely how helpful. The same point can be made about tax remissions and resistance to tax, rent, and debt payments. Precisely how important were they? Second, it must be acknowledged that the period of unrestricted cheap Japanese imports was relatively brief. First, the colonial regimes, under pressure from depressed metropolitan industries, imposed quotas and tariffs against Japanese goods: and then, from the mid-1930s, inflationary pressures and shortages in the Japanese domestic economy weakened Japan's export expansion.

Deterioration and Opportunity

The argument that the crisis of the early 1930s brought about only a relatively modest deterioration in material conditions in rural South-East Asia, even in those parts of the region where the depression appears to have had a more severe impact, is a major challenge to popular perceptions and to much scholarly writing on the subject. However, the argument may obscure a more substantial issue. The truth must be that within any district, some socio-economic groups found the escape routes more easily than others, or were less vulnerable in the first place. Some suffered more harshly than their fellows, and some gained. The result was a potentially major realignment in the distribution of wealth and power in much of rural South-East Asia. To talk in general terms, to claim baldly that the depression had a severe or a modest impact, is to miss that crucial dimension.

This is a subject that has yet to benefit from thorough research. However, for the Burma Delta, Adas (1974) argues that the category of agriculturist perhaps most harshly affected by the price collapse of the early 1930s was the tenant cultivator. Forced to sell their surplus rice at half the anticipated price, they had severe difficulty paying the wages of their hired labourers, the rents demanded by landowners, or the crop loans extended to them by landowners and moneylenders. In 1930–1 large numbers of tenants were evicted from their holdings, and forced to seek new tenancies on still harsher terms. One colonial report described the condition of the tenant class as 'deplorable' (Adas, 1974: 189). In contrast, in Bikol, according to Owen (1989), the conditions of tenancy did not deteriorate significantly. Most tenant contracts continued on existing terms, and long-established mechanisms of equity and reciprocity remained in place. It is difficult, given the existing state of research, to offer a confident explanation of this sharp contrast in experience. Perhaps the strains imposed on the landlord–tenant relationship by the crisis were more severe in Burma than in Bikol, the price falls more dramatic, the burden of tenant debt far heavier. Alternatively, the relationship itself may have been less resilient in Burma. Owen suggests that Bikolano landlords, far removed from the highly commercialized and impersonal culture of Manila, were less prone to the physical and moral detachment that would reject traditions of reciprocity and equity.

Owen argues that it was the smallholders who were most harshly affected by the 1930s crisis in Bikol. Hit hard by collapsing prices and tightening credit, they defaulted on crop loans and lost their land. As a result, the proportion of cultivated land in Bikol under tenantry increased from 8 per cent in 1918 to around 38 per cent in 1938. Adas, while arguing that the tenant cultivator was most vulnerable in the crisis, notes the same phenomenon in the Burma Delta. The proportion of the total occupied area in Lower Burma held by non-agriculturists, mainly moneylenders who were rapidly foreclosing on small landowners, went up from 31 per cent in 1929/30 to nearly 50 per cent in 1934/5.

Elsewhere, Adas and Owen are in close agreement. The landless labourer may have lost relatively little. In Burma he may even have fared rather well initially, as wage rates in force as the depression struck had been set in more optimistic times. Over the longer term, although there was a decline in cash wages, wages paid in kind appear to have remained near to pre-depression levels. Of course there is also the argument that as labourers' wages were already close to subsistence levels before the crisis, there was little room for further deterioration.

But it is at the other end of the socio-economic scale where, on the evidence of Adas and Owen, the most interesting developments were taking place. In Bikol major landowners now found themselves in a position to buy land from those who had defaulted on loans, to take advantage of low construction costs to put up buildings, or to diversify into new commercial ventures, including mining. In Burma indigenous capitalists took advantage of the financial failures of small landowners to buy up holdings at low prices. For such groups, the depression was not a crisis: it was an opportunity.

This is an important theme in the work of Doeppers (1991) on Manila during the 1930s depression. He suggests that the city's substantial population of government officials, teachers, and middle-class pensioners enjoyed a considerable increase in real income during the crisis, indeed 'an explosion in purchasing power' (Doeppers, 1991: 517), for while prices fell sharply, only one small cut was made in the peso salaries of civil servants, and the pensions of retired government teachers, doctors, and police officers were apparently left untouched. The buying power of fixed salaries 'fairly soared' (Doeppers, 1991: 517). One result was a construction boom in Manila, further fuelled by a substantial reduction in building costs and in loan rates. For Manila's middle class, still in work, these were great times. Other inhabitants of the city, of course, faced considerable hardship.

With the current state of knowledge, this is perhaps as far as this theme can be pushed. Many important questions remain. Precisely how far did socio-economic inequalities widen in rural South-East Asia in these years? What was the exact nature of the realignments in the distribution of wealth and power? To what extent did those who prospered in the depression years use their increased resources to diversify into new forms of economic activity? Did the depression provoke a substantial rural–urban migration, of capital as well as labour? Here are important issues for research, bearing on perhaps the most crucial decade in the modern economic history of the region.

SUGGESTED READING

With few exceptions, each piece on this subject focuses on a part of the region and/or a particular commodity. For example, the experience of the Malayan rubber industry in the decades between the wars is examined in John H. Drabble (1991), *Malayan Rubber: The Interwar Years*, London: Macmillan. The sugar industry on Java in this period is briefly considered in Peter Boomgaard (1988), 'Treacherous Cane: The Java Sugar Industry between 1914 and 1940', in Bill Albert and Adrian Graves (eds.), *The World Sugar*

Economy in War and Depression, 1914–40, London: Routledge, pp. 157–69. The Philippine sugar industry between the wars receives extended treatment in John A. Larkin (1993), *Sugar and the Origins of Modern Philippine Society,* Berkeley: University of California Press, Chapters 5 and 6. Norman G. Owen (1989), 'Subsistence in the Slump: Agricultural Adjustment in the Provincial Philippines', in Ian Brown (ed.), *The Economies of Africa and Asia in the Inter-War Depression,* London: Routledge, pp. 95–114, examines the impact of the depression on the agricultural economy of the Bikol region of south-eastern Luzon. William Joseph O'Malley (1977), 'Indonesia in the Great Depression: A Study of East Sumatra and Jogjakarta in the 1930's', Ph.D. dissertation, Cornell University, offers a harsh assessment of the economic impact of the crisis, while giving strong emphasis to political changes. For the impact of the depression on the urban economy, see also Daniel F. Doeppers (1991), 'Metropolitan Manila in the Great Depression: Crisis for Whom?', *Journal of Asian Studies,* 50(3): 511–35; and, a more severe view, John Ingleson (1988), 'Urban Java during the Depression', *Journal of Southeast Asian Studies,* 19(2): 292–309. The 1930s' crisis in Burma is discussed in Michael Adas (1974), *The Burma Delta: Economic Development and Social Change on an Asian Rice Frontier, 1852–1941,* Madison: University of Wisconsin Press, Chapter 8. Chapter 6 argues the importance of the closing land frontier in the gathering agrarian crisis in Lower Burma. The same concept, applied to the Philippines, is briefly considered in John A. Larkin (1982), 'Philippine History Reconsidered: A Socioeconomic Perspective', *American Historical Review,* 87(3): 595–628.

The argument that the crisis of the early 1930s brought varying degrees of economic distress between the major export-committed rural districts of South-East Asia and, more importantly, that even in the districts more severely hit, the deterioration in material conditions was markedly less severe than is commonly thought, is found in Ian Brown (1986), 'Rural Distress in Southeast Asia during the World Depression of the Early 1930s: A Preliminary Reexamination', *Journal of Asian Studies,* 45(5): 995–1025.

The comparison of land alienation rates as a result of debt foreclosure in Lower Burma and Central Siam in the 1930s can be found in Laurence D. Stifel (1976), 'Patterns of Land Ownership in Central Thailand during the Twentieth Century', *Journal of the Siam Society,* 64(1): 237–74.

For the argument that the early 1930s saw a sharp increase in tax burdens in rural South-East Asia, and that this was a central element in the rebellions and disorder which swept parts of the region in this period, see James C. Scott (1976), *The Moral Economy of the Peasant: Rebellion and Subsistence in Southeast Asia*, New Haven: Yale University Press, particularly Chapter 5. For a contrary analysis, see Michael Adas (1979), *Prophets of Rebellion: Millenarian Protest Movements against the European Colonial Order*, Chapel Hill: University of North Carolina Press, which includes extended discussion of the Hsaya San rebellion in Burma. Pierre Brocheux (1995), *The Mekong Delta: Ecology, Economy, and Revolution, 1860–1960*, Center for Southeast Asian Studies, Monograph No. 12, Madison: University of Wisconsin-Madison, Chapter 6, provides a valuable assessment of the 'desperate years of the depression' in the Mekong Delta.

16
The Green Revolution

THE great expansion in the production of rice for export which took place in mainland South-East Asia from the middle of the nineteenth century was achieved with little or no change in cultivation practices or inputs. There was little improvement in the quality of the seeds sown, little or no application of fertilizer, or mechanization of farming operations. Local administrations committed some resources to agricultural research—experimental rice farms were established in Burma from 1914, in Siam in 1916, and in Cochin-China from 1927—but the impact was barely perceptible. In Burma, in 1929–30, less than 2 per cent of the area under rice was planted with improved varieties. The absence of significant advances should cause little surprise. As long as there were still extensive tracts of wilderness, production could be increased by extending the cultivated area. It should be noted, however, that increasing total production in this way almost certainly meant a decline in average yield per hectare, for in time it involved bringing into cultivation less fertile land with poorer drainage. In Siam the rice yield per hectare in 1941 was virtually 30 per cent below the yield in 1911.

Since the late 1960s circumstances have been radically different in many of South-East Asia's major rice districts. Sharp improvements in the quality of inputs have occurred, and cultivation practices have fundamentally changed. A revolution has taken place. The immediate origins of this revolution lay in Mexico in 1943, in the establishment of an American-directed scientific research programme charged with increasing Mexico's output of wheat. By the early 1950s the repeated cross-pollination of genetically dissimilar lines had produced wheat varieties whose yields were responsive to high applications of fertilizer, that were resistant to disease, and which had a short, strong stem to support the increased weight of grain. Mexican wheat production soared. From importing half its wheat requirements in the 1940s, Mexico was fully self-sufficient by 1956, in spite of a large increase in population. With that success, attention now focused on rice. The International Rice Research Institute (IRRI)—established in Los Bañõs in the Philippines in 1960, with funds from the Rockefeller Foundation, the Ford Foundation, and the United States Agency for International Development (USAID)—released its first high yielding variety (HYV) in 1966.

The new rice seeds produced high yields only in the presence of a number of important complementary inputs: chemical fertilizers, to ensure that there were sufficient nutrients to sustain the full growth of the high-yielding rice plant; a precisely regulated, generous flow of irrigation water; herbicides, to kill the weeds which also throve with the application of fertilizers; and insecticides, to kill the insects, worms, and micro-organisms that fed on the rice plant. These were the biochemical elements of the Green Revolution in rice. There were, in addition, mechanical inputs: tractors, powered reapers and threshers, and combine harvesters. In contrast to the biochemical elements, the machines did nothing to raise yields per hectare. They reduced the time it took to perform certain tasks (ploughing, harvesting) and/or the labour that had to be committed to them. There has been considerable debate about whether the mechanical innovations are an essential component of the Green Revolution, whether it would be possible to adopt the biochemical elements (the seeds, fertilizer, improved irrigation, herbicides, and insecticides, which raise yields) but not the mechanical ones. The implications of that argument are considered below. Two further elements improved the farmers' access to the new methods: agricultural extension services disseminated information, and cheap credit enabled poorer farmers to purchase expensive inputs.

Rice growers in the Philippines, Indonesia, and Malaysia adopted the new inputs with amazing speed. As early as 1971/2, high-yielding varieties, derived from IRRI, accounted for 31 per cent of the rice planted in Indonesia. In 1979/80 that figure stood at 67 per cent. In the early 1980s, almost 82 per cent of rice land in Indonesia was planted with high-yielding varieties. Production soared. Average annual output of rice rose from 19.6 million tons in 1971–5 to 37.6 million tons in 1984–8, an annual average growth of over 5 per cent, far outstripping the growth in population. In the late 1960s Indonesia had been the largest importer of rice in the world. By the mid-1980s the country was technically self-sufficient in rice, had substantial reserve stocks, and was lending rice to Vietnam and the Philippines. In West Malaysia, rice production rose from 695,100 tons in 1967 to 1,996,000 tons in 1976, almost three times over.

But as production soared, the attention of researchers, administrators, and policy-makers was directed towards the impact of the new technology on the distribution of income and wealth in the rice-growing settlements which adopted them. Indeed there has been the most vigorous debate on this crucial issue. The optimists held that virtually all classes of cultivator had, in different ways, benefited from the new inputs and practices, and consequently that patterns of socio-economic differentiation had stayed much the same: if differentiation had increased, it was for reasons other than the introduction of the new rice technology. The pessimists argued that the gains from the Green Revolution had gone overwhelmingly to established landowners, so sharply widening socio-economic disparities. Some of the critics conceded that the poorer, weaker elements in rural society—the marginal landowners, tenants, and wage labourers—had made modest gains, losing ground to the rich and powerful, but still improving their lot in absolute terms. Others insisted that the poor had lost absolutely. The Green Revolution had dispossessed them.

Configurations and Contexts

There is no simple, no single answer here. If there were, there would be no debate. Perhaps the most effective way to proceed would be to explain why the answers are neither simple nor singular. There are three broad points. It will be evident from the discussion above that the Green Revolution is not a single, precisely defined innovation, applied uniformly in all places, but a package of innovations, some tightly interdependent but others arguably quite distinct, applied in different configurations in different localities. The crucial point is that different components of the package will produce different socio-economic outcomes. For example, the introduction of high-yielding seeds and the application of fertilizer will, in ways to be considered below, raise the demand for labour, increasing employment opportunities for wage workers and driving up wage rates. In contrast, the introduction of tractors, harvesters, and threshers will displace labour, reducing job opportunities and cutting wages. The application of herbicides may well have the same effects. In other words, different configurations of the Green Revolution package—the extent to which mechanical innovations are present—will have different consequences for the position and prospects of landless labour. The Green Revolution is a vastly varied phenomenon in another important respect. It did not comprise a single technological leap, cleanly completed. Rather, the Green Revolution has been a process of continuous improvement and refinement—in seed varieties, in chemical inputs, and in machinery—and potentially each advance has had a different socio-economic impact.

If the Green Revolution was ever-varied, so too were the rice districts into which it was introduced—each unique in soil characteristics, water conditions, patterns of landownership, and population density. Soil and water supply conditions would do much to determine the extent to which yields rose with the introduction of the new inputs. Landholding patterns have influenced the configuration of biochemical and mechanical elements: where the land was held by small owner-cultivators, for whom the opportunity cost of labour was low, there was little incentive to invest in labour-saving mechanization; conversely, where there were large holdings, and labour costs were high, mechanization of important agricultural tasks was likely to occur on a considerable scale. Patterns of income and resource distribution may (the issue is a controversial one) influence access to the new rice technology. Only wealthy cultivators were in a position, the argument runs, to purchase fertilizers and machinery. To bring these two points together: as both the new technology and the physical and socio-economic landscapes into which it has been introduced are greatly varied in time and place, the range of outcomes must surely be comparably varied.

At the same time as the Green Revolution was taking hold in rice districts in South-East Asia, other major forces for change were also at work, making it near impossible to determine the specific impact of the new inputs and practices. In other words, the Green Revolution may be condemned or praised for changes that were the result of other factors. Three examples demonstrate the point. First, by sharply increasing yields, the new inputs, it is sometimes argued, encouraged landowners who previously had given over part of their land to tenants or kin, to resume cultivation of the holding or to demand higher rents. As the potential income from the land increased, owners grew reluctant to share it, or to share it on gentle terms. But it is clear that increasing landlessness and more exacting terms might have any number of causes. They might reflect, for example, growing population pressure on limited land.

Second, some observers of contemporary rural Java have argued that the introduction of high-yielding varieties and inputs brought about a major change in the way in which labour was recruited for the harvest. Harvesting had traditionally been a communal undertaking, involving large numbers within the village, each of whom, in return for their labour, received a share of the crop. This arrangement ensured a measure of employment and subsistence for the landless poor of the village. In the new arrangement, the landowner sold the crop still standing in the field to a middleman, leaving to the latter the task of organizing labour for the harvest. The middleman, an outsider with no obligations towards the inhabitants of the village, hired less labour and commonly labour from outside. The local poor were excluded: village-derived employment and subsistence were dramatically weakened. The Green Revolution is said to have brought about this change in two ways. It gave rice cultivation a far more rigorous commercial orientation; that is, landowners were forced by the cost of inputs and encouraged by the increased income to be earned from the land to focus on the bare economics of cultivation and to pay less attention to communal obligations. The second mechanism involved a technical matter. The introduction of the new rice varieties, it is argued, meant the replacement of the traditional small harvesting knife (the *ani-ani*) by the sickle, largely because the sickle is more effective in cutting the shorter, thicker stalk of the new rice varieties. But the sickle, cutting many stalks with a single stroke, demanded less labour than the *ani-ani*, which cut stalks one at a time, and therefore, it was argued, forced landowners to restrict the access of poor labour to harvest work. The new exclusionary arrangement achieved this with the minimum of confrontation.

But the change in harvest labour arrangements could just as easily have been the result of a sharp increase in landlessness, itself a consequence of continued population growth. As landlessness increased, the number of village poor presenting themselves to owner-cultivators at harvest time may have grown to the point where, quite simply, only a small proportion could be accommodated. The communal ties which ensured work and subsistence across the village were overwhelmed, and had to be discarded. Or again, some observers have explained the abandonment of communal ties and the rise of exclusionary labour arrangements on

Java in terms of political intervention. The violent crushing of left-wing elements in the Javanese countryside in 1965–6 is said to have weakened the bargaining power of the rural poor against élite landowners. The importance of factors other than the Green Revolution is confirmed by the observation that exclusionary labour arrangements were in use in parts of Java before the high-yielding seeds and the sickle were introduced, and that elsewhere, communal arrangements persisted even when the new inputs dominated.

The final example involves not a deterioration in socio-economic conditions but a possible improvement. A number of comment-ators have argued that the incidence of poverty in rural Java declined substantially following the introduction of the new rice technology. This decline may indeed reflect the widespread adop-tion of the new inputs and practices, bringing benefit to poorer cultivators. But there were other forces boosting rural incomes. Rapid growth in the urban economy, driven by the oil boom, cre-ated a large number of jobs in manufacturing, construction, and trade, many of which were taken by circular migrants who con-tinued to reside in the village but now earned their living in the town. The oil boom also financed increased government expendi-ture on development in rural areas, creating further employment and income for poorer rural households. It is difficult, if not impossible, to disentangle the impact of those factors from the impact of the Green Revolution.

Having established these important warnings, this chapter now looks in detail at the socio-economic impact of the Green Revolution in South-East Asia, focusing on four central issues.

Access

The first is presented in the form of a question. Did large owner-cultivators have better access to the new inputs than small owner-cultivators? Much of the early research on the Green Revolution suggested that this was the case. Only the large farmers, it was argued, had enough income or credit to buy the fertilizers and pes-ticides that were at the core of the Green Revolution. They, and they alone, had the reserves and resources to experiment with innovations which, although promising much, were still not fully understood. Often it was the large cultivators in the settlement who controlled the flow and dispersal of irrigation water, a crucial element if the full yield of the new seeds was to be realized. On occasion, large farmers were favoured by government agencies. The Bimbingan Massal (BIMAS) programme in Indonesia, providing cultivators with subsidized inputs and credit, focused on the larger operators.

Research undertaken from the late 1970s, however, indicated that small owner-cultivators, if initially rather slow, had now caught up with the new technology. In Java even micro-holdings, a mere fraction of a hectare, were being planted with high-yielding seeds and were applying chemical inputs. Clearly, in the long term at least, access to inputs was not a problem. A number of factors may have been important here. From the late 1970s to the mid-1980s, the Indonesian government, using part of its large oil revenues, increased the subsidy on fertilizer, bringing the price within the range of virtually all cultivators. In the late 1980s, fertilizer accounted for as little as 8 per cent of production costs in areas of intensive cultivation. Indeed, the price was so low as to encourage overapplication. Furthermore, inputs became physically more accessible, as sale outlets sprang up in rural markets across Java. And if, on Java in the 1980s, the small owner-cultivator still found it difficult to gain access to government credit, this was not a serious hindrance: informal credit was widely available, at a price.

But in explaining the commitment of the small farmer to the new rice technology, need may have been more important than ease of access. It was those with the smallest holdings, and therefore the smallest incomes from rice, who had the greatest need to raise production, the greatest need for the new inputs. Two observations are interesting in this context. In Indonesia in the early 1980s, application of fertilizer per unit of land was highest on the very smallest holdings, and fell away sharply on holdings in excess of half a hectare. Similarly, the proportion of land planted with high-yielding varieties was highest on holdings under 2 hectares, falling away steeply on holdings above that size. Second, the intensity of labour input was generally greatest on the smaller holdings. Labour-rich small farmers cultivated their land far more assiduously, and consequently, even with identical applications of fertilizer, yields on smaller holdings were commonly substantially above yields on large ones. Given the heavier applications of fertilizer and greater use of high-yielding seeds on the smallest holdings, presumably the gap in yields was wider still. In Indonesia in the 1970s and 1980s, both yield and net return per unit of land in *sawah* districts were highest on the smallest holdings and declined consistently as farm size increased.

It would be easy to conclude from these observations that the introduction of the new rice technology *narrowed* differences in income between large and small owner-cultivators. However, to draw that conclusion is to misunderstand what has been said. The smallest farmers achieved the highest yields and net returns *per unit of land cultivated*. The largest increases in total income went to those with the largest holdings of land. In other words, in the distribution of the income gains from the Green Revolution, the crucial consideration was not access to the new inputs (in time large and small cultivators had near equality of access) or the intensity with which the inputs were applied, but access to land. The point has been well put by Barker, Herdt, and Rose (1985: 157):

The effect of resource ownership on the distribution of earnings is so great that any effect caused by technological change is marginal.... [Moreover] one cannot expect technological innovations introduced over a period of five years to modify a pattern of resource ownership derived from hundreds of years of history.

This leads to the second crucial aspect of socio-economic change.

Land Distribution

By sharply increasing farm incomes, the Green Revolution is commonly said to have promoted concentration in the ownership and operation of agricultural land. Major landowners who previously had allocated part or all of their holdings to tenants or kin now took on cultivation directly, pushing out those who had relied on them for access to land. Landowners also sought to add to their holdings by purchase or by lease. In the case of the former, they could use their additional position as moneylender to force foreclosure on marginal owners as a prelude to possession. In the latter, their superior financial resources enabled them to outbid small owners and landless cultivators for land available for lease, particularly as rents often had to be paid in advance, in full, in cash. And finally, on occasion, the increased earning capacity of the land attracted the interest of urban professionals—teachers and government officials—seeking a good investment.

South-East Asia's experience frequently fits ill with those broad, unspecific, assertions. In the first place, the writings on South-East Asia often contradict each other. In the Muda district in Malaysia, Wong (1987: 213) found that although access to land had become more restricted, 'no process of land concentration (through sale and acquisition of land) can be detected'. In direct contrast, Ishak Shari and Jomo (1982: 233) argued that 'there has been a tendency for inequalities in landownership ... to worsen'. In Java, Hartmann (quoted in Wong, 1987: 5) referred to an 'accelerated rate of land purchases by wealthier farmers as well as by urban elites', while Manning (1988: 73) observed that 'there is little evidence of ... a general increase in land concentration'. Indeed, he is left wondering why 'larger farmers ... did not accumulate land to a much greater extent' (Manning, 1988: 75), a point to be taken up below. Second, some writers insisted that in parts of South-East Asia, land concentration had *decreased*. Manning (1988: 25) notes that in some parts of Java, large farmers, far from reclaiming land from tenants and sharecroppers for their own cultivation, expanded the area they rented out in order to release themselves from farm work for more remunerative non-agricultural employment. (This is a good example of the point that the impact of change elsewhere in the economy, in this case the growth in manufacturing and construction induced by the oil boom, could override the impact of the new rice technology.) Again, Booth (1988a) claimed that landleasing arrangements, far from leading to more land being operated by large farmers, secured a more equal distribution in farm operation. In general, large landowners leased out, small landowners leased in. The latter had the greater need. Writing on Indonesia, Bose (1982: 54) offers an interesting observation on these conflicts in interpretation. He notes that while village studies indicate that 'fairly rapid concentration of land holdings has been occurring', analysis of macro data, the agricultural censuses, suggests that 'the size distribution of farms had not changed appreciably [in the period 1963–73] and that there was no increase in concentration of land control'.

Perhaps the only safe conclusion that can be drawn is that the concentration in landownership, access, or operation in South-East Asia as a consequence of the Green Revolution, where indeed concentration occurred, was on a more modest scale than the opening presentation of the argument may have implied. For Java, Manning (1988) suggests that as the most important group of larger farmers operated a mere 1 or 2 hectares, they obviously lacked the resources to purchase even the smallest additional plot, particularly given the high cost of *sawah*. (However, if they had had sufficient funds, larger cultivators may have been attracted by more profitable investment opportunities outside agriculture, for example, the purchase of Japanese trucks to transport passengers and freight.) At the same time, marginal owners, in the absence of secure alternative employment away from the land, clung to their tiny holdings with immense ferocity.

There are important arguments to be brought together here. If land-leasing tended to equalize access; if no substantial concentration in landownership occurred; and if, as argued at the end of the previous section, income largely reflected resource allocation, then it seems probable that the new rice technology did not have a major impact on income distribution. Indeed Manning (1988: 78) is sufficiently confident to conclude that in the two decades from the introduction of the Green Revolution to Java, 'major cleavages in income and wealth do not appear to have occurred'.

Labour Absorption, Labour Displacement

The biochemical elements of the Green Revolution—the high-yielding seeds, fertilizer, and irrigation water—undoubtedly increased the demand for labour. Much was required for the intensive weeding of planted fields, for the heavy applications of fertilizer and the more precise regulation of irrigation water encouraged weeds as well as rice to flourish. The application of fertilizer also required a substantial labour input. But above all, the use of fast-maturing varieties and the mechanization of ploughing and harvesting made it possible to plant two or even three crops a year, each planting requiring a substantial labour input. In contrast, the mechanical elements of the Green Revolution—the tractor, the harvester, and the thresher—are commonly said to have displaced labour on a substantial scale.

The South-East Asian experience does not challenge those broad arguments but suggests a number of refinements. Evidence from the Philippines indicates that one biochemical input, that is herbicides, far from absorbing labour, displaced it: by killing weeds, herbicides obviously reduced the need to weed by hand. Second, even were the labour-absorbing and labour-displacing impacts of the new rice technology to cancel out, leaving overall labour use roughly unchanged, the experience of South-East Asia shows that demand for particular kinds of labour may rise, for others will fall. Manning (1988) noted that on Java, the large numbers of rural poor, predominantly women, whose livelihood had depended on hand pounding harvested rice, were displaced by mechanical rice hullers in the late 1960s. This had a devastating impact on many rural households, for there was no obvious

alternative employment in the rice economy. Again, the recruitment of outside contract labour for harvesting displaced the local
poor who, in earlier times, had always been employed to bring in
the village's crop. A shift towards hired labour for a wide range of
cultivation tasks, including weeding, was also evident in rice districts in the Philippines.

As a final observation, there was considerable variation in the
extent to which mechanization displaced labour in the different
rice districts of the region. In the Muda district in Malaysia, Scott
(1985) observed the devastating impact of the arrival of the
combine-harvester in the mid-1970s, abolishing at a blow perhaps
two-thirds of the wage-earning opportunities for small owners and
landless labourers, in cutting the crop and gleaning the fields for
loose grain left after the harvest. 'The direct and indirect impact of
machine harvesting has been enormous. The biggest losers have
been almost exclusively the poorer households, who have seen
their economic security and incomes driven back.' (Scott, 1985:
111–12.) In contrast, in Java, mechanization, and thus labour-
displacement, occurred on only a modest scale, reflecting the very
small size of the majority of holdings, the presence of ample
supplies of family and hired labour, and the high cost of agricultural machinery. However, to return to the previous point, some
kinds of labour, for example, the female rice pounders, lost heavily.

A Biochemical and Mechanical Package?

This leads to the final aspect for consideration. To what extent
could a cultivator or community adopt the biochemical elements
of the Green Revolution without the mechanical ones: to what
degree were the biochemical and mechanical elements an indivis-
ible package? The important issue behind this question should be
clear. A community which sought to protect or expand access to
agricultural work for its poorest households would wish to adopt
those elements of the Green Revolution which absorbed labour,
that is, the high-yielding seeds, fertilizer, irrigation improvements,
but avoid those which displaced it. Put another way, was it possible
to raise the productivity of the land through application of the biochemical elements without then displacing labour through mechanization?

At first sight, the biochemical and mechanical components seem
independent of each other. It should make no difference to the
ability of the new seeds and fertilizers to raise yields whether they

are applied to land prepared by hand-directed ploughs or by diesel tractors, whether the ripened crops are cut by hand or by combine harvester. The new seeds and fertilizer were widely taken up in Java while mechanization made relatively little headway. However, some writers have identified links between the two elements. Writing of the Indian experience, Byres (1981) argues that with the cultivation of two or three crops a year, a regime made possible by the use of high-yielding, fast-maturing seeds, the application of fertilizer, and the more precise regulation of irrigation water, cultivators were under great time pressure to harvest and thresh, and then replough, in order that the next crop could be planted on schedule. Only tractors, mechanical reapers, threshers, and combine harvesters could complete those tasks within the limited time available. Only by mechanization could the cultivator keep within the time constraints 'which are the inevitable concomitants of the biochemical innovations' (Byres, 1981: 412). Byres also suggests that mechanization strengthened the bargaining power of larger cultivators *vis-à-vis* their labourers, at a time when the application of the new rice technology had increased labour demands.

There is some support for these observations in the study by Scott (1985) of the Muda district in Malaysia. In two important respects, the introduction of the new seed–fertilizer–irrigation technology towards the end of the 1960s led inevitably to the arrival of the combine harvester in the mid-1970s. It greatly increased labour inputs and so drove up labour costs: it made possible double or triple cropping. In these circumstances, the mechanization of harvesting became irresistably profitable for the large cultivator. The landless poor in Muda had gained much as a result of the biochemical innovations of the late 1960s: but that gain led to their displacement by machines a few years later.

Conclusion

There are important aspects of the socio-economic impact of the Green Revolution in South-East Asia which have been left out of this analysis or which have been touched on inadequately. It would be fitting to conclude with an aspect which, although it has received relatively little attention in the vast Green Revolution literature, may come to be seen as one of the new technology's most important legacies, that is its impact on the ecology of wet-rice cultivation. There are two points to be made. Stands of high-yielding rice are particularly vulnerable to diseases and insects. In earlier

times, cultivators had improved their crops' resistance by planting
many varieties. If one fell to a particular disease, there was every
possibility that the others possessed a natural resistance. But modern rice breeding programmes have dramatically reduced genetic
diversity, and therefore increased the likelihood of a plant disease
sweeping through an entire crop. In the mid-1970s more than half
the *sawah* in Indonesia was planted with just four closely related
modern varieties. Other factors increased vulnerability still further:
near continuous cultivation through the year; closer spacing of
plants; high applications of fertilizer which encouraged the growth
of pests; the use of insecticides which killed the natural enemies of
the pests threatening the rice plant, allowing the latter to flourish
virtually unchecked. This last was notably important in the outbreaks of brown planthopper which severely damaged rice crops
in Indonesia in the 1970s and mid-1980s. Second, there is substantial evidence that excessive applications of pesticides have
poisoned irrigation and drinking water systems, while heavy applications of fertilizers have left substantial residuals in soil and,
again, water. The ecological consequences of dousing the land
with chemicals in this manner may turn out to be extremely serious.

SUGGESTED READING

This brief guide is divided into two: studies of the Green Revolution which have no specific regional focus or focus on regions
other than South-East Asia; and studies of the Green Revolution in
South-East Asia.

An excellent introduction to the Green Revolution, focused on
India, is provided by T. J. Byres and Ben Crow, with Ho Mae Wan
(1983), *The Green Revolution in India*, U204 Third World Studies,
Case Study 5, Milton Keynes: Open University Press. It includes a
valuable discussion of the science and technology of the Green
Revolution, and an excellent examination of the impact of the new
rice technology, again in the context of India, on the different
classes of cultivator and upon women. Also valuable as an introduction is Randolph Barker and Robert W. Herdt, with Beth Rose
(1985), *The Rice Economy of Asia*, Washington, DC: Resources for
the Future, in particular Chapter 10, 'Who Benefits from the New
Technology'. Jonathan Rigg (1989), 'The New Rice Technology
and Agrarian Change: Guilt by Association?', *Progress in Human
Geography*, 13(3): 374–99, in the course of a survey of the more

recent evidence, concludes that the new rice technology has brought benefits to all classes of cultivator, and that many of the damaging changes underway in rural Asia—growing inequalities and increased landlessness—reflect wider processes of agrarian change and agricultural commercialization. In strong contrast, T. J. Byres (1981), 'The New Technology, Class Formation and Class Action in the Indian Countryside', *Journal of Peasant Studies*, 8(4): 405–54, argues that the Green Revolution has sharply increased income inequalities in rural India. He also identifies important links between the biochemical and mechanical elements of the Green Revolution, the introduction of the former leading almost inevitably to the arrival of the latter. Robert Chambers (1984), 'Beyond the Green Revolution: A Selective Essay', in Tim P. Bayliss-Smith and Sudhir Wanmali (eds.), *Understanding Green Revolutions: Agrarian Change and Development Planning in South Asia*, Cambridge: Cambridge University Press, pp. 362–79, argues, again in the Indian context, that research in the new crop technologies has been directed mainly towards the resources and interests of larger cultivators. For a generally favourable appraisal of the impact of the Green Revolution, see also Michael Lipton with Richard Longhurst (1989), *New Seeds and Poor People*, London: Unwin Hyman. Finally, there is a fascinating account of the scientific research which created the Green Revolution in Peter R. Jennings (1976), 'The Amplification of Agricultural Production', *Scientific American*, 235(3): 181–94.

Turning to the literature on South-East Asia, Chris Manning (1988), *The Green Revolution, Employment, and Economic Change in Rural Java: A Reassessment of Trends under the New Order*, ASEAN Economic Research Unit, Occasional Paper No. 84, Singapore: Institute of Southeast Asian Studies, provides a finely detailed review of the literature on economic change in the rice districts of Java in the 1970s, focusing on the extent to which the Green Revolution contributed to labour displacement and to inequalities in wealth and income. Anne Booth (1991b), 'Regional Aspects of Indonesian Agricultural Growth', in Joan Hardjono (ed.), *Indonesia: Resources, Ecology, and Environment*, Singapore: Oxford University Press, pp. 36–60, includes a valuable, strongly statistical, analysis of the impact of the new technology on agriculture across the archipelago. See also Anne Booth (1988a), *Agricultural Development in Indonesia*, Southeast Asia Publication Series No. 16, Sydney: Allen & Unwin/Asian Studies Association of Australia, notably Chapter 5, 'Modernization of Foodcrop Agriculture'.

James J. Fox (1991), 'Managing the Ecology of Rice Production in Indonesia', in Joan Hardjono (ed.), *Indonesia: Resources, Ecology, and Environment*, pp. 61–84, as its title promises, examines the ecological implications of the new rice technology in Indonesia. Finally on Indonesia, a central question is asked in Swadesh R. Bose (1982), 'Has Economic Growth Immiserized the Rural Poor in Indonesia? A Review of Conflicting Evidence', in Geoffrey B. Hainsworth (ed.), *Village-level Modernization in Southeast Asia: The Political Economy of Rice and Water*, Vancouver: University of British Columbia Press, pp. 53–69. His answer is that it has not. Indeed, national socio-economic surveys indicate a significant improvement in the material condition of the rural poor in Java and in the rest of Indonesia in the first half of the 1970s. However, Bose observes, evidence on labour force employment, wages, and on socio-technical institutional change does not appear to support the view that significant improvement took place.

For Malaysia, a substantial study by Diana Wong (1987), *Peasants in the Making: Malaysia's Green Revolution*, Singapore: Institute of Southeast Asian Studies, argues that the closing of the land frontier in the 1960s and the introduction of double cropping in the 1970s produced very considerable change in rural society, notably an increasing independence of cultivating households from hired or exchange labour, as harvesting was mechanized and broadcast sowing replaced transplanting. James C. Scott (1985), *Weapons of the Weak: Everyday Forms of Peasant Resistance*, New Haven: Yale University Press, is a brilliant field study, conducted in a village in the Muda district of Malaysia, of 'the prosaic but constant struggle between the peasantry and those who seek to extract labor, food, taxes, rents, and interest from them'. It includes a vivid account of the devastating impact on the village poor of the introduction of the combine harvester in the mid-1970s. A critical analysis of the impact of the Green Revolution in Malaysia is also provided by Ishak Shari and Jomo Kwame Sundaram (1982), 'Malaysia's Green Revolution in Rice Farming: Capital Accumulation and Technological Change in a Peasant Society', in Geoffrey B. Hainsworth (ed.), *Village-level Modernization in Southeast Asia: The Political Economy of Rice and Water*, Vancouver: University of British Columbia Press, pp. 225–54.

The volume edited by Geoffrey B. Hainsworth also includes two valuable articles on labour use in Philippine agriculture: Randolph Barker (1982), 'Recent Trends in Labour Utilization and Productivity in Philippine Agriculture (with Comparisons to Other

Asian Experiences)', pp. 141–72; Violeta G. Cordova (1982), 'New Rice Technology and Its Effect on Labour Use and Shares in Rice Production in Laguna, Philippines, 1966–78', pp. 191–206. The former concludes that the introduction of the new rice technology increased the demand for labour; the latter that the use of hired labour rose substantially but that of family labour declined.

17
The State-commanded Economy:
Burma and North Vietnam

IN the post-war years, all the newly independent states in South-East Asia bar two retained the market-determined, capitalist systems which had flourished in the late colonial period, although the economic policies they pursued and the objectives they sought were in most respects radically different. The two exceptions were the Union of Burma and the Democratic Republic of Vietnam [North Vietnam] which turned instead to different forms of state-commanded economy, in which the state either owned the means of production or tightly directed economic activity while retaining private or co-operative ownership. It is now widely accepted that these experiments failed. At the time of writing, the reunified Socialist Republic of Vietnam is firmly committed to the introduction of a market economy: the pace and direction of change in the Union of Myanmar is more hesitant. This chapter considers the reasons why Burma and North Vietnam rejected the capitalist route, examines the economic strategies they adopted, and seeks to understand why those strategies have proved so unsuccessful.

Different Paths

Why did the political leaders of newly independent Burma and North Vietnam reject capitalism? In the case of Vietnam, the explanation seems quite straightforward. The Vietnamese who took power in the north on the departure of the French were communists, for whom Marxism-Leninism and the international communist movement had long provided the ideology, the instruction in revolutionary strategy, and the material assistance which enabled them to challenge and then, in 1954, to remove the colo-

nial regime. For a number of reasons, the economic strategy
pursued by North Vietnam's new leaders clove to the model for
the creation of the socialist state then being propounded by the
Soviet Union and China. In the decade before the Pacific War,
many Vietnamese revolutionaries had lived in exile in Moscow. Ho
Chi Minh taught at the Lenin Institute and was actively involved
in Moscow-dominated international communist organizations,
although in the 1920s and from 1938 he had closer links with the
Chinese Communist Party. When the communists took power in
northern Vietnam in the mid-1950s and began the huge task of
economic reconstruction, the Soviet Union was still the dominant
force in the international communist movement, and as such its
analyses and strategies were enormously influential. Moreover, the
Soviet Union and China provided North Vietnam with the
resources for economic reconstruction and, within a short time, for
the struggle for reunification in the south. So powerful was the
Soviet model that deviation from it, even when it clearly fitted
badly with Vietnamese circumstances, was near impossible for
North Vietnam's new leaders.

The economic vision of Burma's post-independence leaders was
shaped by a more diverse range of influences. In the late colonial
period, a few élite Burmese encountered Fabian socialism in the
course of their education in England. Also important was the traditional Burmese–Buddhist concept of an ideal polity as one in
which the state protected the material prosperity of the population.
A still more powerful influence was Burma's peculiarly bitter colonial experience. In emerging from a colonial system in which the
unhindered play of market forces had placed control of the economy almost entirely in the hands of foreigners, notably British
firms and Indian moneylenders, leaving large numbers of Burmese
near-impoverished by their toil in the rice delta, not surprisingly
Burma's new leaders saw foreign interests and market relationships
as inherently exploitative. Here lay the origins of a strong xenophobia, a fierce ambition to shun the outside world.

There were, of course, substantial differences in the policies and
strategies pursued by the North Vietnamese and Burmese administrations in this period. This was evident not least in their contrasting approaches to the agricultural sector. Between 1953 and 1956,
North Vietnam's new leaders carried out a major land reform campaign. One aim was to abolish landlordism and to redistribute land
to small cultivators. But the campaign also sought the removal of
landlords from the Party and the promotion of poor cultivators and

labourers to positions of authority in the countryside, measures intended to increase the state's control over agricultural production and the agricultural surplus. In its first aim, land reform enjoyed reasonable success. At the Tenth Central Committee Plenum (Second Congress) held in September 1956, it was reported that 810 000 hectares had been confiscated or expropriated for redistribution to 2,104,138 households, involving 72.8 per cent of the rural population. But with respect to the second, eliminating landlords and rich peasants from Party ranks, the policy was arguably ill-conceived and certainly badly executed. Far too frequently, the cadres charged with carrying out the land reform acted with excessive zeal, identifying even poor cultivators and labourers as hostile elements and attacking them accordingly. Almost invariably former landlords were left with smaller holdings than anyone else in the village, and might well lose their home as well. It is widely argued that around 5,000 individuals were executed during the land reform campaign, although some writers put the figure at well over 15,000. By mid-1956, the leadership of the Party had realized that 'dangerous excesses' were taking place, and on 29 October 1956 General Vo Nguyen Giap, the architect of the French defeat at Dien Bien Phu, publicly admitted that errors had been made. In late 1956 and through the following year, the majority of those who had been identified as landlords during land reform were reclassified, part of the property confiscated was returned, and most of the individuals who had been expelled from the Party were readmitted. For some, of course, it was too late. The political objective of land reform, to fashion a strong Party apparatus in the countryside, firmly loyal to the central leadership, was thus largely thwarted. Indeed the excesses and errors of the campaign may have intensified the resistance of rural communities to the exactions of the state, a popular theme in Vietnamese history. This was to have an important impact on the ability of Vietnam's leadership to achieve its economic ambitions, as will be shown below.

Land reform in the mid-1950s was a prerequisite for the collectivization of North Vietnam's agriculture, begun in late 1958 but greatly accelerated the following year. By the end of 1959, more than 45 per cent of all cultivating families were in collectives. That figure was 86 per cent at the end of 1960. In this initial stage, most households were in elementary collectives, in which individuals pooled their land, draught animals, and tools, while retaining private ownership. The following years saw the creation of physically larger and functionally more advanced collectives, in which land, animals, and tools were common property and individuals were remunerated solely according to the work they undertook for the collective. The proportion of cultivating households in advanced collectives rose from 12 per cent in 1960 to 65 per cent in 1965, and to 93 per cent in 1975.

An important aim in collectivizing agriculture was, once again, to strengthen the ability of the state to extract the agricultural surplus. The collectives, it was argued, would stop cultivators from consuming their surplus production instead of selling it to the state at low prices. It must be added, however, that 5 per cent of the collective's land was formally allocated to private plots, used for the cultivation of high-value crops, notably vegetables, for sale on the free market at prices substantially above those offered by the state. Beresford (1985) has suggested that the plots brought significant benefits to the collective, in that they supplied the basic subsistence needs of the cultivator, thus freeing more of the collective's output for further investment. However, the majority of writers on this subject, including Fforde and Paine (1987), Vo Nhan Tri (1990), and Wiegersma (1988) disagree, arguing that the larger incomes which cultivators could earn from their private plots inhibited voluntary participation in collective production. In the 1970s it was observed that the average working day on a collective was a mere 4–5 hours, and that longer hours, and certainly more effort and diligence, were devoted to the private plots. The state responded by increasing the formal powers of the collective managers. However, according to Fforde and Paine (1987), instead of acting as obedient agents of the state, most collectives acted to protect local private interests against its demands. Thus a collective would officially report a decline in cultivated area in order to mask an illegal increase in the size of its private plots. In this and other ways, private land came to occupy perhaps 15 or even 20 per cent of the total cultivated area in North Vietnam. Fforde and Paine (1987: 108) see in the period 1960–75 'a broad secular shift against participation in collective production and the supply of surplus staples to the state, and therefore in favour of freely marketed output produced on the expanded private-plots'. By 1975 over two-thirds of sales by members of collectives were to the free market. To put a comparable point, in the same year, the state procured barely 14 per cent of reported domestic rice production.

In Burma, the agricultural sector was organized in very different ways. Instead of setting up collectives, the state tightly regulated the conditions of private land ownership and the terms of production and trade. The central aim of the state was to see land in the possession of the cultivator, in order to build a strong direct relationship between itself and the rural producers. This required two major measures. The first was the abolition of tenancy. This was a huge task. At independence in 1948 it was estimated that of the total of more than 11 million acres in cultivation in the rice delta of Lower Burma no less than 42 per cent was in the possession of non-resident landlords, a further 9 per cent being owned by resident landlords. The first attempts at reform were not successful. The 1948 Land Nationalization Act was rapidly abandoned, while progress under a second act, introduced in 1953, was very slow. As late as 1963 there were still 350,000 landlords in Burma, of whom one-third were not nationals of the country. The military regime which came to power following a coup on 2 March 1962 abolished all rents on cultivable land in 1965, an action which, in the words of the government, marked 'the destruction of the last line of land-lordism' (Steinberg, 1981a: 127). This was an optimistic claim. In 1971 *government* figures showed that tenants still comprised 41.8 per cent of cultivators in Burma, farming 36.6 per cent of land. Since 1974 government statistics have omitted data on tenancy. It is unlikely that it has been eradicated. It may well have been driven underground.

The second measure was to curb or prevent new accumulations of land. This could be achieved in part by severely limiting, perhaps removing completely, the freedom of the individual to dispose of his land. Under the 1953 Land Nationalization Act, holdings taken from landlords for redistribution to small cultivators became the property of the state. The cultivator possessed only cultivation rights, periodically approved or denied by a village committee. Such land could not be mortgaged, sold, or rented, but worked only by the approved cultivator. One source (Hill and Jayasuriya, 1986) claims that land sales are now illegal: another (Steinberg, 1981a) suggests that even the right of inheritance to land has been removed. But new accumulations of land could also be discouraged by depressing the income which cultivators received from the sale of their crops. If there is little profit in the land, there is neither the incentive or the capacity to accumulate more.

The regulation of agricultural production and trade by the state has taken a number of different forms since independence. A State Agricultural Marketing Board, established in 1948, assumed responsibility for all rice exports, displacing the British, Indian, and Chinese firms which had dominated the trade in the colonial period. The Board's procurement price was held constant from 1948/9 to 1960/1, despite substantial increases in world prices. Inevitably, this retarded agricultural expansion. *Padi* production, which had been 8.05 million long tons in 1938/9, crept up from 5.54 million in 1947/8 to 6.92 million in 1959/60. Rice exports in 1961/2, at 1.676 million tons, were just over half the volume achieved in 1940/1. In January 1963, under the new military regime, the State Agricultural Marketing Board became the Union of Burma Agricultural Marketing Board, with substantially increased functions. It was responsible for all procurements of *padi*, whether for the domestic or external market. By the following year, private trade in rice in the domestic market was prohibited: the purchase of *padi* was a state monopoly. With the procurement price still kept far below world prices, the impact was near disastrous. *Padi* production was 7.544 million tons in 1962/3, 7.241 million in 1972/3, a decade in which Burma's population had increased by some 6 million. In 1967 domestic shortages and high prices provoked urban riots. Meanwhile exports collapsed, from 1.521 million tons in 1962/3 to a mere 204,000 tons in 1972/3. In 1973/4, as part of a major reassessment of its economic strategy, the government more than doubled the procurement price of rice. Smaller increases followed in 1978/9 and 1980/1.

For the beginning of the 1974/5 cultivation season, the government introduced a new procurement system, which required each cultivator to supply, at a fixed price, an individually determined quota of *padi*. A cultivator's quota, which might account for as much as a third of his production, was set by the area he had under rice, the national average yield per acre, family size, and the volume of *padi* paid out to hired labour. The cultivator could sell the remainder of his production on the free market, where much higher prices prevailed. But cultivators with smaller plots, far from having a surplus to sell, were often forced to purchase rice on the open market, at great cost, in order to meet their quota and have sufficient food and seed for themselves. This procurement system drove the rice economy into an even deeper crisis in the 1980s. *Padi* production held roughly constant over the decade (13.923 million tons in 1981/2, 13.553 million in 1988/9) while population rose by over 5 million. Exports collapsed, falling to a paltry 49,000 tons in 1988/9. And the free market retail price of rice soared, to more than 12 times the government procurement price in 1987/8.

Industry, as well as agriculture, took markedly divergent paths in North Vietnam and Burma. For North Vietnam's new leaders, the rapid creation of an industrial base constituted development. Their industrialization drive, which gathered real momentum under the First Five-Year Plan of 1961–5, was built on a very considerable inflow of aid from the Soviet bloc and China, including deliveries of industrial plant. As early as 1965, a substantial, relatively well-equipped industrial sector had been established, built around some 200 state enterprises, managed by ministries within the central government. Production was remarkably diverse, and included the manufacture of cast iron, lathes, diesel generators, water pumps, bicycles, chemical fertilizer, antibiotics, cement, thermos flasks, cigarettes, textiles, and toothpaste. Between 1960 and 1965, the industrial labour force increased by 27 per cent, the value of fixed industrial capital by 116 per cent, and the real value of industrial output by 89 per cent. By 1975 industrial output was approaching three and a half times the level of 1960, in real terms. Industry accounted for 18.6 per cent of produced national income in 1960, 27.9 per cent in 1975. This was an impressive expansion, not least because in 1967–8 and 1972, North Vietnam's industrial centres were heavily bombed by the United States air force.

There was, however, one central weakness. Following the Soviet model, North Vietnam's leaders focused almost exclusively on the rapid growth of fixed capital, trusting to the assumption that the complementary inputs needed to keep that expanding capacity fully employed could be smoothly acquired through direct administrative command. They could not. Consequently, capacity utilization in industry was commonly extremely low, less than 50 per cent. Fforde and Paine (1987: 4) put the point firmly: 'Modern industry was precociously overdeveloped. The levels of fixed capacity installed by the aid program ... far exceeded the economy's ability to supply the requisite complementary inputs'. This severe imbalance manifested itself in a number of ways, notably in domestic inflationary pressures, which threatened real wages, and in a sharply increasing, eventually chronic dependence on imports for essential industrial raw materials, basic foodstuffs, and consumer goods. From approximate self-sufficiency in food in the early 1960s, in the mid-1970s North Vietnam was importing perhaps 10–15 per cent of its food requirements. Consumer goods accounted for 13 per cent of imports in 1960, but virtually 27 per cent in 1975. In 1960 the total value of imports was equivalent to approximately 11 per cent of national income: in 1975 the figure was just over 23 per cent. In that same period, just 15 years, North Vietnam's trade deficit grew more than 14 times over. Here was a most serious block on the country's industrialization.

Burma, in contrast, 'has one of the least developed industrial sectors in South and East Asia' (Hill and Jayasuriya, 1986: 49). Not only did industry account for a notably small proportion of gross domestic product (a mere 9.3 per cent in 1986/7) but it was largely restricted to the manufacture of simple consumer goods and the basic processing of primary materials. In 1978 the manufacture of food products, beverages, and tobacco products accounted for 36.8 per cent of value-added in manufacturing, while the simple processing of wood products, non-metallic minerals, and non-ferrous metals accounted for a further 33.8 per cent. In contrast, machinery and transport equipment accounted for a mere 1.4 per cent of value-added in manufacturing.

In one respect at least, this position might cause some surprise, for in the decade following the March 1962 coup, the new military rulers gave high priority to industrial growth. In August 1962 the local Imperial Chemical Industries plant was nationalized, followed in January 1963 by the Burma Oil Company. In February the same year, Ne Win announced that no new private industrial concerns would be permitted. As a consequence, the state's share of processing and manufacturing output rose from 28.6 per cent in 1961/2 to 42.2 per cent in 1970/1. Almost all large industrial concerns were now in state ownership. The military administration invested heavily in industry, that sector attracting 37 per cent of state capital expenditure in 1970/1 compared to under 4 per cent a decade earlier. The returns were disappointing: the output of state industry increased by only 3.4 per cent per year in this period. In the early 1970s, the government abandoned its emphasis on industrial growth, and turned its attention to the far larger agricultural sector.

As in North Vietnam, the state's industrial concerns worked far below capacity. In 1983/4, average capacity utilization in state-owned industry was just 67.9 per cent. It then fell sharply towards the end of the decade, to 34.4 per cent in 1988/9. This was in part a consequence of a severe shortage of foreign exchange, which stopped factories obtaining essential raw materials, spare parts, and fuel oil. But it also reflected the failure of a highly centralized decision-making structure, in which the management of state enterprises possessed so little autonomy (despite a measure of reform in the early 1970s) that decisions on even minor matters were routinely referred to the highest political level. Perhaps not surprisingly, the system proved incapable of co-ordinating the activities of the large number of units comprising the state-commanded economy—aligning production targets with input flows, output with market demands, labour requirements with labour supply.

A final comparison contrasts the external economic relationships of Burma and North Vietnam, their divergent attitudes towards the outside world. Vietnam, as noted above, looked firmly outside, to the development model created by the Soviet Union in the 1920s and 1930s. This provided not only the basic principles but also, frequently, the fine detail of administration and implementation. Second, the considerable industrial growth achieved in North Vietnam from the early 1960s rested on the inflow of aid from the Soviet bloc and from China. The share of foreign economic aid in total budget revenues rose from 22.4 per cent in 1960 to 42.3 per cent in 1965, and to 67.6 per cent in 1970. Indeed by 1975, the economic demands of the war had left North Vietnam utterly dependent on the Soviets and the Chinese. In contrast Burma's leaders sought to insulate their country from the outside world. They adopted no foreign development strategy but attempted to fashion their own Burmese path to economic progress. Foreign commercial interests were banished. The British, Indian, and Chinese firms which had dominated the colonial rice trade were pushed aside when the state imposed its monopoly on exports in 1948. The wave of nationalization that followed the March 1962 coup saw the removal of all foreign banks, Imperial Chemical Industries, and Burma Oil. And exports fell away. Foreign sales of rice, 3.123 million tons in 1940/1, still 1.676 million in 1961/2, had withered to 166,000 tons in 1974/5. (In that last, dismal, year, rice and rice products still accounted for 40 per cent of total export value!) In the 1950s, exports averaged around 18 per cent of gross domestic product. The figure for 1975 was 4.3 per cent, just 2.2 per cent for 1987 and 1988.

However, this stark picture of external disengagement and collapse is in parts overdrawn. First, a considerable smuggling trade must be added to Burma's recorded commerce. Most was with Thailand, although it also took place on a considerable scale with India, Bangladesh, China, Malaysia, and Singapore. Illegal imports were dominated by consumer items, including textiles, bicycles, medicines, cosmetics, and household electrical goods.

Smuggled exports included precious stones, pearls, jade, rice, and teak. Hill and Jayasuriya (1986) suggest that in the early 1980s, the value of non-legal trade was equivalent to over one-quarter of official imports. Writing of a slightly earlier period, Steinberg (1981a) indicates that the value of transactions on the black market was equivalent to more than half the value of Burma's legal foreign trade. Second, although there have been periods of fierce xenophobia, notably in the decade from 1962, at other times the Burmese government has sought, albeit with frequent unease and reservation, a greater economic openness. Having rejected significant foreign borrowing for most of the 1960s, in 1973 Burma joined the Asian Development Bank: in 1976, a Burma Aid Consultative Group was established, to include representatives of the World Bank, the International Monetary Fund, and the United Nations Development Program, as well as seven major industrial nations. There followed a substantial rise in external borrowing. In 1983 foreign grants and loans accounted for 26 per cent of gross domestic capital formation and 40 per cent of public sector investment. Thirdly, towards the end of the 1970s there was a substantial, if temporary, surge in exports, built largely on a recovery in rice exports and a more thorough exploitation of Burma's forests. The value of merchandise exports, in current prices, rose from US$162 million in 1975 to US$531 million in 1981. More recently, a small number of joint projects were established with multinationals, notably in oil exploration.

Yet in the 1980s, Burma's re-engagement with the international economy ran into severe difficulties. Within the regime, suspicion of international business and its ways, fear of the capacity of international capitalism to manipulate a host economy in its own interests, clearly persisted. A more serious constraint was the vulnerability of Burma's export position. In 1983 no less than 71 per cent of export earnings came from forest products and rice, both commodities whose value fluctuated widely year-by-year. Indeed from the middle of the decade, rice exports virtually collapsed, largely in consequence of a failure of the government's procurement mechanism. They were down to less than 50,000 tons in 1988/9. Overlying the collapse in volume was a fall in price. The severe contraction in export values damaged Burma's development drive in two ways. It forced a sharp cut in imports, including imports of capital goods: and with Burma having borrowed abroad on a substantial scale from the mid-1970s, it created a serious debt-servicing problem which undermined future attempts to borrow. It is possible that debt-servicing absorbed as much as three-quarters of Burma's export earnings in the late 1980s.

Common Failings

This chapter has drawn attention to the substantial differences in development strategy and policy between North Vietnam and Burma, both state-commanded economies, in the first decades of independence. The conclusion, in contrast, focuses on two common weaknesses, which are of central importance in explaining the failure of their development ambitions. Neither North Vietnam or Burma had the administrative capacity—the bureaucratic expertise and experience—to run a command economy effectively. The result was rampant inefficiency and a damaging lack of basic co-ordination. Steinberg (1981a: 144) notes with respect to Burma that 'there was very little coordination between the planning of new industries and the allocation of resources, including foreign exchange, necessary for raw materials. Thus plants were constructed and operated at far less than capacity, perhaps averaging half of capacity for the first decade' of military rule. In agriculture little attempt was made to relate rice procurement prices to the costs of cultivation inputs.

It seems clear that the political leaders of both North Vietnam and Burma were too ambitious in seeking such a high degree of control over their economies. In North Vietnam, it is worth recalling, the state sought direct administrative control over all modern industry, the collective farms, and the distribution of virtually all important goods. No bureaucracy, however sophisticated and experienced, could run such a highly complex command network without creating inefficiencies and misallocations. To make matters worse, the political élites in both Burma and North Vietnam failed to make the most effective use of the administrative resources that they did possess. In Burma, in the years following its seizure of power in March 1962, the military forcibly retired the established core of skilled and experienced civilian administrators which it strongly distrusted. Too often, appointments to senior administrative positions reflected political favour or the exercise of patronage. Moreover, the pressure for ideological correctness, reinforced by the practice of referring virtually all important decisions to the highest political level, inhibited effective administration. Fear of initiative and innovation paralysed the bureaucracy.

As the administration malfunctioned, individuals and organizations were forced outside the state-commanded economy simply to keep going. In North Vietnam, managers of state enterprises made arrangements with local agricultural collectives, under which food for the factory workforce or industrial raw materials were swopped for consumer goods in short supply. Some state enterprises produced anything they could, irrespective of plan or instruction, simply to give their workers something to do. In Burma, few individuals or enterprises survived without resorting to the non-legal economy.

The second weakness struck at the heart of the development strategies pursued in North Vietnam and Burma. As both economies were overwhelmingly agricultural, the ability of the two states to achieve, by direct intervention and command, sustained industrialization rested on their capacity to extract surplus resources from that sector. In theory this could be achieved either by taxing agricultural land and production heavily or by forcing rural producers to sell their output to the government at prices far below market levels. In practice neither mechanism worked effectively. In Burma, the tax-raising powers of the newly independent state were so weak in the countryside that in 1956–7, the land tax provided only 4 per cent of tax revenue and a mere 2 per cent of state income. On the other side, in both Burma and North Vietnam, low, rigid procurement prices led cultivators either to conceal their full production from the state, deflecting much of their output into non-legal markets, or to cut their acreage. They were encouraged in this by the inability of the state-commanded economy to deliver adequate supplies of simple consumer goods on which they might spend their modest earnings. In North Vietnam, villagers were particularly well-versed in stratagems to avoid or deflect the unwelcome intrusions of the state, a response which possibly had been strengthened by the failure of land reform in the 1950s to dislodge hostile elements in the countryside. In the absence of material incentives for cultivators, indeed with the presence of powerful disincentives, agriculture stagnated—at best.

If the state's ability to extract resources from the agricultural sector was weak, then the strategy of rapid state-commanded development could be sustained only with very considerable external assistance. This was North Vietnam's experience. But, as was explained above, it soon led to a massive, unsustainable trade deficit, dramatically exacerbated by the economic demands of the war. If, on the other hand, the outside world was shunned, the prospect of achieving sustained growth through industrialization evaporated. During its most fiercely xenophobic phase, the first decade of military rule following the 1962 coup, Burma went through an economic contraction which 'has few parallels in recent economic history' (Hill and Jayasuriya, 1986: 7). From the mid-1970s, external assistance made respectable growth possible for a time: then the debt repayments crisis intervened. For all their political authoritarianism and military weight, in economic terms Burma and North Vietnam were weak regimes relative to the tasks they set themselves.

SUGGESTED READING

For North Vietnam, an excellent introduction to economic policy in the period from independence to reunification with the south is provided by the opening chapter of Vo Nhan Tri (1990), *Vietnam's Economic Policy since 1975*, Singapore: Institute of Southeast Asian Studies, ASEAN Economic Research Unit, 'Legacy of the Development Model of North Vietnam, 1955–75'. This is a strongly critical analysis. The author was a senior economist in Hanoi and then, after reunification, in Ho Chi Minh City before he left Vietnam in 1984. Adam Fforde and Suzanne H. Paine (1987), *The Limits of National Liberation: Problems of Economic Management in the Democratic Republic of Vietnam, with a Statistical Appendix*, London: Croom Helm, offers a most detailed account of economic policy in this period. It too is highly critical, arguing that the commitment of North Vietnam's leaders to the Soviet development strategy forged in the 1920s and 1930s led to the creation of an economy riddled with 'severe macro-imbalances and horrendous micro-level inefficiencies in resource use'. This very densely argued book repays close reading. The extremely valuable statistical appendix, running to almost 100 pages, presents data from a major collection published during 1978 by the Statistical Office in Hanoi. Note should also be made of the first chapter of Adam Fforde (1989), *The Agrarian Question in North Vietnam, 1974–1979: A Study of Cooperator Resistance to State Policy*, Armonk, New York: M. E. Sharpe; and Andrew Vickerman (1986), *The Fate of the Peasantry: Premature 'Transition to Socialism' in the Democratic Republic of Vietnam*, Southeast Asia Studies, Monograph No. 28, New Haven: Yale University. The land reform campaign in the mid-1950s is well covered in Edwin E. Moise (1976), 'Land Reform and Land Reform Errors in North

Vietnam', *Pacific Affairs*, 49(1): 70–92. Nancy Wiegersma (1988), *Vietnam: Peasant Land, Peasant Revolution: Patriarchy and Collectivity in the Rural Economy*, London: Macmillan, notably Chapters 7 and 8, argues that in the 1960s, control over rural labour rested more with family patriarchs than with the newly created agricultural collectives, with the result that the influence of the collective was undermined, its production held back. Melanie Beresford (1985), 'Household and Collective in Vietnamese Agriculture', *Journal of Contemporary Asia*, 15(1): 5–36, argues, in contrast, that in North Vietnam the expansion of private agricultural plots brought important benefits to the collective.

Perhaps the most valuable brief introduction to the recent economic history of Burma is Hal Hill and Sisira Jayasuriya (1986), *An Inward-looking Economy in Transition: Economic Development in Burma since the 1960s*, Occasional Paper No. 80, Singapore: Institute of Southeast Asian Studies. A more detailed analysis of the period from the military take-over in 1962 to the late 1970s can be found in David I. Steinberg (1981a), *Burma's Road toward Development: Growth and Ideology under Military Rule*, Boulder: Westview Press. See also David I. Steinberg (1981b), 'Burmese Economics: The Conflict of Ideology and Pragmatism', in F. K. Lehman (ed.), *Military Rule in Burma since 1962: A Kaleidoscope of Views*, Singapore: Maruzen Asia, pp. 29–50. A number of substantial passages in Robert H. Taylor (1987), *The State in Burma*, London: C. Hurst, consider the economic and financial administration of the independent state. One important conclusion is that, with respect to the economy, 'the state has developed power sufficient to inhibit initiative, but insufficient to impel developments on the planned lines' (p. 353). Some useful comments can be found in Josef Silverstein (1977), *Burma: Military Rule and the Politics of Stagnation*, Ithaca: Cornell University Press, Chapter 6, 'The Economy before and after the Coup and Some Political Implications'. Finally, Louis J. Walinsky (1962), *Economic Development in Burma, 1951–60*, New York: Twentieth Century Fund, provides an extremely detailed account of economic policy-making and administration in the 1950s, written by the chief economic adviser to the government at that time. For the other end of this period, there are a number of valuable papers in Mya Than and Joseph L. H. Tan (eds.) (1990), *Myanmar, Dilemmas and Options: The Challenge of Economic Transition in the 1990s*, Singapore: Institute of Southeast Asian Studies, ASEAN Economic Research Unit.

18
Modern Industrialization

THE most striking feature of economic change in the capitalist states of South-East Asia in the decades since independence has surely been the expansion of manufacturing industry. The contribution of manufacturing to gross domestic product in Malaysia was 9 per cent in 1965 but 32 per cent in 1990; in Indonesia it was 8 per cent in 1965 and 20 per cent in 1990; in Thailand, 14 per cent and then 26 per cent. Again in Thailand, the manufacturing sector accounted for just 2.4 per cent of total export value in 1961 but, remarkably, 68.6 per cent in 1989. In Malaysia, the proportion of the employed population working in manufacturing was 11.4 per cent in 1970 and 20.1 per cent in 1991, when the sector employed 1.374 million people. Singapore achieved the position of a newly industrial country (NIC) some years ago, and is now firmly placed with the East Asian economic dragons, South Korea, Taiwan, and Hong Kong. Considerable popular and academic speculation surrounds the possibility that Thailand and Malaysia will become NICs in the near, or more distant future. In 1991 the Malaysian prime minister announced that Malaysia would aim to become a developed industrial country by the year 2020. Here indeed is a fundamental shift.

This chapter explores two questions. Which factors account for the dramatic expansion in manufacturing industry in modern capitalist South-East Asia? And is that growth leading to the transformation of the region's states into advanced industrial economies: will they each become NICs? A third issue lies beneath these two questions. What has been the nature of modern capitalist South-East Asia's industrialization? Given the very considerable differences between the states of the region, in territorial and demographic size, natural resource endowment, political structure, historical experience, and ethnic balance, the precise answers must differ case by case. But there are also some important common themes.

The Causes of Industrial Transformation

An important part of the explanation for modern capitalist South-East Asia's dramatic industrial growth lies in the changes that have taken place in the advanced industrial economies, the effect of which has been to encourage the relocation of entire industries or particular industrial processes to the Third World. Rising wages in the advanced economies reduced their international competitiveness in labour-intensive industries where labour costs formed a major part of total costs. At the same time rapid technological innovation led to the development not only of a vastly increased range of more complex manufactures, the production of which involved increasingly capital-intensive investment in the industrial core, but also of highly standardized manufacturing processes. The latter made it possible to remove particular stages of production to distant locations, retaining the manufacture of advanced components in the industrial core but siting the labour-intensive, low-skilled assembly work in a developing economy.

In the late 1960s a number of American electronics firms, including Texas Instruments and Hewlett-Packard, built factories in Singapore to assemble components, particularly semiconductors. Assembly work was later extended to Malaysia, Thailand, and the Philippines. In other lines the advanced economies virtually abandoned production altogether, as new enterprises, commonly owned in full or in part by local interests, were established in the Third World. Entire industries were relocated, not simply particular industrial processes. An important example was the textile industry, contracting, sometimes to the point of extinction, in the advanced industrial economies and flourishing in the less developed. In Thailand the period from the early 1960s saw the development of two textile and garment groups, under Damri Darakananda whose Saha-Union was incorporated in the early 1970s, and Sukri Bodhiratanangkura whose interests included Thai Blanket Industry and Thai Synthetic Textile Industry. For both men, early expansion involved joint ventures with Japanese firms.

In some countries of South-East Asia, manufacturing relocated from the industrial core was predominantly for the export market. This was clearly so with the assembly of household electrical goods, but it was also true for much fully local manufacturing, for example, in textile and garment production. In Thailand, textiles and garments accounted for almost 28 per cent of the value of manufactured exports in 1985.

The relocation of industry involved not only the older industrial economies of western Europe and North America but also the industrial economies of North-East Asia, first Japan but then the new industrial states of South Korea, Taiwan, and Hong Kong, to which Singapore should be added. Indeed by the mid-1980s that last group had come to play a central role in the relocation of manufacturing to South-East Asia. One measure of this was the flow of foreign investment. In 1988, 31 per cent of foreign investment in Indonesia, Malaysia, the Philippines, and Thailand came from the East Asian NICs, exceeding investment from Japan. In 1990, Hong Kong, Singapore, and Taiwan accounted for 42 per cent of net direct foreign investment in Thailand, Japan for 30 per cent. It was North-East Asia, largely alone, that was responsible for the staggering increase in net direct foreign investment in Thailand from an annual average of US$268 million in 1980–5 to US$2,442 million in 1990. North-East Asia's dramatic industrial restructuring from the 1960s, and the sustained high growth that was integral to it, provided a crucial foundation for capitalist South-East Asia's own industrialization drive.

The crucial question is: what were the internal conditions that enabled capitalist South-East Asia to respond to the opportunities created by restructuring in the industrial core? Why was the response commonly so powerful: and in what circumstances was it constrained or undermined? Once again, despite substantial differences in individual circumstances, there was much common experience.

One crucial condition, prominent in all the capitalist economies of South-East Asia in this period, was the presence of a copius supply of cheap, largely unskilled, and essentially docile labour. This all-important resource made it possible for these economies to move into the labour-intensive manufacturing processes then being vacated by the advanced industrial core under the pressure of rising labour costs. A substantial part of the rapidly growing industrial labour force comprised young women, in part because, so it was said, their dextrous fingers and patient temperament fitted them for such repetitive, minutely detailed tasks as electronic component assembly or garment production. In addition, young women workers appeared willing to accept lower wages and inferior conditions, and were certainly worse organized among themselves. In Malaysia the proportion of women in the manufacturing labour force rose from 11 per cent in 1957 to 45 per cent in 1985. In that last year, no less than 92 per cent of those employed in the electronics industry were female.

This rich labour endowment was the result of high population growth since the early twentieth century, in some parts of the region from much earlier, exacerbated by a sharp contraction in new employment opportunities in agriculture. In the middle of the nineteenth century, much of South-East Asia had a pronounced shortage of labour relative to land. The open agricultural frontier provided ample opportunities for local communities, even as their size and number increased. But in the middle of the twentieth century, the frontier in South-East Asia was closed or closing, and with population continuing to grow at a high rate, surplus labour needed employment outside agriculture. Industrial capitalists were in a strong position to dictate terms. Labour union organization was weak, in some industries non-existent, a situation frequently reinforced by government intervention. In Singapore in the early 1960s, the government moved sharply to break the power of the independent labour movement and to secure the rise of a compliant labour organization firmly under its control. In fact Singapore's National Trade Union Congress, established in 1961, was part of the government structure: its general-secretaries held Cabinet rank. In Malaysia, prior to 1988 labour unions were excluded from the electronics industry by the government: in that year, in-house unions only were permitted.

In addition, the capitalist economies of South-East Asia were resource-rich, with the notable exception of Singapore. In this respect, and others, they provided a strong contrast with the East Asia NICs. This rich endowment gave the region's capitalist economies a decisive advantage in the production of a number of manufactures, notably wood products and processed foods but also cement, chemical fertilizer, and paper, which involved intensive use of local inputs. In 1985 the value of Indonesia's exports of plywood was US$941 million, 46 per cent of the value of the country's manufactured exports. In the same year, processed foods accounted for 21 per cent of the value of Thai manufactured exports. In addition, for the two South-East Asian economies with large oil and natural gas resources, Malaysia and Indonesia, the price hikes of the 1970s generated huge revenues to force industrial growth. It should be added, however, that these revenues were often used to protect and subsidize inefficient local manufacturing, a strategy which in the longer term undermined industrialization. This is an important point which will be taken up later.

Finally, each of the capitalist states of South-East Asia possessed communication, commercial, and administrative infrastructures which were adequate for a substantial modern industrial sector. Some were far more than adequate. They were the legacy of an earlier age of spectacular export growth, when roads, ports, railways, commercial districts, and modern bureaucracies channelled vast volumes of primary commodities on to the world market. Of course, modern states have invested heavily in extending and improving infrastructures, none more so than Singapore which from the early 1960s built industrial, transport, and service facilities that are clearly unrivalled in South-East Asia, indeed have few equals anywhere in the world.

Cheap labour, rich natural resources, and, commonly, high quality infrastructures were the crucial pre-conditions that made it possible for the capitalist states of South-East Asia to respond to the new opportunities created by restructuring in the advanced industrial core. The mere existence of those advantages, however, does not explain why South-East Asia responded so vigorously. To answer that central question requires an examination of the complex structures of political, economic, and bureaucratic interests in the states of the region, an attempt to understand the ways in which those interests have related and functioned. As those structures and relationships were markedly different in each country, the outcomes, in terms of the pace and character of industrialization, were also diverse.

Ersatz Capitalism

In *The Rise of Ersatz Capitalism in South-East Asia*, published in 1988, Yoshihara Kunio put forward two important criticisms of the region's modern industrialization. The first was that modern manufacturing in capitalist South-East Asia was entirely dependent on foreign technology. Little or no industrial research took place locally, or the basic science research that so frequently underpinned it. The Malaysian car, the Proton Saga, which began production in 1986, depended for its technology on a Japanese partner, Mitsubishi. The technology employed in local assembly

plants, producing vehicles or household electrical goods, was similarly provided by a foreign partner or by the foreign parent company. Yoshihara blamed the absence of an industrial research and
development capacity on two factors: the trader origins of many of
the region's most important industrial capitalists, so that 'they
have neither technical training nor interest in technical matters'
(Yoshihara, 1988: 113); and the region's 'low overall level of technical competence' (Yoshihara, 1988: 114), itself a reflection of
government's minimal interest and investment in science and technology. Without a technological and scientific research base, the
South-East Asian economies are unable to make independently the
advances in industrial technology—the development of more
efficient manufacturing processes, the creation of new products—
that are essential if a strong export capability is to be maintained in
fiercely competitive world markets. Modern industry in South-
East Asia depends entirely on foreign technology to upgrade its
processes and products. Should access to technological innovation
be denied, for whatever reason, the prospects for the region's
manufacturing would be sharply diminished.

Yoshihara's second argument was that many South-East Asian
business leaders were more interested in speculative ventures with
the prospect of immediate high returns than the creation of
efficient industrial empires, a process for which the time-horizon
was long and profits, at least in the early stages, were almost certainly low. South-East Asia's entrepreneurs were strongly drawn
towards property development, including the construction of
hotels, shop and office complexes, financial dealing, and retail
chains. Perhaps more significantly, they sought out business ventures whose profitability, or very existence, rested on state intervention. They were drawn into manufacturing for the domestic
market when governments imposed high tariffs or tight quotas.
Businessmen sought from the government monopoly rights or
commercial privileges: a logging or mining concession, an essential
licence, a low interest loan, an advantageous contract, a manipulation of building or land-use regulations. Each, in a different way,
provided the businessman with an important measure of commercial security, of protection against rivals. It followed that South-
East Asia's business leaders devoted a considerable part of their
energy and resources to building connections with politicians,
senior bureaucrats, and prominent military figures, because their
commercial survival depended on those alliances. For their part,
politicians, bureaucrats, and generals were richly rewarded by

businessmen for their interventions. In this way, a binding dependence between business leaders and state managers was established.

Using alliances with the state to secure their business interests, South-East Asia's capitalists were, in Yoshihara's terminology, 'rent-seekers'. In this context rent is the difference between the market value of a state-controlled resource (for example, a logging concession) or of administrative sanction for a commercial activity which the state regulates (a factory licence, an import permit, building permission) and the amount which the businessman pays for it, either officially to the government or surreptitiously to his contacts within the administration. To be a rent-seeker implies securing monopoly control over a resource or commercial activity, such that profits are extracted without productive investment. In Yoshihara's view, the modern economic landscape of capitalist South-East Asia is heavily populated with rent-seekers. In the Philippines during the period of martial law, cronies of President Marcos received loans from the Central Bank on extremely generous terms, preferential low duties on imported materials, and monopoly trading and processing rights for certain agricultural commodities. In Thailand in the 1950s and 1960s, high-ranking military officers in government built up substantial business interests and connections. In Malaysia, many of the Malay business leaders who came to the fore in the 1970s under the New Economic Policy had begun their careers in government service, now, apparently, using those connections to advance their business interests.

Yoshihara's analysis raises a crucial question. If his claims are true, why has rent-seeking been such a prominent feature in modern South-East Asia? Why have the region's business leaders so often sought protected or monopoly positions through alliance with the state rather than trying to build efficient industries? Or, to approach the relationship from the opposite direction, why have politicians, senior bureaucrats, and the military been such eager accomplices in rent-seeking? On this important point, Yoshihara is far less confident. Indeed one critic has dismissed his explanation of the behaviour of state managers as 'implicitly moral in nature, reducing politics to acts of consciousness and will and, in a very Confucian way, to the moral quality of the officials and leaders of the state' (Robison, 1989: 122). In fact Yoshihara offered two main observations. He noted the considerable degree of insecurity felt by many South-East Asian capitalists of Chinese origin, notably in Malaysia and Indonesia, in the face of discriminatory policies driven by narrow economic nationalism. In response they have sought out short-term speculative ventures with quick returns, as well as protective alliances with the state, systematically avoiding long-term business commitments. More importantly, Yoshihara saw the apparent prevalence of rent-seeking in South-East Asia as a consequence of political authoritarianism. In a dictatorship there is little or no constraint on government as it releases the nation's natural resources for commercial exploitation, or on its ambition to intervene in the economy. Moreover, for much of the post-independence period, South-East Asia's authoritarian regimes have had very substantial revenues and resources at their disposal, in terms of natural endowments (notably petroleum) but also economic and military aid as well as easy access to external borrowing. For Indonesia, although clearly the comment was also to apply elsewhere, Yoshihara argued that from 'the viewpoint of aspiring capitalists, rent-seeking has been the most logical strategy' (Yoshihara, 1988: 87). Here indeed is the central issue, although, as will be argued later, Yoshihara's treatment of it was seriously deficient.

In brief, modern South-East Asian capitalism is an ersatz capitalism, a substitute, a fake capitalism. The region's capitalists could not independently secure the advances in industrial technology which are essential for maintaining a strong export capability. And as rent-seekers they showed little interest in building efficient, internationally competitive industries, but rather hid their inefficiencies behind tariff barriers, preferential loans, and monopoly concessions, each secured through deals with state managers. They cannot act as the vanguard for fundamental economic change, spearheading the generation of sustained, securely founded economic growth. For their part, state managers, in tying their interests to those of rent-seeking capitalists, find it near impossible to address national economic concerns in a long-term, constructive manner.

A well-argued attack on Yoshihara's analysis was provided by Robison (1989). Robison pointed out that there is no inherent reason why an internationally competitive industrial sector could not be maintained in the absence of a strong, independent, science and technology base. After all, there are perhaps no more than a dozen countries in the world which possess that capacity. The fact is that 'up-to-date technology bought off the shelf can be combined with effective systems of management and work organization to produce internationally competitive products' (Robison, 1989: 123). In addition, the relocation of manufacturing outside the advanced industrial economies need not remain restricted to labour-intensive assembly processes. With further restructuring and technological advance in the industrial core, more sophisticated processes and industries could be relocated to South-East Asia. Robison's culminating thrust was his denial that enduring economic growth must always be constructed on an advanced industrial sector. It could equally well be built on banking and financial services, or on the export of processed primary products. In other words, Yoshihara's definition of 'real' capitalism, of 'real' capitalist growth, was far too narrow.

Moreover, as noted above, Robison rejected Yoshihara's explanation for the alleged enthusiastic connivance of South-East Asian state managers in rent-seeking, as 'implicitly moral in nature'. Rather Robison argued that their behaviour will reflect 'the system of options and constraints within which they operate, a system built around such factors as class power, political history and the international economic environment' (Robison, 1989: 122). Certain political and economic circumstances would indeed draw capitalists into rent-seeking and entice state managers into collusion with them, not only in South-East Asia but in any part of the world. Crucially, however, circumstances change, and with them, the ambitions and actions of businessmen, politicians, and bureaucrats. Yoshihara had neglected that capacity for change. In many parts of capitalist South-East Asia, Robison concluded, it is clear that important transformations are taking place: the region's industrial capitalism is far from static.

In some cases that transformation has had a quite specific cause. Robison noted how the sharp fall in world oil prices in the 1980s greatly reduced the ability of the state in Indonesia and Malaysia to sustain rent-seeking capitalists. Subsidies and concessionary loans to business cronies, together with large-scale, state-funded industrial projects were cut back. The protection of import-substitution manufacturing was reduced. The cheap disposal of valuable natural resources to client capitalists was curtailed. In general terms, the state patronage which earlier had nourished the inefficiencies and narrow vision of local capital now flowed much less richly. Also important was a recognition by government, in Singapore in the mid-1960s, in Malaysia, the Philippines, and Thailand from the end of that decade, and in Indonesia in the early 1980s, of the failings of heavily protected import-substitution industrialization. The need to import capital and intermediate goods on a substantial scale in order to service local industry threatened balance of payments crises. The generous investment incentives associated with import-substitution industrialization favoured the adoption of more capital-intensive manufacturing processes, which implied only a modest increase in employment. And of course the expansion of industrial production was limited by the size of the domestic market: while the flourishing of inefficiency behind high tariffs made a later assault on foreign markets extremely difficult.

More deep-rooted forces may also have been at work. In an important paper published in 1992, Ruth McVey identified in many parts of capitalist South-East Asia a clear shift in the attitude of political–military–bureaucratic élites towards business. In the 1950s business was simply squeezed. Political–military leaders and high-ranking bureaucrats supplied, in ways energetically described by Yoshihara, protection and preference to client capitalists in return for a substantial share of the profits. By the 1980s, however, state managers were more likely to encourage, indeed to be part of, the local business class than bleed it. As McVey (1992: 26) put it, 'We can see signs of the gradual crystallization of entrepreneurial attitudes, a shift in weight from bureaucratic and political to business values, and the emergence of more long-term commitment'. Sons of high officials were seeking entry to business schools rather than to the military or civil service academies which their fathers had attended.

A number of factors appear to have contributed to this shift in attitudes and interests. The rich inflow of foreign capital into South-East Asia in this period created real business opportunities that were simply too good to ignore. More interesting, however, political–military–bureaucratic power-holders had come to realize that their interests would be better served if they took on serious business roles and loosened their dependence on squeeze. It had become clear, for example, that unless the political/bureaucratic patron had a detailed knowledge of the business he was protecting, he could not be sure he was receiving an appropriate cut. Indeed 'were people who spent their days in the pursuit of power likely to remain uninterested in gaining control of the sources of [their] wealth?' (McVey, 1992: 23). A further consideration was concern over the 'vulnerability of riches based on office holding' (McVey, 1992: 23). The politician/bureaucrat could bleed business only as long as he held power. But power could be lost overnight—on retirement, through a coup, by bureaucratic transfer. Moreover, having lost office, the politician/bureaucrat could find that his accumulated wealth was vulnerable to seizure by vengeful rivals, claiming that it had been acquired illicitly. It was far more prudent to secure wealth through serious business ventures, built independently of office. Skilfully handled, these could provide 'a safe landing in case of political adversity and a guarantee of continuing family fortune' (McVey, 1992: 23). McVey referred to the career of Phin Choonhavan, a senior figure in the first military clique to come to power in post-war Thailand. In the 1950s he began to withdraw from politics in order to develop his business interests. Phin's faction was overthrown by a coup in 1957, but, although removed from power, it managed to retain a major part of its considerable wealth and influence through the astute investments and extensive business contacts built up earlier.

It would be easy to push this argument too far, and suggest that the shifts in attitude and interest were more widespread and clearcut than in fact they were. McVey herself recognized the difficulty of telling 'where the line between rent-seeking and real entrepreneurship has been crossed, and whether investment in new enterprise is spurred by speculation or prestige seeking rather than a serious aim at development' (McVey, 1992: 26). Moreover, it is clear that there are still substantial areas of the South-East Asian political–economic landscape where government and business remain bound to the protection of inefficient vested interest, to the defence of monopoly and preference, and where speculation and short-term profit-taking are rife. The implications of this observation will be explored in the following section.

Future NICs?

In the opening paragraph, reference was made to an issue which has attracted considerable academic interest and much popular speculation. Within a brief period beginning in the mid-1960s, Singapore became a modern industrial-trading state, firmly grouped with East Asia's formidable economic dragons. Has the rapid industrial growth in Malaysia, Indonesia, Thailand, and the Philippines in the same period set those economies on the same path? Are they shaping up as future NICs? Alternatively, are their industrial sectors likely to remain dominated by low-technology, low value-added, labour-intensive processes? Indeed, could they lose even that?

The future industrial prospects of Malaysia, Indonesia, Thailand, and the Philippines will be shaped, like their past achievements, by an interaction of external and domestic influences. Externally, four considerations might prove to be particularly important. The first is the fear that, in a prolonged period of recession, the advanced Western industrial economies would resort to trade protection to defend domestic employment in those industries, notably textiles, footwear, garment manufacture, hit hard by imports from the new, low-cost producers in the developing world. The constriction of these major markets would clearly threaten the continued expansion of South-East Asia's manufactured exports. On the other hand, to the extent that western Europe and North America imposed trade barriers specifically against imports from the more advanced East Asian economies, industrial South-East Asia could well benefit as East Asian multinationals relocated production in the region in an attempt to circumvent those restrictions. However, in some industries, NICs and Japanese multinationals are more likely to relocate not in South-East Asia but in Europe and North America itself, so coming inside the tariff wall. In general, increased protection in the advanced economies and a slower growth in world trade must harm the prospects for South-East Asian industry.

Second, technological innovation in the advanced industrial core may include the development of robotic machinery to replace human labour in highly repetitive, unskilled manufacturing processes. In that event, South-East Asia's comparative advantage, founded mainly upon a rich supply of low-wage, unskilled labour, would be rapidly eroded, raising the prospect of a repatriation of some industries, perhaps textiles, or some industrial processes, component assembly, back to the advanced economies.

Third, the prospects for continued industrial growth in capitalist South-East Asia rests upon continued industrial upgrading in the East Asian NICs, which itself requires the most advanced industrial economies to continue to pursue restructuring. If South Korea, Taiwan, Hong Kong, and Singapore vacate the moderately low technology, less labour-intensive industries and industrial processes, the opportunities for South-East Asia's industries to upgrade will clearly increase. Working in the opposite direction is the prospect that the region's present labour-intensive industries will face increasing competition from industrial newcomers, notably China but also Vietnam and, perhaps in time, Myanmar, not forgetting the countries of South Asia and Latin America. That

competition could be extremely fierce, given very low wage-costs
in those countries and the foot-loose character of much multina-
tional investment. Indeed, in a worst-case scenario, South-East
Asia's industrial sectors might find themselves both blocked by the
NICs from upgrading and crowded out of their existing specialization by powerful, even lower-wage newcomers. In those circumstances, the region's export-directed industrialization could be in
serious difficulties.

The external environment is clearly important. But the determining factor will be, as it has been, domestic circumstances. It
would be a relatively simple matter to run through a list of potentially damaging internal flaws in the NIC-aspirant economies of
South-East Asia: poor physical infrastructure, concern over the
long-term stability of the political order, administrative inefficiency,
and corruption. All undermine the ability of the economy to meet
the challenges of the changing external environment. At the same
time, the success or failure of government in correcting these
weaknesses reflects the extent to which a consensus exists within
the political and business élites on the overriding importance of
creating an economy driven by an efficient industrial sector, a consensus which ensures that government pursues that vision without
being deflected or thwarted by powerful sectional interests. Two
related arguments are important here. A dynamic industrial sector
can be built only if its production is directed principally towards
external markets. Industry serving the domestic market alone and
strongly protected against imports will at some point hit serious
difficulties. A heavy dependence on imports for essential machinery and raw materials will, given the neglect of the export
market, create balance of payments problems; local prices of protected manufactures will be substantially above world market
levels, so reducing domestic real income; protected from competition, domestic industry will be under little pressure to improve
either the efficiency of its production or the range and quality of
the goods it produces; and, of course, expansion will be limited by
the size of the domestic market. Second, in the long term at least,
there is an incompatibility between the protection of domestic production and encouraging industry to export. As profit margins on
foreign sales, which face fierce competition, are lower than those
on domestic sales, which are sheltered from competitive imports,
maintaining substantial protection means that industrial capital
and enterprise will inevitably be lured towards the more rewarding,

and less demanding, internal market, weakening the commitment to export growth.

In contemporary capitalist South-East Asia that domestic consensus, the growth coalition, has often been undermined. In some states the commitment to rapid industrialization has been weakened by other ambitions. In Malaysia, although the government has long pursued rapid industrial growth, since the early 1970s it has been at least equally concerned with the redistribution of wealth and economic power in favour of the Malays. This has involved placing restrictions on Malaysian Chinese entrepreneurs, the most powerful element within the local capitalist class, so inhibiting, it has been argued, the drive for rapid growth. One Malaysian scholar has suggested that 'ethnic obsessions may have undermined the most feasible and viable options for industrialisation under domestic auspices' (Jomo, 1993: 297). In Indonesia the pursuit of rapid industrial growth has been checked by a considerable ambivalence towards capitalism and the profit-motive, a suspicion of market-forces and foreign intrusion, in part a legacy of fierce political and ideological struggles in the 1950s and early 1960s. A final factor is the continued presence of political and business interests determined to maintain protection and privilege. Those interests remain particularly strong in the Philippines, where the mutually protecting power of political–business élites, richly enhanced during a lengthy period of import-substitution industrialization from the 1950s, has proved to be extremely difficult to confront.

All this suggests, rather obviously, that domestic circumstances are more favourable in some countries than in others. Thailand may be better placed than most: there is considerable political and business élite cohesion and consensus, apparently undisturbed by frequent coups; the Chinese business class is well integrated into the political, social, and economic order, so that questions about the distribution of the rewards from rapid industrial growth have not had a damaging ethnic dimension; economic nationalism has been markedly constrained in the modern period. This in turn suggests that the capitalist economies of South-East Asia may now be set on divergent paths, leading to sharper economic divisions within the region. Singapore's role as an advanced industrial–financial–trading fulcrum appears to be secure, below which might be arranged a hierarchy of greater and less sophisticated industrial economies.

SUGGESTED READING

This subject is comprehensively explored in Mohamed Ariff and
Hal Hill (1985), *Export-oriented Industrialisation: The ASEAN
Experience*, Sydney: Allen & Unwin, which provides thorough
economic analysis and a substantial body of statistical data. The
authors are strongly committed to free-market solutions, urging
deregulation and the removal of subsidies and protection. A highly
critical view of South-East Asia's modern industrial expansion,
focusing on the lack of an independent science and technology
base and on the alleged preference of local capitalists for short-
term speculative ventures ahead of serious industrial initiatives, is
provided by Yoshihara Kunio (1988), *The Rise of Ersatz Capitalism
in South-East Asia*, Singapore: Oxford University Press. A pen-
etrating review of this book by Richard Robison (1989) appeared
in the *Bulletin of Indonesian Economic Studies*, 25(1): 119–24. Many
of Yoshihara's views are also voiced, in a very lively manner, in
James Clad (1989), *Behind the Myth: Business, Money and Power in
Southeast Asia*, London: Unwin Hyman.

The political dimensions of rapid economic growth in modern
South-East Asia are considered in a number of publications.
In a valuable essay, Ruth McVey (1992), 'The Materialization
of the Southeast Asian Entrepreneur', in Ruth McVey (ed.),
Southeast Asian Capitalists, Southeast Asia Program, Ithaca:
Cornell University, pp. 7–33, points to the emergence of new
entrepreneurial attitudes and business values among political
and bureaucratic élites in many parts of modern South-East
Asia, as a vital element in the region's economic transformation.
J. A. C. Mackie (1988), 'Economic Growth in the ASEAN Region:
The Political Underpinnings', in Helen Hughes (ed.), *Achieving
Industrialization in East Asia*, Cambridge: Cambridge University
Press, pp. 283–326, in reviewing the experience of Thailand, the
Philippines, Indonesia, Malaysia, and Singapore, argues that the
forging of an élite consensus on the principal objectives of economic policy, the creation of a growth coalition, appears to be 'a
crucially important condition of successful economic performance'
(p. 325). It should be added that in Thailand, Malaysia, Indonesia,
and the Philippines, Mackie finds none of the 'single-minded drive
towards maximizing growth, raising productivity all round and
eliminating inefficiencies' so prominent in the NICs (p. 324). A
useful survey of the principal political economy approaches to
understanding economic change in contemporary South-East Asia

is provided by Richard F. Doner (1991), 'Approaches to the Politics of Economic Growth in Southeast Asia', *Journal of Asian Studies*, 50(4): 818–49.

Two related volumes of essays offer valuable radical critiques of contemporary economic change in the region: Richard Higgott and Richard Robison (eds.) (1985), *Southeast Asia: Essays in the Political Economy of Structural Change*, London: Routledge & Kegan Paul; and Richard Robison, Kevin Hewison, and Richard Higgott (eds.) (1987), *Southeast Asia in the 1980s: The Politics of Economic Crisis*, Sydney: Allen & Unwin. Finally there are a number of excellent country volumes: Jomo K. S. (ed.) (1993), *Industrialising Malaysia: Policy, Performance, Prospects*, London: Routledge; Peter G. Warr (ed.) (1993), *The Thai Economy in Transition*, Cambridge: Cambridge University Press; Medhi Krongkaew (ed.) (1995), *Thailand's Industrialization and Its Consequences*, London: Macmillan; Yoshihara Kunio (1994), *The Nation and Economic Growth: The Philippines and Thailand*, Kuala Lumpur: Oxford University Press; Anne Booth (ed.) (1992), *The Oil Boom and After: Indonesian Economic Policy and Performance in the Soeharto Era*, Singapore: Oxford University Press; Richard Robison (1986), *Indonesia: The Rise of Capital*, Southeast Asia Publication Series No. 13, Sydney: Allen & Unwin/Asian Studies Association of Australia; W. G. Huff (1994), *The Economic Growth of Singapore: Trade and Development in the Twentieth Century*, Cambridge: Cambridge University Press, Chapter 11.

19
Conclusion: Two Perspectives

THESE final pages explore two perspectives on economic change in South-East Asia in the modern period. The first is best introduced by means of a question. In what respects is the modern economic history of South-East Asia distinctive, compared with the modern economic history of other parts of Asia, or other parts of the non-European world as a whole? This is a variation on an old question. In what respects is South-East Asia a distinct region—what, if anything, unites Myanmar (Burma), Thailand, Laos, Cambodia, Vietnam, Malaysia, Singapore, Brunei, Indonesia, and the Philippines, and distinguishes them, *as a group*, from the rest of Asia? The stock answer usually involves reference to such features as social structure, political organization, religious practice, linguistic grouping. Here the focus is on economic experience.

The question above can be placed in another context. In what respects is the modern economic history of South-East Asia distinctive in relation to the region's earlier economic past? This involves a return to the central issue which underlay the discussion in the first chapter: to what extent, and in what respects, is there continuity between the early modern and modern economic histories of South-East Asia?

In terms of economic structure, the distinctiveness of South-East Asia lay, and lies, in two directions. First, throughout its history the region has been critically involved in long-distance maritime trade. At heart this is a reflection of the region's physical geography, a fragmented land mass penetrated by the sea, astride the main sea routes between China and Japan to the east, and India, the Middle East, and Europe to the west. As even a hurried glance at a map makes clear, there are relatively few parts of South-East Asia's great southern arc, stretching down the Malay Peninsula through the archipelago to the Philippine Islands, which are far from the sea. Even before the development of the railway and the macadam road, the bulk of that area had access to the sea, by rivers which ran off central mountain ranges, through lowlands to the coast. In mainland South-East Asia too, the major rivers—the Irrawaddy, the Chao Phraya, the Mekong, and the Red River—each with extensive tributary networks, brought vast interiors close to the sea and to the world that lay beyond. An important part of this argument is the fact that, in almost all circumstances and in almost all periods, water has provided the cheapest, frequently the only, means to transport large bulk/low value commodities such as rice, textiles, or sugar on a large scale, and until the development of rail, road, and then air transport in the twentieth century, often the most secure way to move substantial volumes of high value articles over long distances, although piracy was a considerable problem until recent times. Over the centuries, the proximity of the sea has drawn South-East Asia into long-distance trade on a dramatic scale.

As a result, the rhythm of economic life in South-East Asia has, in the main, been externally driven. When the world economy has enjoyed sustained growth—the boom of the long sixteenth century, the extraordinary expansion of the industrial–imperial age from the middle of the nineteenth century, the post-war Asian economic boom, driven principally by Japan's arrival as an economic super-power—South-East Asia has experienced impressive expansion. When the world economy has undergone sustained contraction—the crisis of the seventeenth century—its prosperity has disintegrated. South-East Asia has been, and remains, remarkably open to the stimuli and crises of the world economy.

The other economic characteristic which defines South-East Asia is the presence of extremely powerful immigrant commercial minorities, principally Indians and, of course, the Chinese. Throughout the early modern and modern periods, the commercial Chinese, in the roles of moneylender, trader, port-official, merchant, revenue-farmer, banker, industrialist, were frequently the crucial driving force determining the pace and nature of economic change in the region, in ways which have been made clear in almost every chapter in this book. The contribution of the Chinese here lay not only in their numerical strength. More important was the fact that, in general, the immigrant entrepreneurial classes were left relatively unhindered by the state in the pursuit of their commercial ambitions. Indeed the state in South-East Asia has regularly used the immigrant commercial minorities to advance its interests: Chinese merchant-officials conducted the foreign trade of the traditional courts; Chinese revenue-farmers collected a major part of the revenues of the colonial state until the early twentieth century; and Chinese capitalists, commonly in close alliance with state interests, have been at the heart of South-East Asia's modern industrialization. The influence of the Chinese commercial communities was also a reflection of their organizational structure. Each substantial commercial concern was part of a network, built upon kin, clan, or dialect ties, which commonly embraced the major commercial centres of South-East Asia and southern China. In the conduct of regional trade, in raising capital, in pooling managerial experience, these networks were a source of very considerable strength for the Chinese.

In seeking the distinguishing features of the South-East Asian economy, an answer may also have been provided to the question, to what extent was there continuity between the early modern and modern periods in the region's economic history? The two features above—the extensive involvement in long-distance trade and the presence of remarkably powerful immigrant commercial communities—were fully evident in both periods. They were more pronounced in the nineteenth and twentieth centuries than they had been in the sixteenth to the eighteenth: but this was only a matter of degree, not a change of direction. Two brief examples will illustrate the point. In committing himself to specialized production for external markets, the late nineteenth-century South-East Asian cultivator was not embarking on a new form of economic activity, making a decisive break with the past, but simply doing on a much larger scale what he, or she, had always done. In the early modern period, individuals and communities had commonly practised a marked degree of occupational and crop specialization, produced surpluses, and exchanged and sold in both local and distant markets. In the modern period, they merely seized the opportunity to serve larger markets on a larger scale, to exploit more thoroughly the advantages of specialization. Again, when the modern Chinese entrepreneur builds his industrial/financial empire by bargaining monopoly advantages from state managers, in essence he, or she, is behaving no differently than the late nineteenth-century Chinese revenue-farmer or the sixteenth-century court-trader, although almost certainly to greater effect.

The second perspective on South-East Asia's modern economic history is a personal one. When I first began studying the subject, as a postgraduate student in London at the end of the 1960s, in large part the scholarly literature portrayed the region's modern economic experience as a series of failures. Decades of colonial rule had condemned each of the economies of South-East Asia to an extreme dependence on the export of just one or two primary commodities, on increasingly disadvantageous terms. They had been left with little prospect of significant structural change. Large sectors of export production in South-East Asia had been overwhelmingly the preserve of Western capital, which had drained vast profits from the region while conferring little benefit on local factors: for example, it had been common for Western companies to recruit immigrant, not local, labour, whose earnings too, although miserably low, had been largely repatriated. Local agriculturists had been held in a fierce grip by the rapacious Chinese moneylender and middleman, who, once again, had remitted huge profits from the region. Colonial rule had impoverished South-East Asians, dramatically so in Java, by that classic instrument of colonial exploitation, the Cultivation System.

The tone of the present book has been very different. It has stressed the sharp responsiveness of the South-East Asian cultivator to rapidly expanding market opportunities. It has suggested that for substantial numbers of the rural population, close engagement in the world economy brought improvement in material welfare, at least through to the 1920s. The Cultivation System, it is now claimed, led to a marked expansion and diversification of economic opportunity for many poor rural Javanese. Even the depression decade of the 1930s has been portrayed, for certain classes, as a period not of crisis but of opportunity. And perhaps most dramatically, the Chinese commercial minority has been presented not as a rapacious drain but as a uniquely powerful driving force in economic change: in Ruth McVey's marvellous phrase, the Chinese entrepreneur has been transformed from 'pariah to paragon' (McVey, 1992).

There is nothing disturbing in this radical change of focus. All written history reflects the circumstances and concerns of the time in which it is written, and there is little doubt that the extraordinary pace of economic change in South-East Asia since the 1960s, together with substantial shifts in our understanding of the processes of economic change in historical perspective, has profoundly influenced the way in which this modern economic history of the region has been written. It was therefore inevitable that the harsh elements in the economic experience of South-East Asia since the early nineteenth century—the widespread poverty, inequality, exploitation, and oppression—were played down or ignored here. But perhaps it is also inevitable that, should the late twentieth-century South-East Asian economic transformation falter or fail, the next generation of economic historians of the region will once again focus on that dark side.

Bibliography

Adas, Michael (1974), *The Burma Delta: Economic Development and Social Change on an Asian Rice Frontier, 1852–1941*, Madison: University of Wisconsin Press.

_____ (1979), *Prophets of Rebellion: Millenarian Protest Movements against the European Colonial Order*, Chapel Hill: University of North Carolina Press.

Alatas, Syed Hussein (1977), *The Myth of the Lazy Native: A Study of the Image of the Malays, Filipinos and Javanese from the 16th to the 20th Century and Its Function in the Ideology of Colonial Capitalism*, London: Frank Cass.

Alexander, Paul (1984), 'Women, Labour and Fertility: Population Growth in Nineteenth Century Java', *Mankind*, 14(5): 361–72.

Arasaratnam, Sinnappah (1979), *Indians in Malaysia and Singapore*, rev. edn., Kuala Lumpur: Oxford University Press.

Aung Tun Thet (1989), *Burmese Entrepreneurship: Creative Response in the Colonial Economy*, Stuttgart: Steiner Verlag Wiesbaden GMBH.

Badriyah Haji Salleh (1985), 'Malay Rubber Smallholding and British Policy: A Case Study of the Batang Padang District in Perak (1876–1952)', Ph.D. dissertation, Columbia University.

Barker, Randolph (1982), 'Recent Trends in Labour Utilization and Productivity in Philippine Agriculture (with Comparisons to other Asian Experiences)', in Geoffrey B. Hainsworth (ed.), *Village-level Modernization in Southeast Asia: The Political Economy of Rice and Water*, Vancouver: University of British Columbia Press, pp. 141–72.

Barker, Randolph and Herdt, Robert W., with Beth Rose (1985), *The Rice Economy of Asia*, Washington, DC: Resources for the Future.

Barlow, Colin (1978), *The Natural Rubber Industry: Its Development, Technology, and Economy in Malaysia*, Kuala Lumpur: Oxford University Press.

Bassford, John Louis (1984), 'Land Development Policy in Cochinchina under the French (1865–1925)', Ph.D. dissertation, University of Hawaii.

Bauer, P. T. (1948), *The Rubber Industry: A Study in Competition and Monopoly*, London: Longmans, Green.

Bell, Peter F. (1970), *The Historical Determinants of Underdevelopment in Thailand*, Economic Growth Center, Discussion Paper No. 84, New Haven: Yale University.

Beresford, Melanie (1985), 'Household and Collective in Vietnamese Agriculture', *Journal of Contemporary Asia*, 15(1): 5–36.

Boomgaard, Peter (1981), 'Female Labour and Population Growth on Nineteenth-century Java', *Review of Indonesian and Malaysian Affairs*, 15(2): 1–31.

―――― (1987), 'Morbidity and Mortality in Java, 1820–1880: Changing Patterns of Disease and Death', in Norman G. Owen (ed.), *Death and Disease in Southeast Asia: Explorations in Social, Medical and Demographic History*, Southeast Asia Publication Series No. 14, Singapore: Oxford University Press/Asian Studies Association of Australia, pp. 48–69.

―――― (1988), 'Treacherous Cane: The Java Sugar Industry between 1914 and 1940', in Bill Albert and Adrian Graves (eds.), *The World Sugar Economy in War and Depression, 1914–40*, London: Routledge, pp. 157–69.

―――― (1989), *Children of the Colonial State: Population Growth and Economic Development in Java, 1795–1880*, Centre for Asian Studies Amsterdam, Monograph No. 1, Amsterdam: Free University Press.

―――― (1990), 'Why Work for Wages? Free Labour in Java, 1600–1900', *Economic and Social History in the Netherlands*, 2: 37–56.

―――― (1991a), 'The Javanese Village as a Cheshire Cat: The Java Debate against a European and Latin American Background', *Journal of Peasant Studies*, 18(2): 288–304.

―――― (1991b), 'The Non-agricultural Side of an Agricultural Economy, Java, 1500–1900', in Paul Alexander, Peter Boomgaard, and Ben White (eds.), *In the Shadow of Agriculture: Non-farm Activities in the Javanese Economy, Past and Present*, Amsterdam: Royal Tropical Institute, pp. 14–40.

Booth, Anne (1988a), *Agricultural Development in Indonesia*, Southeast Asia Publication Series No. 16, Sydney: Allen & Unwin/Asian Studies Association of Australia.

―――― (1988b), 'Living Standards and the Distribution of Income in Colonial Indonesia: A Review of the Evidence', *Journal of Southeast Asian Studies*, 19(2): 310–34.

―――― (1991a), 'The Economic Development of Southeast Asia: 1870–1985', *Australian Economic History Review*, 31(1): 20–52.

―――― (1991b), 'Regional Aspects of Indonesian Agricultural Growth', in Joan Hardjono (ed.), *Indonesia: Resources, Ecology, and Environment*, Singapore: Oxford University Press, pp. 36–60.

―――― (ed.) (1992), *The Oil Boom and After: Indonesian Economic Policy and Performance in the Soeharto Era*, Singapore: Oxford University Press.

―――― (1994), 'Japanese Import Penetration and Dutch Response: Some Aspects of Economic Policy Making in Colonial Indonesia', in

Sugiyama Shinya and Milagros C. Guerrero (eds.), *International Commercial Rivalry in Southeast Asia in the Interwar Period*, Southeast Asia Studies, Monograph No. 39, New Haven: Yale University, pp. 133–64.

Bose, Swadesh R. (1982), 'Has Economic Growth Immiserized the Rural Poor in Indonesia? A Review of Conflicting Evidence', in Geoffrey B. Hainsworth (ed.), *Village-level Modernization in Southeast Asia: The Political Economy of Rice and Water*, Vancouver: University of British Columbia Press, pp. 53–69.

Breman, Jan (1982), 'The Village on Java and the Early-Colonial State', *Journal of Peasant Studies*, 9(4): 189–240.

———(1988), *The Shattered Image: Construction and Deconstruction of the Village in Colonial Asia*, Centre for Asian Studies Amsterdam, Comparative Asian Studies, No. 2, Dordrecht: Foris Publications.

Brocheux, Pierre (1995), *The Mekong Delta: Ecology, Economy, and Revolution, 1860–1960*, Center for Southeast Asian Studies, Monograph No. 12, Madison: University of Wisconsin-Madison.

Brown, Ian (1986), 'Rural Distress in Southeast Asia during the World Depression of the Early 1930s: A Preliminary Reexamination', *Journal of Asian Studies*, 45(5): 995–1025.

———(1988), *The Élite and the Economy in Siam, c.1890–1920*, Singapore: Oxford University Press.

——— (1989), 'Some Comments on Industrialisation in the Philippines during the 1930s', in Ian Brown (ed.), *The Economies of Africa and Asia in the Inter-War Depression*, London: Routledge, pp. 203–20.

——— (1992), *The Creation of the Modern Ministry of Finance in Siam, 1885–1910*, London: Macmillan.

Brown, Rajeswary Ampalavanar (1994), *Capital and Entrepreneurship in South-East Asia*, London: Macmillan.

Bùi Minh Dũng (1995), 'Japan's Role in the Vietnamese Starvation of 1944–45', *Modern Asian Studies*, 29(3): 573–618.

Butcher, John G. (1979), *The British in Malaya, 1880–1941: The Social History of a European Community in Colonial South-East Asia*, Kuala Lumpur: Oxford University Press.

———(1983), 'The Demise of the Revenue Farm System in the Federated Malay States', *Modern Asian Studies*, 17(3): 387–412.

——— (1993), 'Revenue Farming and the Changing State in Southeast Asia', in John Butcher and Howard Dick (eds.), *The Rise and Fall of Revenue Farming: Business Élites and the Emergence of the Modern State in Southeast Asia*, London: Macmillan, pp. 19–44.

Butcher, John and Dick, Howard (eds.) (1993), *The Rise and Fall of Revenue Farming: Business Élites and the Emergence of the Modern State in Southeast Asia*, London: Macmillan.

Byres, T. J. (1981), 'The New Technology, Class Formation and Class Action in the Indian Countryside', *Journal of Peasant Studies*, 8(4): 405–54.

Byres, T. J. and Crow, Ben, with Ho Mae Wan (1983), *The Green Revolution in India*, U204 Third World Studies, Case Study 5, Milton Keynes: Open University Press.

Caldwell, J. A. M. (1964), 'Indonesian Export and Production from the Decline of the Culture System to the First World War', in C. D. Cowan (ed.), *The Economic Development of South-East Asia: Studies in Economic History and Political Economy*, London: George Allen & Unwin, pp. 72–101.

Chakravarti, Nalini Ranjan (1971), *The Indian Minority in Burma: The Rise and Decline of an Immigrant Community*, London: Oxford University Press.

Chambers, Robert (1984), 'Beyond the Green Revolution: A Selective Essay', in Tim P. Bayliss-Smith and Sudhir Wanmali (eds.), *Understanding Green Revolutions: Agrarian Change and Development Planning in South Asia*, Cambridge: Cambridge University Press, pp. 362–79.

Changing Economy in Indonesia: A Selection of Statistical Source Material from the Early 19th Century up to 1940, initiated by W. M. F. Mansvelt, continued by P. Creutzberg, and edited by Peter Boomgaard, Amsterdam: Royal Tropical Institute.

———, Vol. 1, 1975, *Indonesia's Export Crops, 1816–1940*, initiated by W. M. F. Mansvelt, re-edited and continued by P. Creutzberg, The Hague: Martinus Nijhoff.

———, Vol. 2, 1976, *Public Finance, 1816–1939*, initiated by W. M. F. Mansvelt, re-edited and continued by P. Creutzberg, The Hague: Martinus Nijhoff.

———, Vol. 3, 1977, *Expenditure on Fixed Assets*, initiated by W. M. F. Mansvelt, re-edited and continued by P. Creutzberg, The Hague: Martinus Nijhoff.

———, Vol. 4, 1978, *Rice Prices*, initiated by W. M. F. Mansvelt, re-edited and continued by P. Creutzberg, The Hague: Martinus Nijhoff.

———, Vol. 5, 1979, *National Income*, initiated by W. M. F. Mansvelt, re-edited and continued by P. Creutzberg, The Hague: Martinus Nijhoff.

———, Vol. 6, 1980, *Money and Banking, 1816–1940*, edited by J. T. M. van Laanen, The Hague: Martinus Nijhoff.

———, Vol. 7, 1987, *Balance of Payments, 1822–1939*, edited by W. L. Korthals Altes, Amsterdam: Royal Tropical Institute.

———, Vol. 8, 1987, *Manufacturing Industry, 1870–1942*, edited by W. A. I. M. Segers, Amsterdam: Royal Tropical Institute.

———, Vol. 9, 1989, *Transport, 1819–1940*, edited by Gerrit J. Knaap, Amsterdam: Royal Tropical Institute.

———, Vol. 10, 1990, *Food Crops and Arable Lands: Java, 1815–1942*, edited by P. Boomgaard and J. L. van Zanden, Amsterdam: Royal Tropical Institute.

———, Vol. 11, 1991, *Population Trends, 1795–1942*, edited by P. Boomgaard and A. J. Gooszen, Amsterdam: Royal Tropical Institute.

_____, Vol. 12a, 1991, *General Trade Statistics, 1822–1940*, edited by W. L. Korthals Altes, Amsterdam: Royal Tropical Institute.

_____, Vol. 12b, 1992, *Regional Patterns in Foreign Trade, 1911–1940*, Adrian Clemens, J. Thomas Lindblad, and Jeroen Touwen, Amsterdam: Royal Tropical Institute.

_____, Vol. 13, 1992, *Wages, 1820–1940*, edited by Nico Dros, Amsterdam: Royal Tropical Institute.

_____, Vol. 14, 1993, *The Cultivation System: Java, 1834–1880*, edited by Frans van Baardewijk, Amsterdam: Royal Tropical Institute.

Chatthip Nartsupha and Suthy Prasartset (1978), *The Political Economy of Siam, 1851–1910*, Bangkok: Social Science Association of Thailand.

Chatthip Nartsupha, Suthy Prasartset, and Montri Chenvidyakarn (1978), *The Political Economy of Siam, 1910–1932*, Bangkok: Social Science Association of Thailand.

Cheng Siok-Hwa (1968), *The Rice Industry of Burma, 1852–1940*, Kuala Lumpur: University of Malaya Press.

Clad, James (1989), *Behind the Myth: Business, Money and Power in Southeast Asia*, London: Unwin Hyman.

Cordova, Violeta G. (1982), 'New Rice Technology and Its Effect on Labour Use and Shares in Rice Production in Laguna, Philippines, 1966–78', in Geoffrey B. Hainsworth (ed.), *Village-level Modernization in Southeast Asia: The Political Economy of Rice and Water*, Vancouver: University of British Columbia Press, pp. 191–206.

Day, Clive (1966), *The Policy and Administration of the Dutch in Java*, Kuala Lumpur: Oxford University Press; first published in 1904.

Dhiravat na Pombejra (1993), 'Ayutthaya at the End of the Seventeenth Century: Was There a Shift to Isolation?', in Anthony Reid (ed.), *Southeast Asia in the Early Modern Era: Trade, Power, and Belief*, Ithaca: Cornell University Press, pp. 250–72.

Dick, Howard (1989), 'Japan's Economic Expansion in the Netherlands Indies between the First and Second World Wars', *Journal of Southeast Asian Studies*, 20(2): 244–72.

_____ (1993), 'A Fresh Approach to Southeast Asian History', in John Butcher and Howard Dick (eds.), *The Rise and Fall of Revenue Farming: Business Élites and the Emergence of the Modern State in Southeast Asia*, London: Macmillan, pp. 3–18.

Dixon, Chris (1991), *South East Asia in the World-Economy*, Cambridge: Cambridge University Press.

Doeppers, Daniel F. (1991), 'Metropolitan Manila in the Great Depression: Crisis for Whom?', *Journal of Asian Studies*, 50(3): 511–35.

Doner, Richard F. (1991), 'Approaches to the Politics of Economic Growth in Southeast Asia', *Journal of Asian Studies*, 50(4): 818–49.

Drabble, John H. (1973), *Rubber in Malaya, 1876–1922: The Genesis of the Industry*, Kuala Lumpur: Oxford University Press.

_____ (1991), *Malayan Rubber: The Interwar Years*, London: Macmillan.

Elson, R. E. (1978), *The Cultivation System and 'Agricultural Involution'*,

Centre of Southeast Asian Studies, Working Paper No. 14, Melbourne: Monash University.

_____ (1984), *Javanese Peasants and the Colonial Sugar Industry: Impact and Change in an East Java Residency, 1830–1940*, Southeast Asia Publication Series No. 9, Singapore: Oxford University Press/Asian Studies Association of Australia.

_____ (1985), 'The Famine in Demak and Grobogan in 1849–50: Its Causes and Circumstances', *Review of Indonesian and Malaysian Affairs*, 19(1): 39–85.

_____ (1986a), 'Aspects of Peasant Life in Early 19th Century Java', in David P. Chandler and M. C. Ricklefs (eds.), *Nineteenth and Twentieth Century Indonesia: Essays in Honour of Professor J. D. Legge*, Centre of Southeast Asian Studies, Clayton: Monash University, pp. 57–81.

_____ (1986b), 'Sugar Factory Workers and the Emergence of "Free Labour" in Nineteenth-century Java', *Modern Asian Studies*, 20(1): 139–74.

_____ (1989), 'The Mobilization and Control of Peasant Labour under the Early Cultivation System in Java', in R. J. May and William J. O'Malley (eds.), *Observing Change in Asia: Essays in Honour of J. A. C. Mackie*, Bathurst: Crawford House Press, pp. 73–93.

_____ (1990), 'Peasant Poverty and Prosperity under the Cultivation System in Java', in Anne Booth, W. J. O'Malley, and Anna Weidemann (eds.), *Indonesian Economic History in the Dutch Colonial Era*, Southeast Asia Studies, Monograph No. 35, New Haven: Yale University, pp. 24–48.

_____ (1994), *Village Java under the Cultivation System, 1830–1870*, Southeast Asia Publication Series No. 25, Sydney: Allen and Unwin/ Asian Studies Association of Australia.

Falkus, Malcolm (1991), 'The Economic History of Thailand', *Australian Economic History Review*, 31(1): 53–71.

Fasseur, C. (1978), 'Some Remarks on the Cultivation System in Java', *Acta Historiae Neerlandicae*, 10: 143–62.

_____ (1986), 'The Cultivation System and Its Impact on the Dutch Colonial Economy and the Indigenous Society in Nineteenth-century Java', in C. A. Bayly and D. H. A. Kolff (eds.), *Two Colonial Empires: Comparative Essays on the History of India and Indonesia in the Nineteenth Century*, Dordrecht: Martinus Nijhoff, pp. 137–54.

_____ (1991), 'Purse or Principle: Dutch Colonial Policy in the 1860s and the Decline of the Cultivation System', *Modern Asian Studies*, 25(1): 33–52.

Fast, Jonathan and Richardson, Jim (1979), *Roots of Dependency: Political and Economic Revolution in 19th Century Philippines*, Quezon City: Foundation for Nationalist Studies.

Feeny, David (1979), 'Competing Hypotheses of Underdevelopment: A Thai Case Study', *Journal of Economic History*, 39(1): 113–27.

_____ (1982), *The Political Economy of Productivity: Thai Agricultural Development, 1880–1975*, Vancouver: University of British Columbia Press.

_____ (1993), 'The Demise of Corvée and Slavery in Thailand, 1782–1913', in Martin A. Klein (ed.), *Breaking the Chains: Slavery, Bondage, and Emancipation in Modern Africa and Asia*, Madison: University of Wisconsin Press, pp. 83–111.

Fegan, Brian (1982), 'The Social History of a Central Luzon Barrio', in Alfred W. McCoy and Ed. C. de Jesus (eds.), *Philippine Social History: Global Trade and Local Transformations*, Quezon City: Ateneo de Manila University Press; Sydney: George Allen & Unwin, pp. 91–129.

Fernando, M. R. (1986), 'Dynamics of Peasant Economy in Java at Local Levels', in David P. Chandler and M. C. Ricklefs (eds.), *Nineteenth and Twentieth Century Indonesia: Essays in Honour of Professor J. D. Legge*, Centre of Southeast Asian Studies, Clayton: Monash University, pp. 97–121.

Fernando, Radin (1980), *Famine in Cirebon Residency in Java, 1844–1850: A New Perspective on the Cultivation System*, Centre of Southeast Asian Studies, Working Paper No. 21, Clayton: Monash University.

Fforde, Adam (1989), *The Agrarian Question in North Vietnam, 1974–1979: A Study of Cooperator Resistance to State Policy*, Armonk, NY: M. E. Sharpe.

Fforde, Adam and Paine, Suzanne H. (1987), *The Limits of National Liberation: Problems of Economic Management in the Democratic Republic of Vietnam, with a Statistical Appendix*, London: Croom Helm.

Fisher, Charles A. (1964), 'Some Comments on Population Growth in South-East Asia, with Special Reference to the Period since 1830', in C. D. Cowan (ed.), *The Economic Development of South-East Asia: Studies in Economic History and Political Economy*, London: George Allen & Unwin, pp. 48–71.

Fox, James J. (1991), 'Managing the Ecology of Rice Production in Indonesia', in Joan Hardjono (ed.), *Indonesia: Resources, Ecology, and Environment*, Singapore: Oxford University Press, pp. 61–84.

Freedman, Maurice (1959), 'The Handling of Money: A Note on the Background to the Economic Sophistication of Overseas Chinese', *Man*, 59(89): 64–5.

Furnivall, J. S. (1939), *Netherlands India: A Study of Plural Economy*, Cambridge: Cambridge University Press.

_____ (1948), *Colonial Policy and Practice: A Comparative Study of Burma and Netherlands India*, Cambridge: Cambridge University Press.

Gardiner, Peter and Oey, Mayling (1987), 'Morbidity and Mortality in Java, 1880–1940: The Evidence of the Colonial Reports', in Norman G. Owen (ed.), *Death and Disease in Southeast Asia: Explorations in Social, Medical and Demographic History*, Southeast Asia Publication Series No. 14, Singapore: Oxford University Press/Asian Studies Association of Australia, pp. 70–90.

Geertz, Clifford (1956), 'Religious Belief and Economic Behavior in a Central Javanese Town: Some Preliminary Considerations', *Economic Development and Cultural Change*, 4: 134–58.

———— (1963), *Agricultural Involution: The Processes of Ecological Change in Indonesia*, Berkeley: University of California Press.

———— (1984), 'Culture and Social Change: The Indonesian Case', *Man*, New Series, 19(4): 511–32.

Gran, Guy (1975), 'Vietnam and the Capitalist Route to Modernity: Village Cochinchina, 1880–1940', Ph.D. dissertation, University of Wisconsin-Madison.

Hanks, Lucien M. (1972), *Rice and Man: Agricultural Ecology in Southeast Asia*, Chicago: Aldine.

Hewison, Kevin (1989), *Bankers and Bureaucrats: Capital and the Role of the State in Thailand*, Southeast Asia Studies, Monograph No. 34, New Haven: Yale University.

Higgott, Richard and Robison, Richard (eds.) (1985), *Southeast Asia: Essays in the Political Economy of Structural Change*, London: Routledge & Kegan Paul.

Hill, Hal (1993), *Southeast Asian Economic Development: An Analytical Survey*, Research School of Pacific Studies, Economics Division, Working Paper, Canberra: Australian National University.

Hill, Hal and Jayasuriya, Sisira (1986), *An Inward-looking Economy in Transition: Economic Development in Burma since the 1960s*, Occasional Paper No. 80, Singapore: Institute of Southeast Asian Studies.

Hirschman, Charles (1994), 'Population and Society in Twentieth-century Southeast Asia', *Journal of Southeast Asian Studies*, 25(2): 381–416.

Huff, W. G. (1994), *The Economic Growth of Singapore: Trade and Development in the Twentieth Century*, Cambridge: Cambridge University Press.

Hugo, Graeme J.; Hull, Terence H.; Hull, Valerie J.; and Jones, Gavin W. (1987), *The Demographic Dimension in Indonesian Development*, Singapore: Oxford University Press.

Ingleson, John (1988), 'Urban Java during the Depression', *Journal of Southeast Asian Studies*, 19(2): 292–309.

Ingram, James C. (1964), 'Thailand's Rice Trade and the Allocation of Resources', in C. D. Cowan (ed.), *The Economic Development of South-East Asia: Studies in Economic History and Political Economy*, London: George Allen & Unwin, pp. 102–26.

———— (1971), *Economic Change in Thailand, 1850–1970*, Stanford: Stanford University Press.

Ishak Shari and Jomo Kwame Sundaram (1982), 'Malaysia's Green Revolution in Rice Farming: Capital Accumulation and Technological Change in a Peasant Society', in Geoffrey B. Hainsworth (ed.), *Village-level Modernization in Southeast Asia: The Political Economy of Rice and Water*, Vancouver: University of British Columbia Press, pp. 225–54.

Jennings, Peter R. (1976), 'The Amplification of Agricultural Production', *Scientific American*, 235(3): 181–94.

de Jesus, Ed. C. (1980), *The Tobacco Monopoly in the Philippines: Bureaucratic Enterprise and Social Change, 1766–1880*, Quezon City: Ateneo de Manila University Press.

Johnston, David Bruce (1975), 'Rural Society and the Rice Economy in Thailand, 1880–1930', Ph.D. dissertation, Yale University.

_____ (1976), 'Opening a Frontier: The Expansion of Rice Cultivation in Central Thailand in the 1890s', *Contributions to Asian Studies*, 9: 27–44.

Jomo Kwame Sundaram (1986), *A Question of Class: Capital, the State, and Uneven Development in Malaya*, Singapore: Oxford University Press.

_____ (ed.) (1993), *Industrialising Malaysia: Policy, Performance, Prospects*, London: Routledge.

Kathirithamby-Wells, Jeyamalar (1993), 'Restraints on the Development of Merchant Capitalism in Southeast Asia before *c*.1800', in Anthony Reid (ed.), *Southeast Asia in the Early Modern Era: Trade, Power, and Belief*, Ithaca: Cornell University Press, pp. 123–48.

Knight, G. R. (1982), 'Capitalism and Commodity Production in Java', in Hamza Alavi et al., *Capitalism and Colonial Production*, London: Croom Helm, pp. 119–58.

_____ (1988), 'Peasant Labour and Capitalist Production in Late Colonial Indonesia: The "Campaign" at a North Java Sugar Factory, 1840–70', *Journal of Southeast Asian Studies*, 19(2): 245–65.

_____ (1990), 'The Peasantry and the Cultivation of Sugar Cane in Nineteenth-century Java: A Study from Pekalongan Residency, 1830–1870', in Anne Booth, W. J. O'Malley, and Anna Weidemann (eds.), *Indonesian Economic History in the Dutch Colonial Era*, Southeast Asia Studies, Monograph No. 35, New Haven, Yale University, pp. 49–66.

Kratoska, Paul H. (1983), '"Ends That We Cannot Foresee": Malay Reservations in British Malaya', *Journal of Southeast Asian Studies*, 14(1): 149–68.

Larkin, John A. (1972), *The Pampangans: Colonial Society in a Philippine Province*, Berkeley: University of California Press.

_____ (1982), 'Philippine History Reconsidered: A Socioeconomic Perspective', *American Historical Review*, 87(3): 595–628.

_____ (1993), *Sugar and the Origins of Modern Philippine Society*, Berkeley: University of California Press.

Leiberman, Victor (1993), 'Was the Seventeenth Century a Watershed in Burmese History?', in Anthony Reid (ed.), *Southeast Asia in the Early Modern Era: Trade, Power, and Belief*, Ithaca: Cornell University Press, pp. 214–49.

Lim Chong-Yah (1967), *Economic Development of Modern Malaya*, Kuala Lumpur: Oxford University Press.

Lim, David (ed.) (1975), *Readings on Malaysian Economic Development*, Kuala Lumpur: Oxford University Press.

290   BIBLIOGRAPHY

Lim Teck Ghee (1977), *Peasants and Their Agricultural Economy in Colonial Malaya, 1874–1941*, Kuala Lumpur: Oxford University Press.

_____ (1984), 'British Colonial Administration and the "Ethnic Division of Labour" in Malaya', *Kajian Malaysia*, 2(2): 28–66.

Lipton, Michael, with Richard Longhurst (1989), *New Seeds and Poor People*, London: Unwin Hyman.

McCoy, Alfred W. (ed.) (1980), *Southeast Asia under Japanese Occupation*, Southeast Asia Studies, Monograph No. 22, New Haven: Yale University.

McCoy, Alfred W. and de Jesus, Ed. C. (eds.) (1982), *Philippine Social History: Global Trade and Local Transformations*, Quezon City: Ateneo de Manila University Press; Sydney: George Allen & Unwin.

MacIntyre, Andrew (1991), *Business and Politics in Indonesia*, Southeast Asia Publication Series No. 21, Sydney: Allen & Unwin/Asian Studies Association of Australia.

Mackie, J. A. C. (1988), 'Economic Growth in the ASEAN Region: The Political Underpinnings', in Helen Hughes (ed.), *Achieving Industrialization in East Asia*, Cambridge: Cambridge University Press, pp. 283–326.

McLennan, Marshall S. (1980), *The Central Luzon Plain: Land and Society on the Inland Frontier*, Quezon City: Alemar-Phoenix Publishing House.

_____ (1982), 'Changing Human Ecology on the Central Luzon Plain: Nueva Ecija, 1705–1939', in Alfred W. McCoy and Ed. C. de Jesus (eds.), *Philippine Social History: Global Trade and Local Transformations*, Quezon City: Ateneo de Manila University Press; Sydney: George Allen & Unwin, pp. 57–90.

McVey, Ruth (1992), 'The Materialization of the Southeast Asian Entrepreneur', in Ruth McVey (ed.), *Southeast Asian Capitalists*, Southeast Asia Program, Ithaca: Cornell University, pp. 7–33.

Mahathir bin Mohamad (1970), *The Malay Dilemma*, Singapore: Donald Moore for Asia Pacific Press.

Manning, Chris (1988), *The Green Revolution, Employment, and Economic Change in Rural Java: A Reassessment of Trends under the New Order*, ASEAN Economic Research Unit, Occasional Paper No. 84, Singapore: Institute of Southeast Asian Studies.

May, Glenn Anthony (1980), *Social Engineering in the Philippines: The Aims, Execution, and Impact of American Colonial Policy, 1900–1913*, Contributions in Comparative Colonial Studies No. 2, Westport: Greenwood Press.

Medhi Krongkaew (ed.) (1995), *Thailand's Industrialization and Its Consequences*, London: Macmillan.

Mohamed Ariff and Hill, Hal (1985) *Export-oriented Industrialisation: The ASEAN Experience*, Sydney: Allen & Unwin.

Moise, Edwin E. (1976), 'Land Reform and Land Reform Errors in North Vietnam', *Pacific Affairs*, 49(1): 70–92.

Murray, Martin J. (1980), *The Development of Capitalism in Colonial Indochina (1870–1940)*, Berkeley: University of California Press.

Mya Than and Tan, Joseph L. H. (eds.) (1990), *Myanmar, Dilemmas and Options: The Challenge of Economic Transition in the 1990s*, Singapore: Institute of Southeast Asian Studies, ASEAN Economic Research Unit.

Ngô Viñh Long (1973), *Before the Revolution: The Vietnamese Peasants under the French*, Cambridge, Mass.: MIT Press.

Nitisastro, Widjojo (1970), *Population Trends in Indonesia*, Ithaca: Cornell University Press.

Nørlund, Irene (1991), 'The French Empire, the Colonial State in Vietnam and Economic Policy: 1885–1940', *Australian Economic History Review*, 31(1): 72–89.

O'Malley, William Joseph (1977), 'Indonesia in the Great Depression: A Study of East Sumatra and Jogjakarta in the 1930's', Ph.D. dissertation, Cornell University.

Owen, Norman G. (1971a), 'Philippine Economic Development and American Policy: A Reappraisal', in Norman G. Owen (ed.), *Compadre Colonialism: Studies on the Philippines under American Rule*, Michigan Papers on South and Southeast Asia No. 3, Ann Arbor: University of Michigan, pp. 103–28.

────── (1971b), 'The Rice Industry of Mainland Southeast Asia 1850–1914', *Journal of the Siam Society*, 59(2): 75–143.

────── (1982), 'Abaca in Kabikolan: Prosperity without Progress', in Alfred W. McCoy and Ed. C. de Jesus (eds.), *Philippine Social History: Global Trade and Local Transformations*, Quezon City: Ateneo de Manila University Press; Sydney: George Allen & Unwin, pp. 191–216.

────── (1984), *Prosperity without Progress: Manila Hemp and Material Life in the Colonial Philippines*, Berkeley: University of California Press.

────── (ed.) (1987a), *Death and Disease in Southeast Asia: Explorations in Social, Medical and Demographic History*, Southeast Asia Publication Series No. 14, Singapore: Oxford University Press/Asian Studies Association of Australia.

────── (1987b), 'Measuring Mortality in the Nineteenth Century Philippines', in Norman G. Owen (ed.), *Death and Disease in Southeast Asia: Explorations in Social, Medical and Demographic History*, Southeast Asia Publication Series No. 14, Singapore: Oxford University Press/Asian Studies Association of Australia, pp. 91–114.

────── (1987c), 'The Paradox of Nineteenth-century Population Growth in Southeast Asia: Evidence from Java and the Philippines', *Journal of Southeast Asian Studies*, 18(1): 45–57.

────── (1987d), 'Toward a History of Health in Southeast Asia', in Norman G. Owen (ed.), *Death and Disease in Southeast Asia: Explorations in Social, Medical and Demographic History*, Southeast Asia Publication Series No. 14, Singapore: Oxford University Press/Asian Studies Association of Australia, pp. 3–30.

———— (1989), 'Subsistence in the Slump: Agricultural Adjustment in the Provincial Philippines', in Ian Brown (ed.), *The Economies of Africa and Asia in the Inter-War Depression*, London: Routledge, pp. 95–114.

———— (1992), 'Economic and Social Change', in Nicholas Tarling (ed.), *The Cambridge History of Southeast Asia*, Vol. 2, *The Nineteenth and Twentieth Centuries*, Cambridge: Cambridge University Press, pp. 467–527.

Parkinson, Brien K. (1967), 'Non-economic Factors in the Economic Retardation of the Rural Malays', *Modern Asian Studies*, 1(1): 31–46.

Pelzer, Karl J. (1978), *Planter and Peasant: Colonial Policy and the Agrarian Struggle in East Sumatra, 1863–1947*, 's-Gravenhage: Martinus Nijhoff.

Penders, Chr. L. M. (1977), *Indonesia: Selected Documents on Colonialism and Nationalism, 1830–1942*, St. Lucia: University of Queensland Press.

Peper, Bram (1970), 'Population Growth in Java in the 19th Century: A New Interpretation', *Population Studies*, 24(1): 71–84.

Popkin, Samuel L. (1979), *The Rational Peasant: The Political Economy of Rural Society in Vietnam*, Berkeley: University of California Press.

Post, Peter (1995), 'Chinese Business Networks and Japanese Capital in South East Asia, 1880–1940: Some Preliminary Observations', in Rajeswary Ampalavanar Brown (ed.), *Chinese Business Enterprise in Asia*, London: Routledge, pp. 154–76.

Purcell, Victor (1965), *The Chinese in Southeast Asia*, 2nd edn., London: Oxford University Press.

Purwanto, Bambang (1992), 'From Dusun to the Market: Native Rubber Cultivation in Southern Sumatra, 1890–1940', Ph.D. dissertation, University of London.

Rambo, A. Terry (1973), *A Comparison of Peasant Social Systems of Northern and Southern Viet-Nam: A Study of Ecological Adaptation, Social Succession, and Cultural Evolution*, Center for Vietnamese Studies, Monograph Series No. III, Carbondale: Southern Illinois University at Carbondale.

Reid, Anthony (1987), 'Low Population Growth and Its Causes in Pre-colonial Southeast Asia', in Norman G. Owen (ed.), *Death and Disease in Southeast Asia: Explorations in Social, Medical and Demographic History*, Southeast Asia Publication Series No. 14, Singapore: Oxford University Press/Asian Studies Association of Australia, pp. 33–47.

———— (1988), *Southeast Asia in the Age of Commerce, 1450–1680*, Vol. 1, *The Lands below the Winds*, New Haven: Yale University Press.

———— (1990a), 'An "Age of Commerce" in Southeast Asian History', *Modern Asian Studies*, 24(1): 1–30.

———— (1990b), 'The Seventeenth-century Crisis in Southeast Asia', *Modern Asian Studies*, 24(4): 639–59.

———— (1992), 'Economic and Social Change, c.1400–1800', in Nicholas Tarling (ed.), *The Cambridge History of Southeast Asia*, Vol. 1, *From Early Times to c.1800*, Cambridge: Cambridge University Press, pp. 460–507.

────── (1993a), *Southeast Asia in the Age of Commerce, 1450–1680*, Vol. 2, *Expansion and Crisis*, New Haven: Yale University Press.

────── (ed.) (1993b), *Southeast Asia in the Early Modern Era: Trade, Power, and Belief*, Ithaca: Cornell University Press.

Ricklefs, M. C. (1986), 'Some Statistical Evidence on Javanese Social, Economic and Demographic History in the Later Seventeenth and Eighteenth Centuries', *Modern Asian Studies*, 20(1): 1–32.

Rigg, Jonathan (1989), 'The New Rice Technology and Agrarian Change: Guilt by Association?', *Progress in Human Geography*, 13(3): 374–99.

────── (1991), *Southeast Asia: A Region in Transition: A Thematic Human Geography of the ASEAN Region*, London: Unwin Hyman.

Robequain, Charles (1944), *The Economic Development of French Indo-China*, London: Oxford University Press.

Robison, Richard (1986), *Indonesia: The Rise of Capital*, Southeast Asia Publication Series No. 13, Sydney: Allen & Unwin/Asian Studies Association of Australia.

Robison, Richard; Hewison, Kevin; and Higgott, Richard (eds.) (1987), *Southeast Asia in the 1980s: The Politics of Economic Crisis*, Sydney: Allen & Unwin.

Sandhu, Kernial Singh (1969), *Indians in Malaya: Some Aspects of Their Immigration and Settlement (1786–1957)*, Cambridge: Cambridge University Press.

Sansom, Robert L. (1970), *The Economics of Insurgency in the Mekong Delta of Vietnam*, Cambridge, Mass.: MIT Press.

Sato Shigeru (1994), *War, Nationalism and Peasants: Java under the Japanese Occupation, 1942–1945*, Southeast Asia Publication Series No. 26, Sydney: Allen & Unwin/Asian Studies Association of Australia.

Scott, James C. (1976), *The Moral Economy of the Peasant: Rebellion and Subsistence in Southeast Asia*, New Haven: Yale University Press.

────── (1985), *Weapons of the Weak: Everyday Forms of Peasant Resistance*, New Haven: Yale University Press.

Sharp, Lauriston and Hanks, Lucien M. (1978), *Bang Chan: Social History of a Rural Community in Thailand*, Ithaca: Cornell University Press.

Shepherd, Jack (1941), *Industry in Southeast Asia*, New York: Institute of Pacific Relations.

Silverstein, Josef (1977), *Burma: Military Rule and the Politics of Stagnation*, Ithaca: Cornell University Press.

Skinner, G. William (1957), *Chinese Society in Thailand: An Analytical History*, Ithaca: Cornell University Press.

Smith, P. C. and Ng Shui-Meng (1982), 'The Components of Population Change in Nineteenth-century South-east Asia: Village Data from the Philippines', *Population Studies*, 36(2): 237–55.

Somers Heidhues, Mary F. (1992), *Bangka Tin and Mentok Pepper: Chinese Settlement on an Indonesian Island*, Singapore: Institute of Southeast Asian Studies.

Sompop Manarungsan (1989), *Economic Development of Thailand, 1850–1950: Response to the Challenge of the World Economy*, Institute of Asian Studies, Monograph No. 42, Bangkok: Chulalongkorn University.

Stanley, Peter W. (1974), *A Nation in the Making: The Philippines and the United States, 1899–1921*, Cambridge, Mass.: Harvard University Press.

Steinberg, David I. (1981a), *Burma's Road toward Development: Growth and Ideology under Military Rule*, Boulder: Westview Press.

—— (1981b), 'Burmese Economics: The Conflict of Ideology and Pragmatism', in F. K. Lehman (ed.), *Military Rule in Burma since 1962: A Kaleidoscope of Views*, Singapore: Maruzen Asia, pp. 29–50.

Sternstein, Larry (1984), 'The Growth of the Population of the World's Pre-eminent "Primate City": Bangkok at Its Bicentenary', *Journal of Southeast Asian Studies*, 15(1): 43–68.

Stifel, Laurence D. (1976), 'Patterns of Land Ownership in Central Thailand during the Twentieth Century', *Journal of the Siam Society*, 64 (1): 237–74.

Stoler, Ann Laura (1985), *Capitalism and Confrontation in Sumatra's Plantation Belt, 1870–1979*, New Haven: Yale University Press.

Storer, Thomas Perry (1970), 'The Philippines', in W. Arthur Lewis (ed.), *Tropical Development, 1880–1913*, Evanston: Northwestern University Press, pp. 283–308.

Suehiro Akira (1989), *Capital Accumulation in Thailand, 1855–1985*, Tokyo: Centre for East Asian Cultural Studies.

Sugiyama Shinya and Guerrero, Milagros C. (eds.) (1994), *International Commercial Rivalry in Southeast Asia in the Interwar Period*, Southeast Asia Studies, Monograph No. 39, New Haven: Yale University.

Swift, M. G. (1964), 'Capital, Saving and Credit in a Malay Peasant Economy', in Raymond Firth and B. S. Yamey (eds.), *Capital, Saving and Credit in Peasant Societies*, London: George Allen & Unwin, pp. 133–56.

Taylor, Robert H. (1987), *The State in Burma*, London: C. Hurst.

Thee Kian-wie (1977), *Plantation Agriculture and Export Growth: An Economic History of East Sumatra, 1863–1942*, Jakarta: National Institute of Economic and Social Research (LEKNAS–LIPI).

Tinker, Hugh (1974), *A New System of Slavery: The Export of Indian Labour Overseas, 1830–1920*, London: Oxford University Press.

Valdepeñas, Vicente B., Jr. and Bautista, Gemilino M. (1977), *The Emergence of the Philippine Economy*, Manila: Papyrus Press.

Van Niel, Robert (1964), 'The Function of Landrent under the Cultivation System in Java', *Journal of Asian Studies*, 23(3): 357–75.

—— (1972), 'Measurement of Change under the Cultivation System in Java, 1837–1851', *Indonesia*, 14: 89–109.

_____ (1981), 'The Effect of Export Cultivations in Nineteenth-century Java', *Modern Asian Studies*, 15(1): 25–58.

Vaughan, J. D. (1971), *The Manners and Customs of the Chinese of the Straits Settlements*, Kuala Lumpur: Oxford University Press; first published in 1879.

Vickerman, Andrew (1986), *The Fate of the Peasantry: Premature 'Transition to Socialism' in the Democratic Republic of Vietnam*, Southeast Asia Studies, Monograph No. 28, New Haven: Yale University.

Vo Nhan Tri (1990), *Vietnam's Economic Policy since 1975*, Singapore: Institute of Southeast Asian Studies, ASEAN Economic Research Unit.

Walinsky, Louis J. (1962), *Economic Development in Burma, 1951–1960*, New York: Twentieth Century Fund.

Warr, Peter G. (ed.) (1993), *The Thai Economy in Transition*, Cambridge: Cambridge University Press.

White, Benjamin (1973), 'Demand for Labor and Population Growth in Colonial Java', *Human Ecology*, 1(3): 217–36.

_____ (1983), '"Agricultural Involution" and Its Critics: Twenty Years After', *Bulletin of Concerned Asian Scholars*, 15(2): 18–31.

Wiegersma, Nancy (1988), *Vietnam: Peasant Land, Peasant Revolution: Patriarchy and Collectivity in the Rural Economy*, London: Macmillan.

Wong, Diana (1987), *Peasants in the Making: Malaysia's Green Revolution*, Singapore: Institute of Southeast Asian Studies.

Wong, John (1979), *ASEAN Economies in Perspective: A Comparative Study of Indonesia, Malaysia, the Philippines, Singapore and Thailand*, London: Macmillan.

Wong Lin Ken (1964), 'Western Enterprise and the Development of the Malayan Tin Industry to 1914', in C. D. Cowan (ed.), *The Economic Development of South-East Asia: Studies in Economic History and Political Economy*, London: George Allen & Unwin, pp. 127–53.

_____ (1965), *The Malayan Tin Industry to 1914*, Association for Asian Studies, Monographs and Papers No. 14, Tucson: University of Arizona Press.

Yip Yat Hoong (1969), *The Development of the Tin Mining Industry of Malaya*, Kuala Lumpur: University of Malaya Press.

Yong, C. F. (1989), *Tan Kah-kee: The Making of an Overseas Chinese Legend*, Singapore: Oxford University Press.

Yoshihara Kunio, (1988), *The Rise of Ersatz Capitalism in South-East Asia*, Singapore: Oxford University Press.

_____ (1994), *The Nation and Economic Growth: The Philippines and Thailand*, Kuala Lumpur: Oxford University Press.

Zelinsky, Wilbur (1950), 'The Indochinese Peninsula: A Demographic Anomaly', *Far Eastern Quarterly*, 9(2): 115–45.

Index

Cinnamon, 21, 98, 102
Cochin-China: rice, 15–8, 41, 160
Coconuts, 15, 21, 27–8, 183
Coffee, 15, 29; in Java, 21–2, 51, 96,
  98, 101–2, 133; in the Malay States,
  145–6, 152
Crop payments [Cultivation System],
  99–101, 108–10, 131–3, 135–7
Cultivation System, 20–2, 89–92,
  96–110, 128, 130–8, 141, 164, 170,
  279

Day, Clive, 96, 163
Debt bondage, 121
Debt foreclosure, 52; in Central Siam,
  221–2; in Lower Burma, 139–40,
  221–2, 226
Deli district, 22, 154–5
Depression [inter-war], 47, 49–54, 56,
  59, 216–27, 279
Doeppers, Daniel F., 227
Drabble, J. H., 147, 151
Dutch East India Company, 5–6, 96–7

Education: in the Malay States,
  168–9; in Siam, 179–81
Electrical and electronic goods
  manufacture, 68–9, 261–3, 265
Elson, R. E., 107–10, 128, 132–7
English East India Company, 6
Ethical Policy [Netherlands East
  Indies], 131
Export-oriented industrialization,
  68–71, 214, 262, 271–3

Falkus, Malcolm, 182–3
Famine, 82, 87, 92; in the Dry Zone of
  Burma, 119; in Java, 88, 132, 136–7;
  in northern Vietnam, 60
Feeny, David, 177–9, 182
Fernando, M. R., 107, 109, 136
Fforde, Adam, 249, 252
Financial services, 71–2
Freedman, Maurice, 165–6
French Indo-China, 47, 50, 60;
  industry, 204–5, 208–11
Furnivall, J. S., 138–40, 164, 169–70,
  172

Geertz, Clifford, 90, 103–10, 165

Gran, Guy, 121
Green Revolution, 72–3, 230–42; in
  Indonesia, 72, 231–2, 234–6,
  238–42; in Malaysia, 72–3, 231–2,
  237–8, 240–1; in the Philippines, 72,
  231, 239–40

Hill, Hal, 250, 253, 255, 258
Ho Chi Minh, 247

Import-substitution
  Industrialization, 68–71, 268–9,
  272–3
Indians: as commercial intermediaries,
  41–5, 160; as labourers, 16–17,
  19–20, 38–42, 146, 160–1, 172;
  migration to South-East Asia, 15,
  19–20, 35–41, 76, 172; as
  moneylenders, 17, 38, 41–2, 45, 160;
  see also Chettiars
Indigo, 21, 28, 96, 98, 102, 131, 133
Indonesia, 63, 66–7, 262, 267; the
  Green Revolution, 72, 231–2, 234–6,
  238–42; industry, 70–1, 260, 263,
  268, 270–1, 273; the oil boom, 71,
  235–6, 238, 263–4, 268
Industry, 54, 56, 68, 76, 203–14,
  260–73, 278; in Burma, 204–5, 209,
  253–4, 257; in French Indo-China,
  204–5, 208–11; in Indonesia, 70–1,
  260, 263, 268, 270–1, 273; in
  Malaysia, 69, 260–1, 263, 268,
  270–1, 273; in the Netherlands East
  Indies, 58, 204, 208–9, 211–13; in
  North Vietnam, 252–3, 257; in the
  Philippines, 57, 68–70, 183, 208–9,
  211–14, 261, 268, 270–1, 273; in
  Siam, 57, 191–3, 203–5, 209,
  211–12, 214; in Singapore, 68–9,
  209, 260–1, 268, 270; in Thailand,
  69, 260–3, 268, 270–1, 273
Ingram, James C., 175, 182
International Rice Research Institute,
  231
International Rubber Regulation
  Agreement [1930s], 50, 57
Irrawaddy Delta, 15–7, 34, 41, 52, 89,
  115, 117–20, 123–5, 129, 138–40,
  164–5, 167, 172, 218–9, 221–2,
  225–7, 230, 247, 250

Sompop Manarungsan, 182
Sophonpanit group, 73
Spice trade, 2, 5, 20
Stanley, Peter W., 185
Steinberg, David I., 250, 255–6
Sternstein, Larry, 93
Stevenson Scheme, 48–50, 57, 150–1, 217
Stifel, Laurence D., 221
Straits Trading Company, 206
Subsistence economy, 8, 10, 87, 89, 91, 122, 124–5, 129–31, 137, 139–41, 148, 155–7, 223
Sugar, 15, 29, 51; Java, 21–2, 25, 52, 96, 98–9, 101–2, 104–5, 107–10, 131, 133, 205–6, 217–20, 223; Netherlands East Indies, 51, 57, 96; Philippines, 21, 26–7, 29, 52, 183–5, 219–22
Sugar Law [Netherlands East Indies, 1870], 22, 102
Sugar mills: Java, 99–102, 108, 110, 131, 205–6; Philippines, 205
Suharto, President, 63, 74
Sukarno, President, 63
Sumatra, 29, 35, 37, 40; petroleum, 23, 25, 207; rubber, 21, 23–5, 49–51, 156, 217; tobacco, 21–3, 25, 41, 154–7, 160, 163, 222
Swettenham, Sir Frank, 163
Swift, M. G., 164

Tan Kah-kee, 56
Tea, 21, 28; Java, 98, 102
Teak, 28, 41, 255
Tenant cultivator [during the 1930s crisis]: Bikol, 226; Burma, 52, 218–19, 225–6
Textile imports, 2, 45, 53, 57–8, 117–18, 134–5, 140, 147, 203, 210–11
Textile manufacture, 57, 68–9, 74, 193, 210–11, 252, 261–3

Thailand, 63, 66–7, 262, 266; industry, 69, 260–3, 268, 270–1, 273; tourism, 71–2
Tin, 15, 28, 38; advance of Western capital in the tin industry, 19, 194–200; Malay States, 18–19, 21, 41, 51, 55, 160, 194–200, 206, 223; Netherlands East Indies, 23–5, 51; Siam, 160, 206
Tin smelting, 206–7
Tobacco, 15; Java, 21, 98, 102, 133; Philippines, 27–8, 183; Sumatra, 21–3, 25, 41, 154–7, 160, 163, 222
Tourism: Thailand, 71–2

U Nu, 65

Van den Bosch, Johannes, 98–9
Van der Heide, J. Homan, 176–9
Van Hoevell, W. R., 132–3
Van Niel, Robert, 101, 136
Vaughan, J. D., 42
Vo Nhan Tri, 249

War (1941–5), 47, 59–60
Western capital: advance in the tin industry in the Malay States, 19, 194–200; in banking and commerce, 43–5; relationship with Chinese capital, 43–5; in rubber plantations in the Malay States, 19–20, 23, 145–7, 149–53, 172, 217
White, Benjamin, 88–91, 103, 108–9
Wiegersma, Nancy, 249
Wong, Diana, 237–8
Wong Lin Ken, 196–9

Yip Yat Hoong, 196–8
Yoshihara Kunio, 264–9

Zelinsky, Wilbur, 83

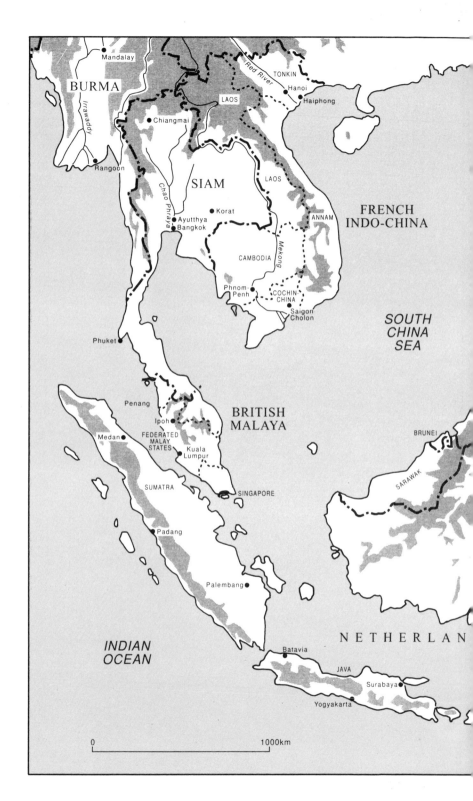

BURMA

Irrawaddy

Mandalay

Chiangmai

Rangoon

Chao Phraya

SIAM

Ayutthya
Bangkok

Korat

LAOS

Red River

TONKIN

Hanoi

Haiphong

LAOS

ANNAM

Mekong

CAMBODIA

Phnom-
Penh

COCHIN
CHINA

Saigon
Cholon

FRENCH
INDO-CHINA

SOUTH
CHINA
SEA

Phuket

Penang

Ipoh

FEDERATED
MALAY
STATES

Medan

Kuala
Lumpur

BRITISH
MALAYA

BRUNEI

SARAWAK

SUMATRA

SINGAPORE

Padang

Palembang

INDIAN
OCEAN

Batavia

JAVA

NETHERLAN

Surabaya

Yogyakarta

0   1000km